ROMANS, CELTS & GERMANS

The German Provinces of Rome

MAUREEN CARROLL

TEMPUS

First published 2001

PUBLISHED IN THE UNITED KINGDOM BY:

Tempus Publishing Ltd
The Mill, Brimscombe Port
Stroud, Gloucestershire GL5 2QG

PUBLISHED IN THE UNITED STATES OF AMERICA BY:

Arcadia Publishing Inc.
A division of Tempus Publishing Inc.
2 Cumberland Street
Charleston, SC 29401
1-888-313-2665

Tempus books are available in France, Germany and Belgium
from the following addresses:

Tempus Publishing Group	Tempus Publishing Group	Tempus Publishing Group
21 Avenue de la République	Gustav-Adolf-Straße 3	Place de L'Alma 4/5
37300 Joué-lès-Tours	99084 Erfurt	1200 Brussels
FRANCE	GERMANY	BELGIUM

British Library Cataloguing in Publication Data.
A catalogue record for this book is available from the British Library.

ISBN 0 7524 1912 9

Typesetting and origination by Tempus Publishing.
PRINTED AND BOUND IN GREAT BRITAIN

Contents

Acknowledgements

The author is grateful to a number of institutions and individuals for supplying photographs and illustrations for the book. These include the Rheinisches Bildarchiv (Cologne), the Römisch-Germanisches Museum (Cologne), the Rheinisches Landesmusuem (Bonn), the Landesmuseum Mainz, the Römisch-Germanisches Zentralmuseum (Mainz), the Museum im Andreasstift (Worms), Museum Burg Linn (Krefeld), the Westfälisches Römermuseum Haltern, the Museum Wiesbaden, the Rijksmuseum van Oudheden (Leiden), the Prähistorische Staatssammlung (Munich), the Landesdenkmalamt Baden-Württemberg, the Rheinisches Amt für Bodendenkmalpflege, the Landesbildstelle Württemberg, Dr Michael Gechter (Overath), Dr Egon Schallmayer (Saalburg), Dr Sebastian Sommer (Stuttgart) and Dr Sven Schütte (Cologne). Credits are given individually with the black and white figures and colour plates.

The plans drawn by David Godden are adapted from the following sources: **6** After Schucany (1999) fig. 3; J.T.J. Jamar, *Heerlen, de Romeinse thermen* (Zutphen: 1981) fig. 2; Petit and Mangin (1994) p. 163, fig. 11; Horn (1987) fig. 363; **8** After A. Becker, H.-J. Köhler and G. Rasbach, *Der römische Stützpunkt von Waldgirmes* (Wiesbaden: 1999) fig. p. 14; **9** After Horn (1987) fig. 396; **10** After Baatz and Herrmann (1982) fig. 208; Filtzinger, Planck and Cämmerer (1986) fig. 64; Horn (1987) fig. 334; **11** After Drack and Fellmann (1988) fig. 306/307; **13** After Horn (1987) fig. 541; **14** After Drack and Fellmann (1988) fig. 392b; **16** After Cüppers (1990) fig. 374; **17, 18** After Drack and Fellmann (1988) fig. 227, 326; **19** After Petit and Mangin (1994) p. 91, fig. 2; **20** After F. Fremersdorf, *Das römische Haus mit dem Dionysosmosaik* (Cologne: 1956) fig. 27; J. Morel, *Bulletin de l'Association Pro Aventico* 36, 1994, fig. 3; R. Laur-Belart, *Führer durch Augusta Raurica* (Basel: 1988) fig. 126; **22** After D. Planck, *Das römische Walheim* (Stuttgart: 1991) fig. 42; **23** After Petit and Mangin (1994) p. 94, fig. 4; **27** After Roymans and Theuws (1991) fig. 22; **28** After S.A. Arora, *Archäologie im Rheinland 1997* (Cologne: 1998) fig. 32; **29** After Drack and Fellmann (1988) fig. 511; Baatz and Herrmann (1982) fig. 116; E. Schallmayer, *Archäologische Ausgrabungen in Baden-Württemberg 1986* (Stuttgart: 1987) fig. 116; **30** After W. Gaitzsch, in H. Hellenkemper, H.G. Horn, H. Koschik and B. Trier (eds.), *Archäologie in Nordrhein-Westfalen. Geschichte im Herzen Europas* (Cologne: 1990) fig. p. 238; **31 and 59** After G. De Boe, in H. Hiller (ed.), *Villa Rustica* (Freiburg: 1988) fig. 11-13; **32** After Horn (1987) fig. 430; **33** After Baatz and Herrmann (1982) fig. 112, 133, 190, 295; **34** After Drack and Fellmann (1988) fig. 418; **35** After C. Ebnöther, *Der römische Gutshof in Dietikon* (Zürich: 1995) fig. 21; **37** After Filtzinger, Planck and Cämmerer (1986) fig. 453; **38** After plan by M. Gechter; **39** After Filtzinger, Planck and Cämmerer (1986) pl. 74; **40** After Petit and Mangin (1994) p. 23, fig. 7; **41** After Drack and Fellmann (1988) fig. 485; **46** After Horn (1987) fig. 209; **57** After Horn (1987) fig. 387; Schucany (1999) fig. 2; Drack and Fellmann (1988) fig. 516; **58** After Rüger (1979) fig. 17.

List of illustrations

Text figures

Colour plates

Preface

Teaching the archaeology of Roman north-west Europe, as I do at the University of Sheffield, is sometimes difficult. Much information on sites and excavated remains is inaccessible, and material published in German, Dutch and French can be daunting not only to students, but also to colleagues and interested readers without the necessary knowledge of these languages. There are, of course, important studies on the Roman north-west provinces in English. These include books by scholars such as Edith Wightman, John Drinkwater, Anthony King and Greg Woolf, but these focus on Roman Gaul and the treatment of the neighbouring German provinces is, of necessity, brief. Prompted by the lack of English language publications on recent archaeological developments in Germany, John Creighton and Roger Wilson edited a compilation of papers delivered by German archaeologists at the Roman Archaeology Conference in Nottingham in 1997 which offered information on selected research themes of current interest. I wanted to do something else, something more comprehensive. Working in various parts of Germany and cooperating with colleagues in the Netherlands, Belgium and Switzerland for many years, I have been able to gain insight into the rich archaeological heritage of the area. Presenting this in a synthesis to a wider public, in English and with numerous illustrations, seemed to me to be a worthwhile undertaking.

This work is meant to be of interest to many people with different backgrounds. Because the scope is broad, the book is designed to supply useful information of a general nature, although several issues are discussed in more detail. The choice of material and themes presented here naturally reflects my own research interests, and it should be said from the beginning that the reader will not find extensive coverage of Roman forts, Roman religion or the Church, except in contexts in which this is relevant to the issues discussed. Some of the material covered in this book is based on my own excavations, particularly in Cologne. Because this site is archaeologically so rich, yet under-represented in the published record, I have included aspects of its archaeology in several chapters and devoted a whole chapter to early Cologne as a case study on cultural relations on the German frontier. I make frequent use of primary Roman sources in the text. They are interesting and often entertaining, and they are the closest we will ever come to hearing voices of the Roman past, even if they always need to be put into the context in which, by whom and for whom they were written. The bibliography is not exhaustive by any means, but I have attempted to include the most relevant studies of recent date on a variety of themes.

I am grateful to Peter Kemmis Betty for so enthusiastically taking up my idea for the book. I owe a huge debt of thanks to David Godden for painstakingly and competently producing the illustrations. Over the years I have profited from stimulating and much appreciated discussions of the Roman West with a number of colleagues, especially Antony Birley (Düsseldorf), Raymond Brulet (Louvain-la-Neuve), Michael Gechter (Bonn), Stefan Neu and Sven Schütte (Cologne), Caty Schucany (Bern), Harry van Enckevort (Nijmegen), Colin Wells (San Antonio) and David Wigg (Frankfurt). My thanks also go to my colleagues at the University of Sheffield, in particular John Collis, Dawn Hadley and John Moreland, who were kind enough to comment on an earlier draft of this book.

Introduction

This book is not about the Roman period in Germany, at least not Germany within its present political boundaries, and it therefore does not have the title 'Roman Germany'. It might seem surprising to find sites in the Netherlands, Belgium, France and Switzerland as well as Germany discussed here, but that is because parts of these modern countries once lay within the Roman political boundaries of Germania Inferior and Germania Superior. These two provinces are the focus of this study (**1**).

Within the German provinces were many disparate landscapes and a wide variety of population groups — Celts (the Greek name) or Gauls (the Latin name), Germans, peoples of mixed Celtic and Germanic origin, and Romans from across the Empire — all joined by Roman external agency into a heterogeneous whole. This book tries to deal with all of them, although admittedly the Romans, who were a significant presence in the region, get the most attention due to the nature of the evidence. What is the evidence? The archaeological material — excavated sites and all manner of artefacts — is abundant. However archaeologists have often focused more strongly on what is recognisable as 'Roman', for example stone-built architecture and certain types of easily recognisable pottery such as terra sigillata, rather than on less tangible timber structures or handmade local pottery which even in the twentieth century was sometimes thought to be pre-Roman. The excavated remains allow us, if properly studied, to assess the complex impact of Rome on various regions and the varying degrees to which the indigenous populations accepted, adapted or rejected Roman culture. Written sources such as Latin historical and geographical treatises have an inherent Roman bias, and their reliability as accounts of the cultural and ethnic diversity of the conquered areas is limited. Nevertheless, they have a great value as contemporary documents from a Roman perspective and can be compared and contrasted with the excavated evidence. Other written sources such as inscriptions, particularly those on funerary monuments, reveal population influx and movement, social structures and identities.

In the multi-ethnic environment of the German provinces, perceived and expressed identities are an important issue. Did the Celts call themselves Celts, did the Germanic peoples identify themselves as Germans, and is it justified to use these terms in this book? The archaeological and historical evidence suggests that these two large groups did not regard themselves as nations, but rather it was the Roman ethnographic tradition derived from earlier Greek accounts that politically and ideologically constructed the larger ethnic communities known as Celts/Gauls and Germans. Diodorus Siculus and Caesar writing in the first century BC acknowledged the diversity of peoples in Gaul, but confirmed that they were all joined together under one name by the Romans as the Gauls. What is now the equivalent of France, Switzerland, Belgium, the Netherlands and Germany west of the

1   Provinces of the western Empire with main administrative centres

Rhine was known as Gaul (*Gallia*), despite the fact that Germanic and mixed Celtic and Germanic peoples lived there. Carved out of the eastern fringes of Gaul were the German provinces where Celtic and Germanic groups also lived side by side. The indigenous peoples under consideration, however, categorised their ethnic ascription on a specific tribal level, identifying themselves as belonging to a particular group and not using a collective name. In using, mainly for the sake of simplicity, the names 'Celt' or 'Gaul' (which I do interchangeably) and 'German' I am using the standard terminology of antiquity which also has an established tradition in modern archaeological and historical research. That there is great diversity in this generalised unity is absolutely clear, and this is taken into account in many ways in the individual chapters of the book.

Archaeological research on the Roman period in the modern states comprising the former German provinces is as diverse as the ancient peoples in them, and attitudes towards the pre-Roman and Roman past vary greatly. Peoples and events have often been selectively chosen to bolster more recent political and ideological structures. The most extreme case of this was exhibited in National Socialist Germany when the Roman past was rejected as foreign and oppressive and the indigenous Germanic peoples were idealised as freedom fighters of racial purity and superiority. Since the Second World War, archaeology in Germany has taken a turn in reaction to this. The Romans are of great interest again, perhaps because issues of race and ethnicity can be more easily avoided, although I find the apparent reluctance in German archaeology to explore ethnic and other identities unfortunate. The Romans are obviously regarded as 'safer', and a study of them need not reopen a Pandora's box of race-historical issues once so negatively exploited and better forgotten. Excavating at sites in Germany in the 1980s and 1990s, which were clearly not of the Roman period or outside the frontiers of the Empire, our excavation teams were inevitably asked by interested members of the public on site whether we had yet found something Roman. The disappointment at being told that this was not the case was tangible. The Romans can also be rather useful politically and ideologically, as in 1992 in Cologne when there was a concerted effort on the part of the city administration to distance itself from any racial prejudice and aversion to foreigners expressed by right-wing groups. One of the mottos of the time was '*Die ersten Kölner waren Ausländer*' ('the first inhabitants of Cologne were foreigners'). In other words, the Romans who founded Cologne were a mixed group from around the then-known world, and this multicultural society was represented as a role model of harmony.

Unlike the archaeology of the Roman period in Britain which is known rather enigmatically and inconsistently as 'Romano-British', that of the same period in Germany is known simply as 'Roman'. The same is true in the Netherlands and in Switzerland. There are no overtones of a particular people or nation at the heart of the period, although interestingly Dutch scholars more frequently than others explore social, cultural and ethnic structures of the pre-Roman and Roman periods, but without nationalistic sentiments. In contrast, Roman-period archaeology in Belgium is alternatively called '*Belgo-Romain*' or '*Gallo-Romain*', both terms alluding to the indigenous population of the Roman period and both implying some kind of national particularism. '*Gallo-Romain*' is also widely used in France, again indicating that the Gauls as indigenous peoples and perceived ancestors of modern France are central to an understanding of the period. The phrase '*nos ancêtres, les Gaulois*' ('our ancestors, the Gauls') was first coined in the sixteenth century, and this sentiment is still expressed today.

In the nineteenth century both France and Germany were guilty of manipulating history for political and nationalistic purposes. Both countries bypassed their common Frankish past to hail either an early Gaulish or Germanic leader as a national hero. In France, Vercingetorix, the Gaulish chieftain of the Arverni who united other tribes in fierce resistance to Caesar in 52 BC, became the manifestation of Gaulish resistance to foreign domination, an issue particularly relevant in the wake of German aggression against France in the Franco-Prussian war of 1870/71. In Germany, Arminius (or Hermann), the Cheruscan chieftain who defeated Varus and his three Roman legions in AD 9, became a symbol of the German love of freedom and of national unification. The latter attitude was largely prompted by the treatment of Germany by Napoleon, the Roman conquest somehow being equated with foreign domination by France. The Germans, of course, could and did point out to the French that Vercingetorix was actually defeated, whereas Arminius was not. Statues were erected to both of them, Vercingetorix at Alesia in 1865 and Arminius near Detmold in 1875. At the same time, the Belgians proclaimed the Gaulish leader Ambiorix of the Eburones, who died fighting Caesar, a national hero, erecting a statue of him in the town centre of Tongeren. These figures were put forward as visible symbols of national unity and a glorification of perceived ancestors, ignoring the disunity and fictitious nationhood of both the Gauls and the Germans in the Iron Age and in the Roman period.

There is no argument that Vercingetorix was a Gaul and Arminius a German, but problems of interpreting identity arise in France and Germany with the late Roman and early Medieval Franks. A catalogue accompanying an exhibition shown in Mannheim in 1996 and Berlin in 1997 entitled *Die Franken — Wegbereiter Europas* or *Les Francs — Précurseurs de l'Europe* tackles, among other things, the identity of the Franks, attempting to place them in a larger context as the creators of a shared European experience from the fifth to eighth centuries. One of the chapters of the catalogue has the apt heading '*Eine Geschichte — Zwei Geschichten*' ('one history — two stories'). To the French, the Merovingian Franks represent Germanic invaders who brought about the destruction of Roman Gaul; to the Germans they represent the triumph of a confederation of Germanic peoples who freed Germany from Roman domination and ruled over Gaul. Since the nation of France rose out of the Germanic kingdom of the Franks this poses a real conflict for the French. The conflict is partly reconciled by an historical event: the conversion of Clovis (French) or Chlodwig (German) to Christianity in 496. With the baptism of Clovis and his army, the barbarian German is perceived to have acknowledged the faith and culture of late Roman Christian Gaul (although not all Gallo-Romans were Christians), thereby unifying the Gallo-Romans and the Franks and becoming the first king of France. In the year of the 1500th anniversary of his conversion, a special church celebration was held by the Pope in Reims where Clovis was baptised, and special issues of history books such as *Clovis. La naissance de la France* or *Clovis ou les origines de la France* were published in 1995 and 1996. The question whether the Franks were French or German, however, does not take into account that their genesis as a people and their establishment as a kingdom is intimately related to the role the Franks played within the context of late Roman history.

These conflicts between Gaulish/Celtic peoples and Germanic peoples, between the French and the Germans, are relevant to a study of the German provinces. The theme of opposition between Gauls and Germans is one occurring already in antiquity, and it goes back to the late second and first centuries BC when the northern Germanic Cimbri and Teutones and later the Suebi from the Elbe region plundered Gaulish territory west of the Rhine. In 58 BC the Gaulish Aedui are said to have feared that 'in a few years all the natives will have been driven forth from the borders of Gaul, and all the Germans will have crossed the Rhine' (Caesar, *De Bello Gallico* 1.31). Caesar made ample use for tactical and ideological reasons of cavalry units recruited from east-bank Germanic tribes, the old enemies of the Gauls, in his campaigns in Gaul (*De Bello Gallico* 7.13, 65, 70), and the Roman general Cerialis, addressing the Lingones and Treveri in AD 69, fuelled old animosities by reminding them of the lust, avarice and aggressiveness of past Germanic neighbours (Tacitus, *Historiae* 4.73).

Exchange and contact between Gauls and Germans was not simply a pre-Roman phenomenon, but relations between Gauls and Germans, both conflicting and friendly, and between both groups and the Romans continued throughout the first few centuries AD. After the Roman conquest of Gaul and the Rhineland, peoples who were ethnically and culturally Gaulish/Celtic on the middle and upper Rhine were politically organised by the Romans into the district of Germania Superior, the name of the province thus not accurately reflecting the character of the population, but perhaps revealing something about the Roman perception of it. Germania Inferior, particularly the north, and the annexed area between the Rhine and the *limes*, encompassed regions in which both ethnic Germans and people of mixed Germanic and Celtic origin lived. In addition to this, a greater degree of physical and social mobility in Roman provincial society enabled many to travel and participate in economic life in areas outside their immediate communities. The opportunities offered by the newly established towns on the Rhine frontier, often heavily populated by the Roman military and its dependants, for example, attracted many Gaulish businessmen and merchants to a predominantly Germanic region. Moreover, the post-Caesarian restructuring of tribes and subtribes west of the Rhine, often involving the resettling of Germanic groups from the east bank of the river to the west bank, meant that during the early Empire the population of the provinces found itself in a state of flux. It was the Romans who united the Gallic and Germanic polities into larger units referred to as *Galli* or *Germani*. Nevertheless, a Gallic or Germanic nation identifying itself with a collective name did not exist, and modern attempts to negate the disunity and disparity of the many groups in Gaul and Germany are nationalistic constructs.

The other essential component in this Gallic-Germanic world were the Romans, themselves a disparate bunch from many localities in the Empire. In what way, for example, was an auxiliary soldier born and raised in the Danube region who retired with Roman citizenship and settled in one of the German provinces a 'Roman'? Why would a 'Roman' soldier of distant, possibly north Italian, origin stationed on the German frontier become a devotee of gods rooted in local, pre-Roman cults of the lower Rhine? And why would some Gaulish peoples invent an origin myth which linked them to Rome through common descent? To varying degrees the Gaulish and Germanic peoples took an active part in internalising Roman culture as it was presented to them and, by the same token, in contributing to a western Roman culture that is very different from that in other parts of the Empire. This is reflected in many ways that are explored in the following chapters.

1 Landscapes and peoples

The Rhine rises in the land of the Lepontii, who inhabit the Alps; in a long, swift course it runs through the territories of the Nantuates, Helvetii, Sequani, Mediomatrici, Triboci and Treveri, and on its approach to the Ocean divides into several streams, forming many large islands (Caesar, *De Bello Gallico* 4.10).

The appearance of the country differs considerably in different parts; but in general it is covered either by bristling forests or by foul swamps (Tacitus, *Germania* 5).

Physical geography of the German provinces

The two German provinces, Germania Inferior and Germania Superior, as they were established in AD 85, stretched from the North Sea coast to the Swiss Alps, each province encompassing a variety of landscapes (**2**). Germania Inferior in the extreme north was bounded by the Rhine river which emptied in three arms, known today as the Neder Rijn, Kromme Rijn and Oude Rijn, into the North Sea. Immediately south of these lay marshy lowlands and the islands in the delta of the Rhine, Maas, Waal and Schelde rivers. The banks of the Oude Rijn provided only a narrow strip of dry land for habitation, in some places only a mile or so (1-2km) in width. The coastline was protected to a degree by sand dunes, but these were prone to shifting and were interrupted where the rivers broke through to enter the sea. The middle part of the province between Nijmegen and Krefeld was characterised by gentle wooded hills, whilst the southern section encompassed both the broad plain of the meandering Rhine and, to the west of the Cologne basin, fertile loess plains. The rugged Eifel and Ardennes mountains rise in the extreme south and south-west respectively to heights between 1600-1900ft (500-600m) above sea level. South of Bonn the valley plain of the Rhine narrows to a small strip of land, the mountainous slopes of the Ahr and Eifel extending in their western limits to the river. Whilst the sandy soils of the northern lowlands were of poor quality for cultivation and in the delta area the land was often flooded with sea water, the fertile soils of the loess regions to the south were ideal for agriculture, in particular cereal cultivation. The Eifel and Ardennes were mined for ores and provided stone of varying kinds ranging from sandstone, limestone and granite to volcanic basalt and tufa. The backbone of the province in the east was the Rhine, and a number of large and small navigable rivers watered the interior and allowed connections between inland regions, the Rhine and the North Sea coast. The province extended in the west slightly beyond the Maas river, sharing a border with neighbouring Gallia Belgica. The rather modest Vinxtbach river formed the southern boundary of Germania Inferior, beyond which lay Germania Superior.

Germania Superior, unlike its sister province, incorporated areas on both sides of the Rhine. In the northern section west of the Rhine, the provincial boundary crossed the Moselle river as well as the Vosges and Hunsrück mountains. Further south, the province extended in the west into the Plateau de Langres, incorporating the sources of the Seine, Marne and Meuse/Maas rivers, and reached its southernmost limit at Lake Geneva. East of the Rhine the border ran eastwards along the back of the Taunus mountains and continued southwards to cross the Main (**colour plate 1**), Neckar and Danube rivers, where it touched that of the neighbouring province of Raetia. It also shared borders on the south with Alpes Poeninae and Gallia Narbonensis, on the west with Gallia Ludgunensis, and on the north-west with Gallia Belgica. The Rhine valley in the northern part of the province, diminished in width by the encroaching Eifel, Voreifel and Pfälzer mountains, opens up west of the river around Mainz to form a broad, fertile landscape as far south as Speyer, whilst the valley floor east of the Rhine slopes gently up to the sandstone Odenwald mountains. Between the Odenwald and the Taunus range to the north, the Wetterau plain was a densely settled agricultural landscape, particularly north of the Main river. The winding Neckar valley south of Wimpfen equally provided fertile slopes for cultivation (**colour plate 2**), and, west of the Rhine, the Moselle was known for its agricultural productivity and vine-clad slopes. The southern part of Germania Superior was altogether more rugged, with densely forested elevations of up to almost 4000ft (1200m) above sea level such as the Black Forest and the Vosges. South of the bend of the Rhine near Basel the limestone ridge of the Jura range stretches from east to west to a height of over 4500ft (1400m), and to the east and north-east of Lake Geneva the Swiss Alps begin in earnest as an inhospitable region. Between these two mountain chains, however, the valley of the Aare was sought out for settlement and cultivation.

From Iron Age to Roman landscapes

The landscapes of the Roman period, in particular those chosen for occupation, differed to some degree from those inhabited by the peoples of the Iron Age. Although not all areas have been scientifically investigated, changes in the environment and the vegetation in some regions are clearly indicated by palynological and palaeobotanical research. These changes reflect differences between the Iron Age and Roman economies. The loess plains west of the Cologne basin is one of the areas that have been studied. In the late Iron Age, from about 250 to 50 BC, the land was farmed intensively for cereals and the woodlands were extensively used for pasturage of sheep and goats, to the point that the mixed tree cover of oak and pine became increasingly encroached upon by heath. On the hill slopes the loess eroded, exposing the sandy subsoil. Due to the disruption of settlement during Caesar's campaigns in the region, certainly accompanied by a population reduction as witnessed by archaeological and written sources, the forests partly regenerated after 50 BC; the heaths were reclaimed by arboreal vegetation, most notably pine, and oak and beech dominated the woodlands. This was the landscape that presented itself to Roman settlers in the early first century AD. They proceeded from the middle of this century to clear the land and farm it again extensively for cereal crops, and they maintained grasslands and hay-meadows for stock farming of cattle. In another landscape, the northern Wetterau in Hessen, palynological analysis shows that here, too, the woodlands in the late Iron Age chiefly had been used for pasturage. The beech forests were thus decimated, leaving pine and oak as tree cover. The central Wetterau was deforested, and the land under cultivation. From the turn of the first century BC to the first century AD, the forests in the northern Wetterau began to regenerate on account of the cessation of woodland pasturing. At the same time, and until about 250, cereal crops, including rye for the first time, were intensively planted and harvested, and there is evidence for the management of hay-meadows. Due to the exploitation of the land by the late Iron Age population, neither in the loess plains of the lower Rhine, nor in the Wetterau, did the Romans find natural, untouched forests upon their arrival. Where dense forests such as those in the Ardennes or the Black Forest were encountered, these remained only marginally populated or were uninhabited. Tacitus' remarks on the appearance of Germany — bristling forests and foul swamps — were exaggerated, partly for dramatic effect. What changed the landscapes of the two provinces more drastically than anything else was the network of new roads, the establishment of towns and villages on a hitherto unknown scale and the dense occupation of the countryside.

Peoples at the time of Caesar

During Caesar's expeditions in Gaul and Germany from 58-50 BC, numerous population groups with regional territories and power centres were encountered by the Romans, many for the first time. The cultural geography of Iron Age and early Roman western Europe was complex, and these peoples were just as diverse as the many landscapes they occupied. Caesar, however, simplistically divided the tribes in north-west Europe into two main groups: Celts or Gauls (*Keltoi* in Greek, *Celtae* or *Galli* in Latin) and Germans (*Germani*). In this survey, only those groups who lived within the areas later corresponding to the provinces of Germania Inferior and Germania Superior or in areas tangential to these provinces will be discussed. Gaul north of the Seine was the territory of the Belgae, who Caesar claimed in the distant past to have migrated to Gaul from beyond the Rhine. Belgic Gaul consisted of a mixture of peoples who were Celtic, as well as others north of the Somme who were either of mixed Celtic and Germanic character or even primarily of Germanic origin. These latter on the lower Rhine were known to Caesar as *Germani cisrhenani* (west-bank Germans). Along the middle Rhine, Germanic and Gallic population groups inhabited both banks of the river, but on the upper Rhine Celtic peoples held sway and formed a bulwark against the Germans in the east.

In the northern part of the Rhineland, the Menapii occupied the marshy lowlands and forests just south of the river, and they are also said to have possessed lands and villages beyond the mouth of the Rhine. Where the boundary between their territory and that of the Frisii in the Dutch coastal area north of the Rhine lay is unknown, and perhaps this and all other boundaries were rather more fluid than the later Roman territorial divisions. The Eburones inhabited the region between the Maas and Rhine, including part of the Eifel, and their territory may have extended northwards to the Kempen area. Their

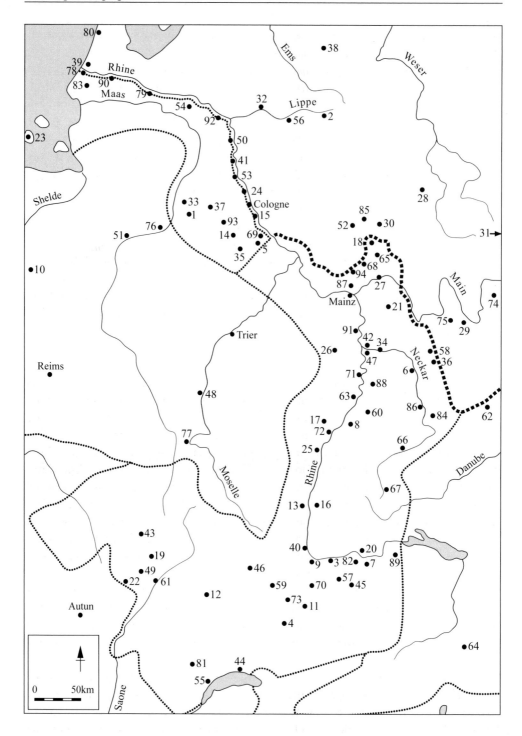

2 *(opposite) Map showing cities, towns, small towns and forts in the German provinces as well as transfrontier sites mentioned in the following chapters.*

1 Aachen; 2 Anreppen; 3 Augst; 4 Avenches; 5 Bad Neuenahr-Ahrweiler; 6 Bad Wimpfen; 7 Baden; 8 Baden Baden; 9 Basel; 10 Bavay; 11 Bern; 12 Besançon; 13 Biesheim; 14 Billig; 15 Bonn; 16 Breisach; 17 Brumath; 18 Butzbach; 19 Dampierre; 20 Dangstetten; 21 Dieburg; 22 Dijon; 23 Domburg; 24 Dormagen; 25 Ehl; 26 Eisenberg; 27 Frankfurt-Heddernheim; 28 Fritzlar-Geismar; 29 Gaukönigshofen; 30 Gießen; 31 Haarhausen; 32 Haltern; 33 Heerlen; 34 Heidelberg; 35 Iversheim; 36 Jagsthausen; 37 Jülich; 38 Kalkriese; 39 Katwijk; 40 Kembs; 41 Krefeld; 42 Ladenburg; 43 Langres; 44 Lausanne; 45 Lenzburg; 46 Mandeure; 47 Mannheim; 48 Metz; 49 Mirebeau; 50 Moers-Asberg; 51 Namur; 52 Naunheim; 53 Neuss; 54 Nijmegen; 55 Nyon; 56 Oberaden; 57 Olten; 58 Osterburken; 59 Péry; 60 Pforzheim; 61 Pontailler sur Saône; 62 Rheinau-Dalkingen; 63 Rheinzabern; 64 Riom-Parsonz; 65 Rödgen; 66 Rottenburg; 67 Rottweil; 68 Saalburg; 69 Sinzig; 70 Solothurn; 71 Speyer; 72 Strasbourg; 73 Studen; 74 Sülzdorf; 75 Tauberbischofsheim-Distelhausen; 76 Tongeren; 77 Toul; 78 Valkenburg; 79 Vechten; 80 Velsen; 81 Villards-d'Héria; 82 Vindonissa; 83 Voorburg-Arentsburg; 84 Waiblingen; 85 Waldgirmes; 86 Walheim; 87 Wiesbaden; 88 Wiesloch; 89 Winterthur; 90 Woerden; 91 Worms; 92 Xanten; 93 Zülpich; 94 Zugmantel

southern neighbours, the Aduatuci, to whom the Eburones were tributary, lived north of the confluence of the Maas and Sambre rivers on the northern fringes of the Ardennes. Both the Eburones and the Aduatuci were *Germani cisrhenani*. Other smaller allied groups belonging to these left-bank Germans were the Condrusi and Caerosi, who dwelt possibly in the Condroz and the northern Eifel respectively, and the Segni and Paemani whose homelands are not exactly known. Both the Caerosi and the Condrusi were dependents (*clientes*) of the Treveri, their southern neighbours. The domain of the Treveri reached from the south-east fringes of the Ardennes and Eifel to the Hunsrück, and the middle and lower Moselle flowed through their land to the Rhine. According to Tacitus, they took pride in their Germanic descent, although their material culture and language was Celtic. East of the Rhine in northern Germany were the Tencteri and Usipetes, and further south the Sugambri. South of the Sugambri lived the Ubii in the Neuwied basin, lower Lahn valley and possibly parts of the Taunus. The last four Germanic groups were under pressure from the Suebi, in Caesar's estimation the largest and most warlike nation among the Germanic peoples. Ethnographically, the middle and upper Rhine on its eastern side had been mainly Celtic until the Suebi advanced from the Elbe to the Rhine in the first half of the first century BC.

South of the Treveri, the lands west of the upper Maas, across the Vosges and up to the upper Rhine in Alsace, belonged to the Celtic Mediomatrici, with the heartland of their territory in Lorraine. Between the Rhône and the Saône in upper Alsace dwelt the Sequani. The Rauraci occupied the left bank of the upper Rhine between the Belfort gap at the southern tip of the Vosges mountains and the Jura range. The Jura range acted as a natural boundary between them and the Helvetii to the south. This latter Celtic group was in constant conflict with the Suebic Germans east of the Rhine, attempting to stem their incursions into Gaul. Helvetian territory was carefully defined by nature (and by Caesar), being bounded by the Rhine, the Jura, Lake Geneva and the Rhône river. This may not have been the original homeland of the Helvetii, however, since Tacitus (*Germania* 28) refers to their territory as once having been situated east of the Rhine up to the Main river. Their position between the Rhine, Jura and Lake Geneva at the time of Caesar may be the end result of migrations forced on them by the Germans. East of the Rhine, at least from the first half of the first century BC, the Germanic Suebi dominated a large territory stretching from the Lahn river to the upper Rhine. Under the Suebian king Ariovistus, seven sub-groups of this large folk, in all 120,000 people, had crossed into Gaul around 70 BC. Numerous Elbe-Germanic finds, which are attributed to the Suebi, begin to appear at this time at sites in the Neuwied basin on either bank of the Rhine, suggesting that these east Germanic peoples were not only present in Aeduan and Sequanian lands, but also Ubian and Treveran territory. Finally, the lands between the Seine and Saône were the domain of the Lingones.

Although Caesar treats the Rhine as a cultural boundary separating Germans from Gauls, the Rhine was never a deterrent for population movement or for trade or contacts of other kinds between groups on either side of the river. As far as migrations are concerned, the direction of movement almost always seems to have been from east to west, resulting in new population influxes and mixed cultures west of the Rhine, particularly on the lower Rhine. Germanic peoples either crossed the Rhine themselves to settle in Gaul or displaced Celtic groups from east of the Rhine who were forced to migrate to the west. Even Caesar confirmed cultural blurring in regard to populations on either side of the Rhine. The proximity of Germany to Gaul, at least on the Rhine, and exposure to Gaulish customs acted, in Caesar's view, as civilising factors on those Germans in riverbank regions (*De Bello Gallico* 4.3). In effect, it is doubtful that he held either group in high esteem, referring often to the Gauls as fickle and the Germans as treacherous and hypocritical. Even a Gaul such as Licinius, who rose high in the ranks of Roman government and became procurator under Augustus, was regarded as suspicious because of his origins and he displayed behaviour which 'combined the greed of the barbarian with something of the dignity of the Roman' (Cassius Dio, *Historia Romana* 54.21).

Pre-Conquest settlements

The villages, settlements and fortresses of these many peoples encountered by Caesar are not equally well known archaeologically, and the state of research on them differs considerably from region to region. Although we need not rely on Caesar for our archaeological enquiry into settlement types, it is worth noting that he mentioned *oppida*, *castella*, *vici* and *aedificia* in his commentaries on the Gallic war. What precisely he meant by these terms is difficult to say, and although they should not be too narrowly defined today, some kind of interpretation, however hesitant, must be offered. *Oppida* are understood here as large fortified settlements which served as regional focal points and power centres, ranging from about 50 to over 250 acres (20-100ha) in size and generally located on hilltops. *Castella* were likely smaller, fortified strongholds, also usually on elevated ground, which may not have been permanently occupied. *Vici* appear to have been clusters of farmhouses, and *aedificia* may have been isolated farmsteads. This brief survey can only be a rough sketch of some of them.

Caesar recorded *vici* and *aedificia*, but no *oppida*, in Menapian and Eburonean territory. In general, the picture that emerges from archaeological research is that these regions were characterised by scattered unfortified agrarian settlements of very modest size, usually encompassing timber-aisled houses and post-built granaries. This does appear to corroborate Caesar's assessment. These peoples had a lower level of social organisation than those in central and southern Gaul, and this is reflected in their settlement structure. In Eburonean settlements, the houses are very similar in size and appearance, suggesting that there was no differentiation between the dwellings of an elite group and the rest of the population. The lack of *oppida* and evidence for recognisable status difference is an indication of an underdeveloped sociopolitical hierarchy, and, indeed, the dual kings of the Eburones had only limited power, as one of them, Ambiorix, lamented. Nevertheless, some kind of exercised authority is suggested by the presence of fortifications at some sites. In Eburonean lands only three fortified settlements, two lowland villages and a hill fort, are known today. One of the former near Hambach-Niederzier has been completely excavated and consisted of roughly 265 post-built structures, including houses and mainly granaries, within an area of about 7 acres (3ha) fortified by a double ditch and timber and earth rampart. No recognisably larger houses were detected, and the square four-, six- and nine-post structures at Niederzier are entirely within the Iron Age building tradition of the loess regions west of the Cologne basin. Occupation began around 120/100 BC, but had ceased by 60/50, presumably during Caesar's campaigns in the area. A hoard of iron ingots, gold jewellery, gold coins (so-called rainbow cups) of the Vindelici on the Danube and gold staters of the northern Gaulish Ambiani indicate far flung exchange networks in this peripheral zone. The second fortified lowland settlement at Eschweiler-Laurenzberg also housed numerous granaries and, like Niederzier, had no larger farmhouses. Both may have functioned chiefly as fortified food storage compounds under local control for the surrounding rural communities. The hill fort of over 12 acres (5ha) near Euskirchen-Kreuzweingarten was situated on an elevation 820-90ft (250-70m) above sea level in the Voreifel mountains. It was defended by a timber-laced stone and earth rampart (*murus gallicus*), and was occupied in approximately the same time period as the settlement at Hambach-Niederzier.

In Treveran territory, six *oppida* and at least eight smaller hill forts built at the beginning of the late La Tène period have been investigated archaeologically. These *oppida* at the Titelberg, Kasselt, Castel, Otzenhausen, the Martberg and the Donnersberg were built on elevated ground and generally enclosed an area approximately 75-106 acres (30-43ha) in size, although the adjoining hills of the Martberg and the Hüttenberg 650ft (200m) above the Moselle enclosed an even larger area of around 170 acres (70ha). These sites were regional centres for trade and craft production, and the political importance of two of them, the Titelberg and the Martberg, is underlined by the existence of mints producing Treveran coinage. The defensive character of the *oppida* is indicated clearly by their location and the massive fortifications surrounding them. Whilst the *oppida* reflect central settlements of tribal groups, the hill forts or *castella* were the seats of power for local lords. That certain of these leaders in Treveran society could possess considerable personal power, leading to conflicts and power struggles within the tribe, is indicated by the existence of political factions headed by aristocrats such as Indutiomarus and Cingetorix who could count on a substantial body of dependent clients. The *castella* generally did not exceed 2-5 acres (1-2ha) in size. The Treveran late Iron Age hill fort Altburg at Bundenbach in the Hunsrück, occupied from about 300 to the mid-first century, contained over 200 buildings, mainly granaries. The largest post-built structures and a polygonal timber building interpreted as a temple were separated from the rest of the settlement by a timber palisade, possibly demarcating the complex of the settlement's elite. The concentration of granaries here suggests that this elite controlled food stores from the region. Fortified upland sites such as that at Bundenbach are numerous in the Hunsrück, usually only 6-9 miles (10-15km) apart. They too may have served as fortified storage compounds or as places of refuge for the population of nearby settlements.

Late Iron Age settlements of the Rauraci in the upper Rhine region on either side of the river were both of the fortified and unfortified type in the period 150-60 BC. The fortified settlements of usually up to 12 acres (5ha) in size, and built in the mountains above the Rhine valley, were not permanently settled, but were laid out for the defence of the individual regions. At such sites, for example Ehrenkirchen-Kegelriss and Sissach-Fluh, markets, political gatherings and religious ceremonies might have been held, but their main purpose will have been as places of refuge. Caesar refers to such *castella* in the Alpine region. Unfortified, open settlements, such as those at Basel-Gasfabrik and Breisach-Hochstetten, on the other hand, were established in the river plain, and at these sites trade, craft production and food storage facilities are in evidence.

In Helvetian territory, the oldest late Iron Age settlements date to the end of the third century BC. These include Bern-Engehalbinsel on the Aare river and Yverdon on the Lac de Neuchâtel. In both cases, fortifications were not added until the early first century, at Bern increasing the area of the settlement from 12 to 346 acres (5-140ha). The large *oppidum* at Altenburg-Rheinau on the Rhine was first built some time before about 120 BC. The defensive measures at these sites may be connected with the threat of Germanic advancement, both from the marauding Cimbri and Teutones at the end of the second century and the Suebi in the early first century BC. The threat from the latter became reality by 58, and the Helvetii abandoned another of their fortified *oppida* at this time, that on Mont Vully between the Lac de Neuchâtel and Lac de Morat near Avenches, burning it to the ground and thereafter setting off on their western migrations in search of safer territory. According to Caesar, the Helvetii had 12 *oppida* and some 400 villages (*vici*) in their homelands. Helvetian society, like that of the Treveri, was based upon leadership by several aristocratic families, which may explain the large number of *oppida* as regional power centres.

In parts of southern Germany, in particular east of the upper Rhine, on either side of the Neckar and along the Danube, flatland areas are dotted with a particular kind of rural settlement, the so-called late Celtic *Viereckschanzen*. These square or rectangular settlements were enclosed by a V-shaped ditch on all four sides, and they often had wells and timber structures within them. Archaeologists do not agree on the function of the

Viereckschanzen, but they are most often interpreted as religious sanctuaries. The wells are accordingly interpreted as cult shafts for ritual deposits and the buildings, particularly the post-built structures often encountered in the corners of the enclosure, are identified as temples. The multi-phased *Viereckschanzen*, however, may have functioned as centralised settlements in which economic, political and religious life was controlled by local rulers. This is supported by sites such as Riedlingen on the upper Danube, where the presence of a large central building, granaries, sunken-floored buildings (*Grubenhäuser*) with evidence of spinning and metalworking as well as a range of finds typical of rural settlements, suggest that the *Viereckschanzen* were established as nucleated rural villages. An exclusively religious function as an enclosed sanctuary seems unlikely, although a temple may well have been one of the elements within the enclosure. For those *Viereckschanzen* in which almost no other structures other than a 'temple' in the corner existed (if they were at all recognised in excavations), the interpretation as a nucleated settlement is difficult. Perhaps the *Viereckschanzen* did not all function in the same way. The fortified post-Caesarian settlement at Westheim on the west bank of the Rhine near the mouth of the Neckar looks for all the world like a *Viereckschanze*, yet excavations within it have revealed that it is clearly a nucleated rural settlement of post-built houses and granaries (**3**). Many of the *Viereckschanzen*, especially those known only through aerial photography, may indeed be just such settlements.

Finally, east of the Rhine in the lands of the Tencteri and Usipetes, small unfortified rural settlements with timber-aisled houses are known which are related to the same type of settlement found in the Netherlands, the lower German Rhineland and northern Belgium. Caesar refers to *vici* and *aedificia* in Sugambrian territory, but no *oppida*. Nevertheless, two fortified hilltop sites (*castella?*) at Königswinter-Petersberg and Bensberg, 13 and 9 acres (5.2 and 3.8ha) in area respectively, do exist which were occupied in the first half of the first century BC. Neither hill fort was permanently occupied, but was used only periodically as a place of refuge. The east-bank Ubii, according to Caesar, had *oppida* into which, in times of trouble, livestock and harvests could be brought for safekeeping. Since the exact borders of Ubian territory are as yet impossible to determine, it is anything but clear whether *oppida* such as that at the Heidetränk in the northern Taunus or the Dünsberg north of the Lahn belonged to the Ubii. Traces of settlements on the Rhine at Neuwied and the mouth of the Lahn near Braubach can, on the other hand, very probably be attributed to them. Cemetery finds indicate a material culture similar to that of the Treveri, although Caesar and Tacitus group the Ubii with the Germans. The close contacts with the Treveri in the Neuwied basin on either side of the confluence of the Rhine and Moselle could explain some cultural similarity.

Pre-Roman religion and social order

The segmentary social structure of Gallic and Germanic societies is reflected in their religious organisation. Although most of our information on Iron Age gods, goddesses and cult organisation stems from Roman sources, both archaeological and textual, cults appear to have been organised on the tribal and subtribal level. At all levels priests were allied to

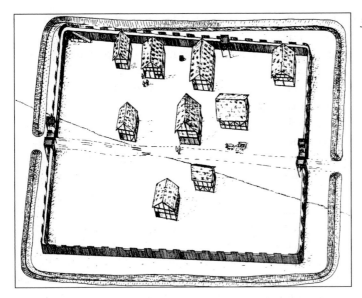

3 *The fortified Romano-Celtic village at Westheim in the later first century BC. From H. Cüppers, Die Römer in Rheinland-Pfalz, 1990, fig. 22*

the cults and performed public rituals. An example of a tribal cult is that of Lenus who was revered as chief god by the Treveri, as was Camulus by the Remi, Caturix by the Helvetii and Segomo by the Sequani, all of these in the Roman period being equated with Mars. Other native Mars gods were worshipped on subtribal levels, for example Loucetius (Mars Loucetius), who was the tutelary god of the Aresaces, a subtribe of the Treveri. The subtribal groups functioned as relatively autonomous cult communities, but they were also part of the larger religious organisation. Cult rituals were executed on the tribal level in which representatives from the districts participated, as they did at the central sanctuary of Lenus Mars at Trier-Irminenwingert. The Germanic Suebi, composed of many subtribes, had a hierarchical religious structure in which one god was seen to be the highest. In this case, the highest ranked god was that of the Semnones who were considered the most ancient and most noble of the Suebian subtribes. Cults were also organised by small local groups, a prime example being the Matronae, or ancestral mothers, worshipped on the lower Rhine by village communities, clans and kin-groups.

In many cases, leadership, wealth, political and religious administration were controlled by the same, often small, group of nobles within society, linking all components in a varied whole. The illusion of a natural line of aristocratic succession and the legend of divine descent of the ancestors of the nobility was passed on from generation to generation. According to Tacitus (*Germania* 2), Mannus, son of the god Tuisto, was the divine ancestor of the Germanic people. His three sons gave their names to three tribes: the Ingaevones, the Herminones and the Istaevones, all of them largely mythical. Tacitus also says that some believed that Mannus had more descendants who founded the tribes of the Marsi, Gambrivii, Suebi and Vandilii. Those with the most ancient and noble genealogy, like the Semnones of the Suebi, and by association the elite of the Semnones, were closest to the divine origin. Power within the tribe and its sub-groups was, thus, passed down through mortal representatives whose claim to superior status was justified and even god-given. Cult rituals confirmed and renewed the validity of this status, since only the elites were entitled to hold the office of priest and perform them. Nevertheless, religion was not simply another means of wielding power for the elites in society. The elites, too, were part of a larger social and ideological community of gods and spirits, and neither institutionalised power nor divine descent and nobility made them immune to internecine struggles and usurpation by others claiming equal distinction.

Since the elites after the Roman conquest played a key role in the spread of Romanisation, their contribution to the assimilation of native and Roman religion should not be underestimated. Cults of syncretised native and Roman gods involved the active participation of native elites who determined which cults were public and which were private, and in their role as magistrates they established the religious calendar of the community. A divine and common ancestry could be constructed to fuse native and Roman religious and political ideologies. Identity could be redefined by making conscious links with Rome through a constructed origin myth. The Remi, for example, in their official public cult of Mars Camulus conceptualised their tutelary deity as a Roman Mars and interwove their myths of origin and Trojan ancestry with those of Rome. Not only the Remi, but also the Aedui and the Arverni incorporated the legendary past of Rome in their own mythological origin. The tribal god of the Batavi, Magusanus, was transformed into Hercules Magusanus, and we can see deliberate constructions linking native groups with Rome in the myth repeated by Tacitus (*Germania* 3) that the Germanic peoples were once visited by Hercules, and even Ulysses. The latter, in his wanderings, was said to have reached the Rhine and founded the town of *Asciburgium*/Moers-Asberg. The appropriation of Roman myths, gods and ideas was not limited to the native elite in their expression of the official *civitas* cults, but is also reflected in the private devotions of members of society on a lower level. Nevertheless, whilst gods such as Mars and Hercules, and double-named versions thereof, were recipients of votive dedications on tribal and subtribal levels in Gallic and Germanic areas, others such as Mercury and Apollo appear to have been of local importance and the object of private veneration.

In the next chapter we will look at the conflicts between indigenous peoples and the Romans and what immediate impact the Roman conquest had on the Gaulish and Germanic regions, particularly in regard to the rearrangement of population groups and transformation of political and territorial structures.

2 Conquest and frontiers

After these events Caesar had every reason to suppose that Gaul was at peace again, for the Belgae were defeated, the Germans driven out, and the Seduni in the Alpine region conquered (Caesar, *De Bello Gallico* 3.7).

(Tiberius) himself had been sent nine times into Germany by the deified Augustus, and he had effected more by policy than by force. Policy had procured the Sugambrian surrender, policy had bound the Suebi and King Maroboduus to keep the peace. The Cherusci and the other rebel tribes, now that enough had been done for Roman vengeance, might similarly be left to their internal strife (Tacitus, *Annales* 2.26).

Caesar's Gallic War and the aftermath

In 59 BC Gaius Julius Caesar became governor of Illyricum and Gallia Cisalpina as well as Gallia Narbonensis for a term of five years. With this post came the command of three legions. All the events of the subsequent years of war in Gaul are recorded only in Caesar's accounts. The obvious bias of information on the conquered provided by the conqueror is not unproblematic and the numbers of people involved in the conflicts may not be reliable, but the sequence of events may be generally accurate. Since the borders of Gallia Narbonensis touched the limits of territory controlled by other Gallic tribes, the Aedui, Sequani and Helvetii, serious trouble brewing between these three was seen as a danger to the Roman state. It was also a welcome opportunity for Caesar to pursue his own personal ambitions under the guise of acting as the saviour of 'his' part of the Empire. In addition, the Germanic search for land in Gaul contributed to the fear of upheaval, a fear that proved to be warranted. In their desire to gain control over the Aedui, the Sequani had engaged German tribes under the Suebian king Ariovistus as mercenaries. In 62 BC, the Aedui were defeated, but Ariovistus turned against the Sequani and demanded one third of their territory in return. In response to this, the Sequani called upon the Romans to assist them in driving out the Germans. The Suebi had already made incursions into Gaul before this, forcing the Helvetii into a compact territory between the Alps and the Rhine. In 58 the Helvetii decided to leave the confines of their lands and migrate further west into Gaul. They burnt all their settlements and took enough provisions with them for the march they were to embark upon through Gallia Narbonensis. The Helvetii persuaded the Sequani to let them pass through their lands, and by the time Caesar appeared on the scene with the necessary number of troops, the Helvetii were already in the territory of the Aedui, pillaging and raiding where they went. In a battle near Bibracte, the Helvetii were routed and forced by the Romans to return to their homes with their allies, the Rauraci, Latobrigi and Tulingi. They were ordered to reoccupy their lands and rebuild their settlements, so as not to leave a dangerous vacuum into which German tribes could slip and gain a further foothold in Gaul. The death toll for the Helvetii and their allies was high. Of the original 368,000 men, women and children who had begun the march, only 110,000 returned. The events following this encounter are summarily described below to illustrate the extent of upheaval in Gaul. They are the events as recorded by Caesar.

Caesar next turned his attention to Ariovistus' army of Seubi, Harudes, Marcomanni, Triboci, Vangiones, Nemetes and Sedusii. Engaging the Suebi and their allies near *Vesontio*/Besançon, the capital of the Sequani, the Romans defeated them soundly, driving the remaining survivors of the battle across the Rhine.

In 57 the Belgic tribes and west-bank Germans, fearing that they would be next on Caesar's list, joined forces for battle. This alliance consisted of the Bellovaci, Suessiones, Nervii, Atrebates, Ambiani, Morini, Menapii, Caleti, Veliocasses, Viromandui, Aduatuci, Condrusi, Eburones, Caerosi and Paemani, some 246,000 men. One by one, the tribes were forced to surrender to the six Roman legions and Treveran auxiliary troops, but the Nervii, Atrebates and Viromandui held out the longest. In a fierce battle, the Nervii were defeated, bringing 'the name and nation of the Nervii almost to utter destruction' (Caesar, *De Bello Gallico* 2.28). The Aduatuci were beaten into submission, with 4000 killed and 53,000 sold into slavery.

After defeating the coastal Veneti in 56, Caesar marched against the Morini and Menapii, but it was not until the following year that they surrendered. In the winter of 55, it was again the Suebi who caused disruption east of the Rhine, driving out the Usipetes and Tencteri who fled to Menapian, Eburonean and Condrusian territories. Somewhere near the Maas a battle took place in which the Romans drove the 430,000 Usipetes and Tencteri back to the Rhine, large numbers of the enemy being killed or drowning in the river. The rest withdrew to the east bank of the Rhine to join the Sugambri. When told to surrender, the Sugambri replied that the Rhine marked the limit of the Roman Empire and that Caesar had no claim to imperial power across the Rhine. Although Caesar crossed the Rhine to hunt down the Sugambri, they retreated to their forests and robbed him of a victory.

After two expeditions to Britain in 55 and 54, Caesar returned to northern Gaul to find that the Eburones had declared war on Rome. Led in battle by Ambiorix and Catuvolcus, the Eburones destroyed one-and-a-half Roman legions. With the Roman forces reduced, the anti-Roman faction of the Treveri gathered allies around them, but the east-bank Germans did not join in. The Romans succeeded in putting down this revolt, leaving Gaul 'somewhat more tranquil' by the end of 54 (*De Bello Gallico* 5.58).

The next year the Treveri, Nervii, Aduatuci, Menapii and all east-bank Germans took up arms again. After subduing the Menapii and routing the Treveri, Caesar crossed the Rhine to seek out potential troublemakers, notably the Suebi, and give assistance to Rome's allies, the Ubii, against them. The whole operation was ineffective, since the Suebi retreated to the forests. His next encounter against the Eburones in 53, however, was very much more successful. Caesar's army scattered the population throughout the countryside and enticed the Sugambri to plunder and raid Eburonean lands, thus further weakening them. With his large force, Caesar set fire to every village and farmstead, drove off cattle and destroyed corn crops. It was not until 51, however, that the Eburones were finally annihilated, after Caesar had successfully fought against a coalition of Gaulish tribes led by the Arvernian Vercingetorix at Alesia in 52. The Roman army killed or captured a large number of the Eburonean population, set fire to and pillaged their land again. After various mopping-up operations against the Treveri and other Gaulish tribes, Caesar returned to Italy in 50, confident that he had left behind a Gaul which would not readily take up war again.

After eight years of war, Gaul was exhausted. Monetary resources were spent, many rebellious tribes had been killed or sold into slavery, some of the *oppida* and *castella* abandoned and rural settlements burnt and plundered. Caesar's departure and the subsequent civil war in Italy, however, hindered Rome for years from annexing and reorganising Gaul.

How are the events of the historical sources reflected in the archaeological evidence? The names of some of the hardest hit tribes in Gaul, particularly the Eburones and Aduatuci, were never heard again. Eburonean settlements, such as those at Niederzier, Eschweiler-Laurenzberg and Euskirchen-Kreuzweingarten, were permanently abandoned according to the excavated evidence. A very few farmsteads in former Eburonean territory west of the Cologne basin are known at which timber-aisled houses and granaries were built in the Germanic tradition, but these do not predate the end of the first century BC, suggesting that whatever percentage of the population had survived the Gallic war, they only very slowly recovered from the devastation. In contrast, continuity of occupation in post-Caesarian times is everywhere in evidence in Treveran territory. Some of the large *oppida*, the Titelberg for example, reached their greatest density of occupation and wealth after the war. Rural farmsteads like that at Mayen north of the Moselle continued to be inhabited throughout the second half of the first century BC, later being converted to a Roman-style villa. Within the territory of the Mediomatrici, farmsteads and accompanying burials from the period between 50 and 10 BC at Speyer, as well as a fortified village at Westheim (*see* **3**), built after the Gallic war, indicate that life went on in the middle Rhine valley. The Rauraci rebuilt their *oppidum* in Basel after 58 BC, but the archaeological evidence indicates that the location of it shifted from Basel-Gasfabrik to the Münsterhügel. The Helvetii did the same, relocating their pre-Caesarian *oppidum* at Mont Vully to the Bois de Châtel, and on the north shore of Lake Geneva at Lausanne a trading settlement developed in the last decades of the first century BC.

Only in the part of Gaul nearest to the province of Gallia Narbonensis were new Roman colonies established. Augst was founded in 44 BC in the territory of the Rauraci on the upper Rhine, and Nyon in Helvetian lands on Lake Geneva in 45. Both were located at geographically strategic points on routes giving access to the rest of Gaul. It was left to Augustus to reorganise Gaul and create a functioning administration.

Despite the destruction of the war, however, not all was quiet in Gaul after Caesar's departure. Recurring incursions of Suebi between the Rhine and the Moselle led M. Vipsanius Agrippa, the governor of Gaul from 39-37 BC, to cross the Rhine as a demonstration of Roman power. Elbe-Germanic material not indigenous to the Neuwied basin has been found in graves between that area and Krefeld-Gellep to the north, suggesting the presence of east Germanic groups, presumably the Suebi, at this time. In

29, further disruption, in which the Treveri were involved, was caused by the Suebi in eastern Gaul. During Agrippa's second period of office in 19, German attacks had to be repelled yet again, and in 17/16 Marcus Lollius and the 5th Legion were soundly defeated by groups of east-bank Sugambri, Usipetes and Tencteri who had crossed the Rhine. At the same time, Alpine tribes took up arms, which action in Roman sources was characteristically referred to as a 'revolt' (Cassius Dio, *Historia Romana* 54.20). Thus Augustus left the capital in 16 to go to Gaul, where he stayed until 13, to settle territorial disputes and plan the invasion of Germany.

Demographic reorganisation under Augustus

One of the most profound changes brought about by Augustus was the reshuffling of the cards in terms of the native population. During his reign, whole tribes were relocated from their old homelands to new ones, Roman strategic interests always determining who went where (**4**). The devastation of Eburonean territory between Ardennes, Eifel, Maas and Rhine, and associated depopulation, even if not total, left a dangerous gap in north-east Gaul. In order to fill this gap, the Germanic Ubii from the Lahn valley east of the Rhine in modern Hessen were transplanted to the old Eburonean homeland. The Ubii had been one of the few tribes during the Gallic War who had shown unflagging loyalty to the Roman cause, supporting Caesar in his endeavours against the other transrhenine Germans. They had asked Caesar for deliverance from the Suebi, but it was not until some time after 39 BC under Agrippa that the Ubii were actually allowed to cross the Rhine and settle there. Tacitus (*Germania* 28) says that Agrippa himself was responsible for protecting the Ubii on their migration into Gaul, and he also reveals why this was done: 'They crossed the river many years ago, and as they had given proof of their loyalty to Rome they were stationed close to the west bank, to keep out intruders, not to be kept under surveillance themselves'. This was the same policy that dictated Caesar's insistence that the Helvetii return in 58 to reoccupy their lands and restore their towns and villages: 'His chief reason for doing so was that he did not wish the district which the Helvetii had left to be unoccupied, lest the excellence of the farmlands might tempt the Germans who dwell across the Rhine to cross from their own into the Helvetian borders, and so to become neighbours to the Province of Gaul and to the Allobroges' (*De Bello Gallico* 1.28).

Other west-bank German tribes associated with the Eburones, such as the Segni, disappear in name, but like the remaining Eburones they were probably absorbed by other larger groups. Some of them were almost certainly absorbed by the Ubii, others are probably to be found with the Tungri who appear as a new group in former Aduatucan territory and who likely included surviving Aduatuci. On the northern fringes of the Ardennes were now the Sunuci, a tribe or subtribe not known to Caesar. They, too, may have been part of the larger group of Eburones. After repeated conflict with the east-bank Sugambri, most recently in 12/11 BC, 40,000 members of this group were resettled on the west bank of the lower Rhine in 8 BC. It is thought that these Sugambri in part made up the Cugerni and Baetasii who from the early first century AD controlled the area opposite the mouth of the Lippe river.

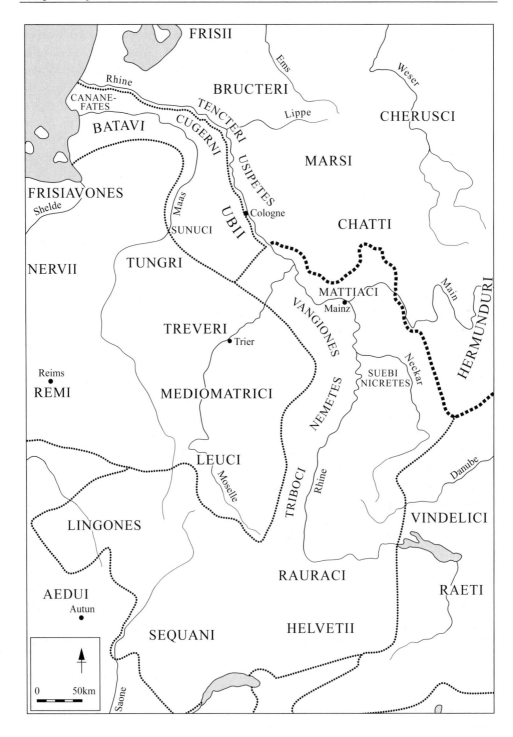

4   *Map showing main tribal territories in the German provinces*

Further population shifts on the lower Rhine and Rhine delta took place in the late first century BC which, if not prompted by official Roman policy, must have occurred with Roman sanction. The Batavi, formerly a segment of the Chatti in Hessen, settled north of the Tungri and Ubii in the eastern Dutch Rhine delta. The favourable treaty conditions negotiated with the Romans suggest that the Batavi had not offered stiff resistance and may have actively sought inclusion within the Empire. The Cananefates, now just west of the Batavi on the Rhine delta, may also have been a sub-group of the Chatti. The Menapii lost part of their northern territory to be replaced by the Frisiavones, however the Sturii and Marsaci who settled on the islands in the Rhine delta may have been Menapian sub-groups.

Among the Suebian Ariovistus' allies in the Gallic war were the Triboci, Nemetes and Vangiones, other east-bank Germans. Tacitus records them in AD 98 as holding the west bank of the Rhine. The earliest Germanic finds related to the Elbe-Germanic culture appear around Speyer (later *civitas Nemetum*) and Worms (later *civitas Vangionum*) in the last decade of the first century BC, suggesting that these groups were resettled at approximately the same time as the Sugambri to hold the border zone. These new territories had to be detached from the Mediomatrici who thereby lost their riverbank lands.

On the other side of the Rhine, the population from south of the Main to around the mouth of the Neckar appears also to have been of Suebian/Elbe-Germanic origin. Their presence from the late first century BC/early first century AD at sites such as Ladenburg and Mannheim-Wallstadt is archaeologically attested. It is assumed that these settlers were placed here under Roman supervision, charged with holding the eastern fringe of Gaul. They later gave their name, *Suebi Nicretes* (Neckar Suebi), to the region. North of the Main settled the Mattiaci, probably also under Roman control. One of their settlements at Hofheim was superceded by a Roman fort built between 20 and 40.

A map showing the tribal distribution in Gaul and Germany at the time of Caesar looks quite different from one reflecting the changes initiated by Augustus (**5**). After the Gallic war, and especially with significant interference from the Roman state, the population found itself in a state of flux. Sub-groups of tribes could disappear, to re-emerge allied with another group, both then appearing under a different name. In many cases it is difficult, if not impossible, to recognise anything in the material remains of late Iron Age and early Roman tribal groups which is characteristic to one or the other of them. We cannot even begin to imagine how disruptive these migrations and transfers were, whether they were as punishment for resistance to the Romans or as rewards for loyal behaviour. It was a tremendous achievement to move so many peoples and seriously alter the demographic structure of northern Gaul and the Rhineland. Whilst the sheer effort of this restructuring by the Romans commands great respect, the toll in disorientation and loss of independence of the native populations should not be forgotten. Uprooted peoples not only had to deal with the removal from their homelands, but also with remnants of possibly antagonistic indigenous populations in the new lands and with the ever-present representatives of the Roman state.

To render the conquered lands and their peoples a controllable part of the Empire, Augustus introduced profound administrative reforms, dividing Gaul into self-governing *civitas* territories and establishing administrative capitals in each of them. Before this was

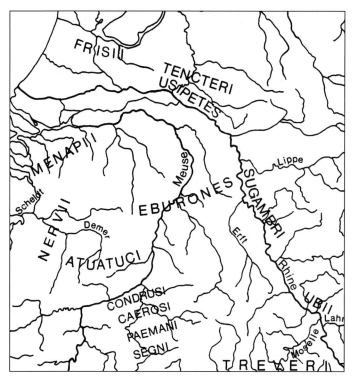

5a Tribal distribution in northern Gaul under Caesar

possible, however, Augustus was compelled to lead military campaigns into regions north of the Alps and to Germany east of the Rhine, which aimed to protect Roman interests and lead to stability.

Roads for the army

It was clear to Augustus that the northern frontier needed to be secured, and in order to do that access from Italy to the north had to be guaranteed. Typically, the Alps were said to be 'filled with wild and barbarous tribes' (Velleius Paterculus, *Historia Romana* 2.90.1). In 25 BC the Alpine passes of Great and Little St Bernard were brought under Roman control, and in 15 BC mountain passes in the east were made accessible after the conquest of Raetia. Through them Roman troops could be shifted to northern Gaul and Germany. Between 15 BC and 12 BC large concentrations of troops were stationed along the Rhine from which military offensives were launched into Germany beyond the Rhine. It was from here that a permanent threat emanated, and a defensive policy of blocking Germanic expansion at the Rhine was not sufficient.

A necessary prerequisite for moving troops was the building of a network of roads. Agrippa had already begun to extend a north-east route from Lyon to the Moselle and beyond that to Cologne and a north-west route to the Atlantic coast via Autun and Beauvais. Another main east-west axis in use from that time went from the Atlantic coast via Bavay to Cologne. These roads were laid out by Roman troops stationed in Gaul, in

5b Tribal distribution in northern Gaul under Augustus

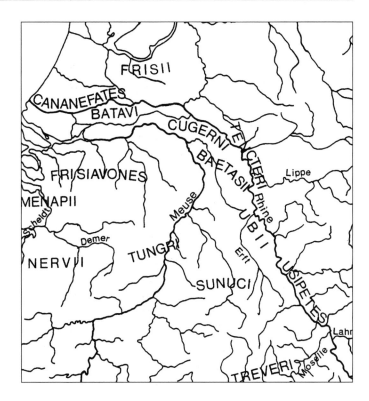

particular in Aquitania and in the lands of the Lingones and Remi. The important Rhine valley route along the west bank began in Vindonissa, passing by Strasbourg, Mainz, Cologne, Xanten and Nijmegen to Katwijk on the North Sea coast. This road connected not only the Alpine region with the North Sea, but also the military bases along the Rhine with each other. There is no compelling reason to assume that the Agrippan building of roads took place as early as his first governorship in AD 39 before the Alpine regions were brought under Roman control. The Bavay-Cologne route was in use from around 20 BC, and archaeological finds at Tongeren and Liberchies on that road date to the second decade of that century. However, it is very difficult to date the road system, and it may be that parts of it do date back to Agrippa's earlier period of office. When Augustus decided that the German threat could only be dealt with by crossing the Rhine and tackling the Germans head on, the Rhine route became extremely important for launching campaigns in that direction.

The network of Alpine roads was not substantially improved or extended until the mid-first century AD by Claudius, and even then many of the roads were only wheel ruts cut into the rock. The earliest milestones along the road through the Great St Bernard pass date to AD 47, and a year before that the route over the Reschenpass into the Alpine foreland to Augsburg was laid out. Although initially the roads in northern Gaul were constructed to facilitate troop movements, they were also the essential line of communication and travel for the civilian population. Early Roman towns such as Billig, Jülich and Heerlen in Germania Inferior, to name only three, owed their existence and importance to their position on overland routes, particularly at the intersection of main roads (**6**). Likewise early Roman settlements like those at Solothurn and Olten on the Aare and Pontailler-sur-Sâone grew up where important rivers were narrow enough to bridge and overland routes crossed them. This trend continued in the second century when new roads were laid out in annexed territory east of the Rhine. Small market settlements like Wiesloch near Heidelberg on the artery parallel to the Rhine are characteristic of this later development.

The state had a vital interest in the security and condition of the roads, and it ensured that communications, travel, transport and the exaction of customs duties proceeded in an orderly and effective manner by posting police units at intervals along the roads. These units consisted of a body of selected legionary soldiers, *beneficiarii*, seconded by the provincial governor for fixed periods of service and posted at road stations to provide security on the roads and oversee tax collection. *Beneficiarii* stations were a compound of buildings within a walled enclosure in roadside locations. Isolated *beneficiarii* stations are known on the road leading from Strasbourg to the Danube (Geislingen, Schenkzell-Brandsteig), on the artery from Basel to Mainz (Friesenheim) and outside many forts on the upper German frontier where military and civilian traffic was heavy. On the road outside the auxiliary fort at Osterburken on this frontier was a complex of timber buildings and a sanctuary within which stood a temple and numerous stone altars dedicated by the *beneficiarii* posted there between 178 and 238. On the lower Rhine such stations were often associated with a small roadside settlement, for example at Jülich, Zülpich and Billig. *Beneficiarii* oversaw activities at the commercially important small town at Ehl on the overland route between Strasbourg and Biesheim in Tribocian territory. *Beneficiarii* posts were also occasionally located outside principal towns such as the colonies of Cologne and Augst where they acted as control points for traffic leading into the town.

Augustan campaigns into Germany

One of the earliest forts associated with the military expeditions against the Germans is the base of the 19th Legion at Dangstetten on the north bank of the upper Rhine. The site was chosen in 15 BC as an ideal starting point for advancing northwards to the Danube and the Neckar. The post-Caesarian Rauracan settlement in Basel-Münsterhügel was cleared around the same time, and a Roman fort erected, possibly also in preparation for the German campaigns.

In 12 BC, attacks against the Germans were launched by Augustus' nephew Drusus. The operational bases of these campaigns were at Mainz on the middle Rhine, *Vetera*/Xanten, Neuss and Nijmegen on the lower Rhine. The base at Mainz was situated opposite the mouth of the Main river, that at Xanten opposite the Lippe, both rivers giving access to the heart of enemy German territory and converging upon the Weser and Elbe rivers. The Augustan forts east of the Rhine were also located on rivers (Lippe, Lahn, Main) to facilitate the transport of foodstuffs and supplies necessary for the campaigns in regions in which, unlike Gaul, an existing supply infrastructure could not be depended upon. In the first two years of the campaigns, the Sugambri and Usipetes were the targets of unsuccessful expeditions. In 11, a base on the Lippe itself and another in the territory of the Chatti, who had moved into former Ubian lands, were established. The Lippe base

6   *Small towns in roadside and*
    riverside locations at Heerlen
    (Netherlands), Kembs (France),
    Olten (Switzerland), and Billig
    (Germany)

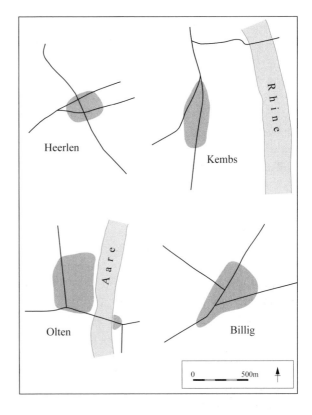

named in the written sources is usually assumed to have been that at Oberaden, whose timber rampart was built from trees felled late in the summer of 11. A fort at Rödgen in the Wetterau was built as a supply depot, probably in 11/10 BC. The launching point for the campaign against the Chatti, Marcomanni and the Cherusci in 9 was the base at Mainz. Drusus marched as far east as the Elbe, without crossing it. Drusus is hailed by Velleius Paterculus (*Historia Romana* 2.97.3) as the great conqueror of Germany, an equally great exaggeration, since the German campaigns had to be resumed some years thereafter.

Augustus' stepson, Tiberius, assumed command of the Rhine army after the death of Drusus. Details of his campaigns in 8 BC are vague, but it is certain that he defeated the Sugambri. According to Velleius (*Historia Romana* 2.97.3), Tiberius was close to making Germany a tributary province of Rome, and although this is an exaggeration, we may understand the remark to mean that many of the troublesome German tribes by then had been defeated or pacified to the point that treaties, however binding, could be struck between them and Rome. Rome, at this point, regarded Germany up to the Elbe as part of the Empire. Tiberius returned in 7 to Rome, and the bases at Dangstetten, Rödgen and Oberaden were abandoned at the same time. We cannot assume, however, that all bases were given up, leaving the newly conquered Germans to their own devices.

This was by no means the end of the story. Campaigns were fought some time after 6 BC against the Hermunduri in Mainfranken, and a battle against the Cherusci from the Weser region was lost. In 3 BC, Domitius Ahenobarbus advanced to the Elbe without a fight, and was the first to finally cross this magical line. For reasons unknown, many

Germanic groups between the Rhine and the Elbe rose up against the Romans in AD 1. Tiberius returned in 4, and in this year and the next fought numerous battles by land and sea against the Cananefates, Bructeri, Cherusci and Chauci. The focal point of these campaigns was clearly the northern regions beyond the Rhine. The new governor, P. Quinctilius Varus, assumed command of the Roman army in 6 or 7, but his lack of military experience and heavy-handedness with the native population cost the Roman Empire dearly. Trusting Arminius, the leader of the Cherusci, Varus and three Roman legions were drawn into their territory in 9 to distribute soldiers to various communities which had asked for their help in establishing peaceful conditions. Once spread out in the inextricable forests and marshes of Cheruscan territory, the 17th, 18th and 19th legions, as well as thousands of auxiliary troops, were ambushed and slaughtered by a tribal federation of Rhine and Weser Germans. This was an unparalleled defeat for Rome, and one which Augustus lamented for many years. The site of the famous battle has now been located at the narrow pass at Kalkriese between hills and marsh, and ongoing excavations have revealed a scattering of finds left by the troops and the Germanic plunderers over a distance of 6 miles (10km).

What of the military bases established in this last phase of the German campaigns? The line of forts along the Rhine, especially the Dutch lower Rhine, was strengthened by new camps, their number increasing from three to ten. A number of camps along the Lippe are known, but none of them can be as securely dated as Oberaden without dendrochronological evidence. The legionary base at Haltern was built between 7/5 BC and AD 1, and Anreppen, the most easterly of the Lippe bases, dates to the early first century AD, possibly the year 4. It was probably established as an operational base for campaigns along the Weser, evidence for which in the form of other camps on the river and even beyond is as yet lacking. That they must exist, however, is clear from the intentions of the Romans to incorporate German territory beyond the Weser to the Elbe and by Florus' remarks that Drusus set up camps on the Maas, Weser and Elbe (*Epitome* 2.30.26). Haltern was built as a permanent base for an occupation army, not a marching one. The base had a stores depot, an auxiliary fort and a harbour fort, an extensive cemetery with high status barrow tombs (**7**) and, most revealingly, a settlement (*canabae*) outside the walls for civilian followers. A base with civilian dependants suggests that the Romans considered the region to be pacified and safe enough to allow this kind of settlement. Moreover, the relatively large number of officers' quarters in the fort has been interpreted as an indication that Haltern was the seat of the military administration for the annexed German territory.

Of great interest in this regard are two recently discovered Augustan bases in northern Hessen. One of these in the Lahn valley at Dorlar was a temporary marching camp, possibly laid out during Drusus' campaigns. Only about a mile (2km) distant from Dorlar, a permanent base was established at Waldgirmes in the first decade of the first century AD, probably to control the Lahn valley and access to the Wetterau. It was so clearly built for permanency that as the excavations progress at the site there is increasing doubt whether Waldgirmes is a fort rather than a civilian settlement. It is currently referred to in publications, rather neutrally, simply as a '*Stützpunkt*' (base). The building originally interpreted as the headquarters building (*principia*) was constructed on stone foundations,

7 *Aerial view of an excavated barrow tomb outside the legionary base at Haltern, Germany.* Courtesy Westfälisches Römermuseum Haltern

not the normal timber of other Augustan forts, and the plan of the building also has greater similarity with a civilian forum (**8**). The stone used in building came from the Metz area on the upper Moselle river. The other buildings flanking the streets bear little resemblance to military barracks. The site even had a water supply system consisting of pipes made of lead from the Eifel, and in some prominent position within the settlement stood a gilt bronze statue, of which fragments survive, possibly of Augustus himself. Taken as a whole, the site clearly must have had a special status and, like Haltern, was deemed to be in an area safe enough for longer-term, comfortable occupation. The very high percentage of handmade, Germanic pottery found at the site suggests that a local population was supplying the troops with at least some provisions and cooperating peacefully with them. One is reminded of Cassius Dio's remarks that at the time Varus became governor of Germany east of the Rhine towns were being founded and the local people were becoming accustomed to hold markets (*Historia Romana* 56.18). Only further excavations can shed light on the nature of the occupation at Waldgirmes.

The creation of the frontier

After the disaster of AD 9, all forts east of the Rhine were given up. Tiberius strengthened the defences along the Rhine and concentrated eight legions on it. The Rhine was divided into two military zones, one on the lower Rhine and one on the upper Rhine. It was not until 15 that further campaigns were undertaken into Germany. All eight legions were then sent from *Vetera*/Xanten and Mainz against the Cherusci and Chatti, but there were many close calls for the Roman forces and there was no decisive battle. After another unsuccessful year of war, Tiberius decided to end all attempts at conquest. The effort and cost of further campaigns were too high. The Germans were to be left, in Tiberius' words,

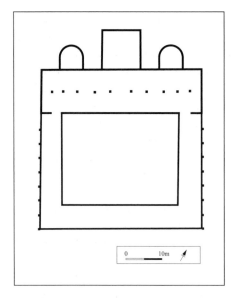

0 _____ 10m

*8 Possible forum building with stone
foundations at the Augustan settlement
at Waldgirmes, Germany*

to their own internal disputes and the Rhine, at least the lower Rhine, was from then on the frontier of the Empire. The strip of land about 6 miles (10km) wide on right bank, however, was still considered to be Roman territory, at the beginning for the use of the military, but by the late first/early second century also allowing Germanic settlements. At Rees opposite Xanten, for example, the late Iron Age settlement, possibly a Sugambrian one, remained unoccupied in the first century AD and was not resettled until the second or third century. The Rhine as a natural frontier was by no means an impenetrable boundary in regard to exchange and contact (chapter 5).

Four legions protected the lower Rhine in *Vetera*, Neuss and Bonn. These were supplemented with about 20,000 auxiliary troops. Under Claudius (41-54), the chain of forts along the Rhine was added to, and any gaps in the chain were finally filled by Vespasian (69-79). By then, the frontier, the function of which was defence, was guarded by four legionary forts, a fleet base and 27 auxiliary forts. On the upper Rhine, the frontier developed in a very different manner.

As part of Tiberius' defensive policy, legionary bases were established at Strasbourg and Vindonissa, the former to guard the Belfort gap giving access to the interior of Gaul, and the latter to control the crossing of the river Aare. The other two legions were stationed at Mainz. A Roman bridgehead was established in the early decades of the first century AD east of the Rhine in the Wetterau, consisting of forts at Hofheim and Wiesbaden. Under Vespasian, new territorial gains were made on the upper Rhine. From Mainz expeditions into the Wetterau were launched and the region south of the Main river militarily occupied with bases at Heddernheim and Friedberg. Forts such as that at Rottweil and Heidelberg were built along the Neckar. Domitian opened his campaigns against the Chatti in 83, but in difficult terrain the Roman forces could not gain the upper hand, even after two years. Nevertheless, after 85 the Chatti were to be separated from east-bank Roman territory in the Wetterau and Taunus and kept out of it by the construction of the *limes*. At this stage, the *limes* was nothing more than a wide strip cleared of trees and controlled by timber observation towers one kilometre apart. After a second war against the Chatti in 89, the *limes* was extended further south from the Main river through the Odenwald and new forts for auxiliary troops as well as fortlets and towers were built. This linear installation has traditionally been attributed to Domitian, but a recent reappraisal of the evidence makes a Trajanic date between 105 and 115 more likely. Contemporaneous with the redeployment of troops from the interior and from the newly won Dacian war to the *limes* was the establishment of new civilian settlements where the army had been (see chapter 3). Under Hadrian (117-38) the *limes* was strengthened by a timber palisade and in a last 'correction' of the frontier under Antoninus Pius (138-61) it was pushed 18 miles (30km) further east. The provision of forts with masonry defensive walls, such as that at the Saalburg, often dates to this period (**colour plate 3**). The timber observation towers were replaced by stone towers in the second half of the second century, and a ditch and bank built between palisade and towers (**colour plate 4**). At the southernmost fort at Lorch, the *limes* turned east to form the Raetian frontier up to the Danube.

The *limes* at all times was a system of interconnected outposts controlling the military road and rivers along the frontier and acting as a line of communications. It was much more a demarcation line than a barrier, and it was never built to withstand serious, large-scale attacks from without. The military road from Strasbourg across the Rhine to the Danube was a major route under the protection of forts and fortlets along the *limes*. Movement from beyond the frontier could be channelled through control points, particularly important for trade and exchange, and enemy activity could be detected and checked. Trade and exchange with Germanic groups outside the *limes* is indicated by frequent Roman imports of the second and third centuries at sites north and east of the *limes* (chapter 5). The *limes* cut off old pre-Roman routes that led from the Rhine to the interior of Germany, but these routes continued to be travelled now under the supervision and control of the military. The maintenance of a zone of peaceful contact and exchange beyond the *limes* was almost certainly part of the Roman frontier policy.

The German lands between the Rhine and the *limes*, known as the *Agri Decumates*, were annexed (the conquest of Germany taking place on a much smaller scale than originally planned), and in the area Gallic settlers were allowed and probably encouraged to live amongst the already present Germans. Tacitus has little to say about these settlers that is positive: 'All the most disreputable characters in Gaul, all the penniless adventurers, seized on a territory that was a kind of no man's land' (*Germania* 29). A Celtic/Gallic substrate in the population of the *Agri Decumates* appears to have remained constant at about 15% from the late first to the third century AD, if the known personal names from the region are a reliable indicator. The roughly equal spacing of the new *civitas* capitals and market villages in between them suggests that the settlement pattern was centrally planned as part of an immigration and occupation programme of the *Agri Decumates* in the early second century.

Even though Tacitus (*Historiae* 1.16) called Gaul in AD 68 an unarmed province and other sources are often silent on the subject of a military presence in the Gallic interior, it would be erroneous to believe that the Roman army was limited to the frontier zone along the Rhine or along the upper German *limes*. If military strength was deemed necessary in Gaul, as it was in the few years following Nero's death, forts were built which rivalled those of the frontier. The legionary base at Mirebeau near Dijon, for example, was planted in Lingonian territory by Vespasian in 70, and it was not until 90 that the garrison, Legio VIII, was transferred from there to Strasbourg and the Mirebeau fort abandoned. Near Dijon a camp at the La Noue site was established around 70, and at Biesheim an army detachment continued to be present after the establishment of the *limes* until the late third century. The legions stationed on the Rhine moreover were just as much designed to check problems in Gaul as they were in Germany. Tacitus' remark that 'the German garrison was ready to cope indifferently with the German or the Gaul' makes this clear (*Annales* 4.5.2).

Augustus and Germany: defence or offence?

Opinion is divided on Augustus' aims and intentions regarding the conquest of Germany. Was he, as Colin Wells asserts, an open imperialist who aimed at permanent conquest of Germany from the beginning, or were his campaigns merely a reaction to the defeat of Lollius and the 5th Legion in 16 BC with the aim of pushing back the Germans to establish a permanent defensive frontier along the Elbe? If Augustus' policy was a defensive one, then it was a very aggressive form of defence. The period from 15 BC to AD 9 was one of large-scale expeditions, massive troop deployment and territorial conquest. The concerted efforts to make a show of strength up to the Elbe, and even beyond by crossing it, tells us that it was an ideologically and strategically important goal for conquest. Although Velleius' remarks that Tiberius by 7 BC had just about made Germany a tributary province proved to be miscalculated they may reflect a situation the Romans perceived to be true. All evidence points to the intention to do just that in the years following. It appears that civilian settlements and cooperation with the local population at Haltern and Waldgirmes did take place. In Cologne a national sanctuary of Rome and Augustus was established around the birth of Christ. This was based on the pan-Gallic sanctuary of 12 BC at Lyon at which delegates from all tribes in Gaul met in annual assemblies. One of the priests of the cult-centre in Cologne in AD 9 was a Cheruscan, suggesting that all German tribes, including those east of the Rhine, were to be united in a larger German province with its political and religious centre in Cologne. Varus was sent not to carry out further military campaigns — he was too inexperienced for this — but to prepare the way for transforming Germany into a Roman province. He had been appointed to impose taxation and expedite the process of making Germany governable. If he proceeded too quickly, it was surely not his fault, but the ultimate responsibility of the state. The whole chain of events, involving preparation for conquest, military campaigns, permanent garrisons of army units, imposition of taxation, is no different from any other attempt to enlarge the Empire through annexation anywhere else.

None of this points to a purely defensive Augustan policy. After the Varian disaster, however, Augustus realised that the annexation of Germany was unrealistic, at least for the time being, advising Tiberius in 14 to leave the boundaries of the Empire where they were. This *was* defensive policy. Enough first-hand experience had been gained to see that the regions between the Rhine and Elbe could not be subjugated or held in the long run. Only in rare cases had the Romans been able to form alliances with the elite of German tribes. The underdeveloped social hierarchy of most of the tribes was not suitable for the kind of cooperation aimed at the top of the pyramid in society which had been successfully applied to Celtic societies. The Germans before Augustus had not been content to stay behind the Rhine, and there was no reason to believe that other German tribes the Romans had only recently encountered, and many more they had not yet even met, were prepared to stay behind the Elbe. By 16, Tiberius had taken the advice given to him by Augustus on his deathbed.

3 Administration and urbanisation

It is well known that none of the German tribes lives in cities and that they do not even allow houses to touch one another. They live separately and scattered, according as spring, meadow or grove appeals to each man. They lay out their villages not after our fashion with buildings contiguous and connected. Everyone keeps a clear space around his house (Tacitus, *Germania* 27).

Were there ever so many cities, inland and maritime? Were they ever so thoroughly modernised? . . . You may contrast the tribe of the past with the city there today. Indeed, it may be said that they were virtually kings of wilderness and fortresses, while you alone govern cities (Aelius Aristides, *To Rome* 93).

Province, *civitas*, town

After the defeat of Varus and his legions in 9 the heavily militarised zone along the Rhine was divided into an upper and lower Rhine district. Between 82 and 90, probably in the year 85, these districts were formally reorganised into two provinces: Germania Inferior and Germania Superior. The boundaries of the provinces have been outlined in chapter 1 (*see* **1**). The creation of the German provinces lagged behind that of the Gallic provinces by decades. Gallia Narbonensis had officially become a province in 27 BC, followed by the division of the rest of Gaul into three provinces, the *Tres Galliae*: Gallia Aquitania, Gallia Lugdunensis and Gallia Belgica. Had Augustus' plans for conquest of Germany proceeded according to plan, however, the German provinces might have come into existence sooner and their boundaries developed along different lines. In fixing the borders of the German provinces, parts of Gaul were separated from the rest, but some of them had already been detached in setting up the military zone under Tiberius. Gallia Belgica lost its Rhineland, and the territories of the Lingones, Sequani and Helvetii now lay within the province of Germania Superior. The administrative capital of Germania Inferior was Cologne, that of Germania Superior Mainz. Both provinces were imperial provinces and under the direct jurisdiction of the emperor rather than the senate. The emperor's representative in each German province had the title of *legatus Augusti pro praetore*, and each legate or governor was not only the commander-in-chief of his provincial army, but also in charge of civil and judicial matters. In the Rhenish provinces, the legates served for periods of two or three years. About 50 of the 85 legates from the first to the third century in Cologne and Mainz are known by name; none of them was native to northern Gaul or Germany.

Gaul had been divided into territories (*civitates*), the Roman political boundaries of which, except for northern Gaul, generally corresponded to the pre-Roman ones. Most of the final touches on the drawing of *civitas* boundaries took place under Augustus. It is doubtful whether the north of Gaul, especially those parts in which peoples such as the Eburones and Aduatuci had been severely reduced in number and scope, was reorganised into *civitates* before the first census of Gaul in 27 BC. The most northerly *civitates* on the lower Rhine may not have been formalised until the later first century. The annexed east-bank lands up to the upper German *limes*, the *Agri Decumates*, were not organised into *civitates* until the time of Trajan, possibly after the *limes* as a line of military installations had been established between 105 and 115. The *civitas Ulpia Sueborum Nicrensium* around Ladenburg, *civitas Ulpia Taunensium* with Heddernheim as its centre and the *civitas Ulpia Mattiacorum* around Wiesbaden belong to this latter group.

Each *civitas* had one central seat of administration, the *civitas* capital. The rational choice of the location of a *civitas* capital was made under consideration of the Roman roads and waterways — an administrative capital had to be accessible — and of its relationship to the pre-Roman settlement pattern. The east-west overland route Bavay-Cologne would have been important for any towns, but especially *civitas* capitals (Arras, Bavay, Tongeren), as would the north-west (Amiens, Beauvais, Senlis) and north-east (Toul, Metz, Trier) roads. Langres, for example, lay on the intersection of the Lyon-Toul-Trier and the Reims-Besançon roads, and at least eight other roads in all directions converged upon the Lingonian *civitas* capital. Many of the *civitas* capitals also lay on rivers or the confluence of rivers (Cologne, Nijmegen, Besançon, Trier). Surprisingly few of the north Gaulish *civitas* capitals were located on the site of a pre-Roman Iron Age settlement. Langres, situated on a plateau, and Besançon on the Doubs river appear to be two of them. Often the site of an earlier settlement was shifted, not by any great distance, political geography determining where the Roman town would be laid out. This is the case, for example, with Avenches, transferred from the hill of Bois de Châtel to a site closer to the valley floor. Capitals such as Cologne, Nijmegen and Xanten were artificial creations with no pre-Roman predecessors. The civilian settlements which had grown up around Roman forts at Wiesbaden, Heddernheim and Ladenburg became the capitals of their *civitates* only after the forts were given up and the garrison moved on to the *limes*.

Within each *civitas* were smaller units, the *pagi*. These were districts corresponding to tribes or subtribal groups. Some of the *pagi* were regrouped under Augustus to become *civitates*, other *pagi* once part of a larger group could be split off and joined with another. This was probably the case with the *pagi* of the Eburones and Aduatuci who were regrouped with the Ubii, Tungri, Sunuci, Cugerni and so on. Likewise, the Aresaces and Caeracates in the area around Mainz were detached sub-groups of the Treveri.

Not all *civitates* were of equal status. Loyal allies like the Remi, Lingones and Ubii received federate status, meaning that they had treaties with Rome establishing their own rights. More neutral groups such as the Treveri were free *civitates*, theoretically exempt from interference by the governor of the province and immune from taxes. Tributary *civitates*, such as that of the Mediomatrici, were neither exempt from tax nor external interference. The three different grades of *civitates* involved these varying privileges, at least originally, but by the time of Tiberius the titles may technically only have been marks of status.

Superior in status to all *civitas* capitals were the full Roman colonies, the earliest being Nyon (45 BC), Augst (44 BC) and Lyon (43 BC). These were planned from the beginning as colonies, Augst and Nyon being built on virgin soil. Some *civitas* capitals could later be promoted to colonies, as was the case with Cologne and Trier under Claudius, Avenches under Vespasian, Xanten under Trajan and Besançon under Marcus Aurelius. This could, but did not necessarily, involve the release of veteran legionaries with full Roman citizenship into the community.

Devolution

The government of cities everywhere was based on a constitution. In the German provinces, self-governing cities were of three types: *coloniae*, *municipia* and *civitas* capitals. A *colonia* was made up of Roman citizens who annually elected senior and junior magistrates with various responsibilities. The two senior magistrates, *duoviri*, supervised the others and oversaw judicial matters. Two junior magistrates, *aediles*, were in charge of public works, and two further ones, *quaestores*, were responsible for financial affairs. The town council, *ordo*, was composed of 100 local senators or *decuriones*. In veteran colonies like Cologne, some of the earliest magistrates recorded were Roman citizens of Italian birth who retired here from the legions, but it is certain that others were members of the Ubian elite, resulting in a mixed group of magistrates. In Avenches, on the other hand, the names of the magistrates are native, suggesting that legionary veterans were not settled here. In a *municipium*, of which only very few examples are known in the German provinces (Rottweil, Voorburg-Arentsburg, Nijmegen and much later Mainz), the administration resembled that of a *colonia*. The difference was that a *municipium* had a greater proportion of non-Roman inhabitants than a colony, and these had Latin rather than Roman rights. The foundation charter included native laws and customs as well. Finally, the *civitas* capital was predominantly made up of people without Roman citizenship, the leading members of whom served as magistrates along the same lines as those in a colony.

In general, those who acted as magistrates in local government had to be wealthy, since much of the public works and maintenance of the *civitates* was paid for by them. Prerequisites for becoming a magistrate were land ownership and personal wealth of at least 100,000 *sesterces*. Any shortfall in the tax revenues assessed by the state had to be topped up by the *duoviri*, but at least in the first and second centuries the financial and social benefits of this post probably outweighed any potential danger of this kind. Although normally only the elite of the *civitas* could take on the responsibility of local government, there were exceptions, and in the third century in Nijmegen and Trier we know of traders and merchants serving as magistrates at a time when businessmen could have accumulated enough wealth to do so. The reasons for taking on the task of magistrate are threefold. Firstly, the native elites by co-operating with the Roman government maintained their position of prominence in society. The old patron-client system of the Iron Age, in which the aristocratic families distributed wealth and gifts to other leading tribal members and kin-groups to increase their status, was retained, only now the elite was spending fortunes on public displays of wealth in the community. Secondly, participation in local government meant that some degree of influence could be exerted upon matters pertaining to the interests of the tribe without leaving government solely to the Roman state. Thirdly, non-Roman magistrates serving in *municipia* and *civitas* capitals were awarded Roman citizenship upon termination of their period of office, a powerful incentive to seek out this distinction.

Apart from the *coloniae*, *municipia* and *civitas* capitals, *vici* existed throughout the provinces, and they took on many forms from villages to fully-fledged towns ranging in size from anywhere between 10-15 acres (4-6ha) (Olten, Basel) to around 250 acres (100ha) (Strasbourg). These small towns named in ancient sources are not always referred to specifically as *vici*. Of the many small towns in the Franche-Comté region in Sequanian territory, for example, only one, Villards-D'Héria, is attested as a *vicus* in an inscription. Districts within a city were referred to as *vici*; we know of a *vicus Lucretius* in Cologne and a *vicus Augustana* in Heddernheim, for example, but cannot identify the location of either. It is generally thought that the *vici* were not self-governing, but some form of local administration certainly existed. A *curator* or financial commissioner, for example, is known from the *vicus* at Mainz, and sometimes votive dedications were made by the inhabitants (*vicani*) of a *vicus* as a corporate body. In some cases, even a *civitas* capital could be a *vicus*, as is the case with all the main towns in the *Agri Decumates* (Wiesbaden, Heddernheim, Dieburg, Ladenburg, Baden-Baden, Wimpfen, Pforzheim, Rottenburg) and those in the west-bank *civitates* of the Triboci (Brumath), Nemetes (Speyer) and Vangiones (Worms). These *vici* certainly had administrative tasks for the whole *civitas*, and were in possession of a complete set of magistrates. The *pagi* also existed as political entities with some degree of administration. Both *vici* and *pagi*, however, were subordinate to the *civitas* capital, unless, of course, the *vicus* **was** the *civitas* capital. The inhabitants of the *vicus* at Zülpich (*vicani Tolbiacenses*), for example, were under the jurisdiction of the provincial capital at Cologne. Even Mainz, the capital of Germania Superior, was nothing more than a *vicus* in the legal sense until the end of the third century when it became a *civitas* capital, and later in the fourth century a *municipium*. Likewise, the large civilian settlement outside the legionary base at Strasbourg legally remained a *vicus* until the *civitas* capital of the Triboci was transferred from Brumath to Strasbourg possibly in the early third century.

The political organisation of government and magisterial offices is also reflected in the structure of cult communities. Cults were organised on various levels, from the level of the Roman state to that of small, local groups. The imperial cult of Rome and Augustus, in which the veneration of the state and the emperor was inextricably interwoven, was organised on state level with directives for its establishment coming from the central Roman government. This cult in the Gallic and Germanic provinces operated on a provincial, pan-tribal scale, the sanctuary of Rome and Augustus for the *Tres Galliae* being established in Lyon and that for the German provinces in Cologne. Priests were drawn from the native aristocracy. Cults of syncretised native and Roman gods were organised on the *civitas* and *pagus* levels. The men who held priestly office for any of these cults were members of the tribal elite who also held important administrative positions in the *civitas*. Furthermore, just as the *vici* were under the political jurisdiction of the *civitas* capitals, the religious administration of small, local cult communities in *vici* and in the countryside near *vici* was in the hands of priests of public cults on *pagus* or *civitas* levels who performed religious rituals at the local sanctuaries. Moreover, these cult communities were managed on a local level by *curiae*, colleges of community groups and kin-groups.

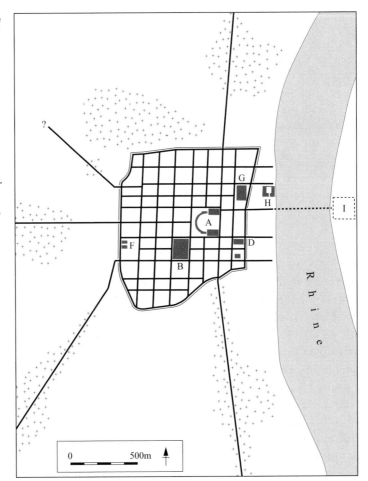

9 *Cologne in the second century.*
A forum;
B baths;
D capitoline temple;
F Gallo-Roman temples;
G governor's palace;
H horrea;
I bridgehead (Deutz).
The bridge and bridgehead date to the early fourth century.
Crosses = graves

Morphology of urban settlements

A regular street grid is a feature of all the colonies of the German provinces. One of the first tasks to be performed in laying out such new towns was the planning of a regular street grid in which a network of streets at right angles to each other divided the city into *insulae* or blocks. The main axes were determined by the overland roads leading to and from distant places and on which the town was to be located. Where the two main streets (*decumanus* and *cardo*) inside the town intersected was the forum. Cologne, for example, had regular intersecting streets, and the town was transected by the Rhine valley road and the Bavay-Cologne road (**9**). The importance of the road network for the existence of a city is clearly illustrated at Nyon too through which the Geneva-Lausanne-Avenches road ran. A 'chessboard' street grid, however, was not generally applied to the planning and development of *municipia, civitas* capitals or *vici*. Any regularity of street plan there usually resulted from the layout of streets set back from, and running parallel to, the main thoroughfare. There are exceptions, however, and the *vici* of Mandeure and its satellite Mathay-Essarté do display orthogonal planning, but without a clearly distinguishable

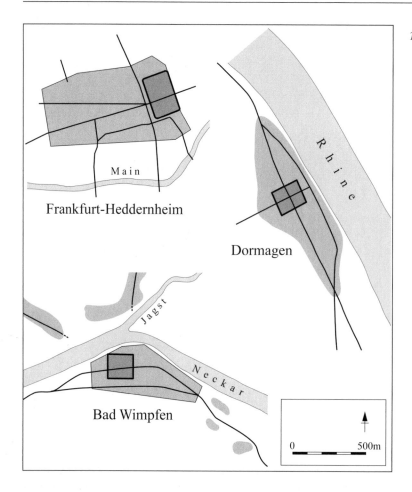

10 *Civilian settlements around Roman forts (dark grey) at Frankfurt-Heddernheim, Bad Wimpfen and Dormagen, Germany*

intersecting *decumanus* and *cardo*. *Vici* such as Heddernheim, Rottweil, Speyer and Wimpfen originally developed slowly as civilian settlements outside a Roman fort. They lay on the access road leading to the fort itself or were located on a road around the fort (**10**). Shops, workshops, tavernas and houses had their frontage on the access road. After the transfer of the garrisons and the abandonment of the forts, these *vici* lived on and flourished to become *civitas* capitals. However even if the simple timber buildings were replaced by more complex ones with stone foundations, and public buildings were added, the towns never had the regular plan of the colonies.

The heart of the colony, the forum, was the site of the most impressive public and religious buildings expressing the town's association with, and allegiance to, Rome. Laid out at the intersection of the main roads, these buildings could not fail to be seen by anyone passing through the town. These included the basilica as the main administrative building at one end of the forum and the principle temple at the other, the entire complex being enclosed by colonnaded halls. This temple was dedicated to the Capitoline Triad (Jupiter, Juno and Minerva). The secular part of the forum (*area publica*) was divided from the religious area (*area sacra*) by a street from which vehicular traffic was usually blocked. This is the classic Gallic forum, of which Augst, the capital of the Rauraci, has the best

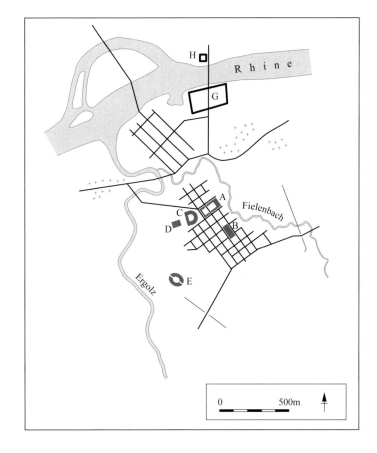

11 *Augst, Switzerland.*
A forum;
B baths;
C theatre;
D Schönbühl
temple;
E amphitheatre;
G late Roman
Kaiseraugst;
H bridgehead at
Wyhlen.
Crosses = graves

preserved example (**11**). Here the council room (*curia*) in which the *ordo* convened is attached to the basilica and takes the form of a semicircular structure 52ft (16m) in diameter with rows of stone seats for the local senators (**12**). The forum of the second half of the first century AD at Cologne was also divided into a secular and religious section, the latter being closed off from the surrounding *insulae* by a semicircular, colonnaded building over 422ft (130m) in diameter with an underground level (*cryptoporticus*). Unlike other Gallic fora, there was no Capitoline temple in the *area sacra* at Cologne, rather the Capitoline temple was located on the river front, its name surviving in the Romanesque church of St Maria im Kapitol built on the same site. Xanten's temple of Jupiter stood in an *insula* of its own, separated from the secular part of the forum in the neighbouring *insula* (**13**). The temple was built around the middle of the second century, and the forum seems to have been refurbished at this time as well with the help of the military who supplied and shipped the stone from quarries near Bonn to Xanten. The temple of Capitoline Jupiter was an expression of Roman state religion and the unity of religion and the state, and its inclusion in the repertoire of public buildings in all colonies with a body of Roman citizens was a political statement and a symbol of allegiance to Rome.

The *municipia* and *civitas* capitals also had their administrative centre in the forum. A central apsidal room 39ft (12m) in diameter in the basilica at the *vicus* and *civitas* capital of Ladenburg is assumed to have been the *curia*. It may have been reserved only for the senior

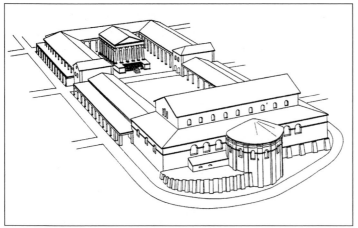

12 *Reconstruction of the forum at Augst.* From W. Drack and R. Fellmann, *Die Römer in der Schweiz*, 1988, fig. 62

13 *Xanten, Germany.*
   A forum;
   B baths;
   D temples;
   E amphitheatre;
   F Gallo-Roman temple to the Matronae.
   Crosses = graves

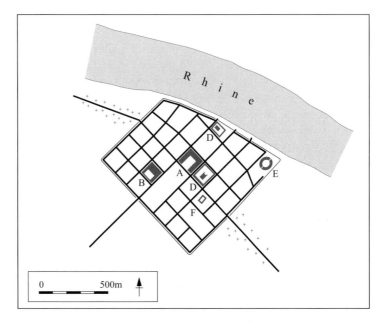

magistrates presiding over council meetings, however, as it is difficult to imagine 100 senators convening in a room of this size. In comparing the sizes of various basilicas, it is quite remarkable to see that the one at Ladenburg was larger (154 x 240ft; 47 x 73m) than those in the colonies of Augst (98 x 220ft; 30 x 67m), Nyon (75 x 194ft; 23 x 59m) and Avenches (90 x 230ft; 27 x 70m). The reasons for this remain obscure. An early example of a forum-like complex has been excavated at the *vicus* at Speyer. This timber-built complex dating to about AD 30 consisted of two long buildings parallel to each other and connected by a portico on the third side from which a simple basilica projected. One of the long buildings was a granary (*horreum*), and its size (20 x 60ft; 6 x 18m) suggests that it would have had storage capacity for a substantial part of the community. If this really is a market forum, it is interesting to see the emergence of such public works at a time when the *vicus* was still attached to a Roman auxiliary fort. It would not be the only example of a forum outside a military base, however, since a forum to the south-west of the legionary fort at Vindonissa was also built in the first century, and it was the largest building at Vindonissa. One might assume that the military was responsible for the infrastructure of the *vicus*; with an eye towards supplying the garrison, a market would have been in the military's own interests.

Although the forum occupied a prominent position on a main road in the *vici*, there is no evidence that there was a Capitoline temple associated with the forum in these towns. In the *vici* and *civitas* capitals the religious needs of the non-Roman population were expressed in the dedication of temples to native deities. These temples, so-called Gallo-Roman temples, had a central room surrounded by an external ambulatory. The religious centre of the *vicus* at Aachen-Kornelimünster, possibly named *Varnenum*, consisted of a complex of buildings including at least two Gallo-Roman ambulatory temples to Sunuxal, the tutelary goddess of the Sunuci, and her male counterpart Varneno. The important point to note is that such religious buildings occupied a central location in the *vici*, and they were probably built as a result of local patronage rather than official state support. The connection between political and religious allegiance to the Roman state, as expressed by Roman citizens in the colonies in the erection of a Capitoline temple, is apparently lacking in the towns of lower status whose population consisted chiefly of non-Roman citizens. The Gallo-Roman temple precinct at Winterthur may have continued to exist after severe fire damage to the *vicus* in the third quarter of the third century, and it occupied a central position in the greatly reduced settlement surrounded by the fortifications built in 294. The main temple in the harbour town (*vicus*) of Lausanne on the northern shore of Lake Geneva was a Gallo-Roman temple, situated on the edge of the loosely organised forum (**14**). At the other end of the forum stood the basilica, and adjacent to that was an enclosed sanctuary with three small chapels. The livelihood of this small town depended on water-borne traffic and it is no coincidence that the main public buildings, including clubhouses of the shippers and traders, were located on the lakeshore in a complex representing the political, economic and religious centre of the *vicus*. However Gallo-Roman temples were not limited to *civitas* capitals or *vici*. They were also built in the colonies, probably with funds from local benefactors rather than state support as the Capitoline temples were. These Gallo-Roman temples to native gods did not occupy a central position in the colonies and they may not always have been planned from the outset. They sometimes appear to have been added later in the life of the colony in response to local cults. This is clearly the case at Cologne, where a double Gallo-Roman temple complex of the second century on the western periphery of the city was preceded by a house of the later first century overlying the remains of early first-century pottery kilns, and at Xanten, where a Gallo-Roman temple to the Matronae was erected in the middle of the second century on top of demolished residential buildings overlying first-century pottery kilns. This perhaps implies that whilst allegiance to the Roman state gods took priority in the early days of a colony, the local population continued to worship its own gods, perhaps in a more private fashion, until these cults were given a more monumental architectural setting.

Public baths, sometimes several of them, were provided in towns of any status. In Cologne we know of at least three baths, ranging from the large complex occupying two

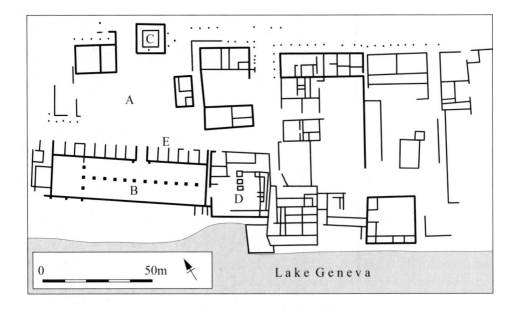

14 Forum and harbour at Lausanne on Lake Geneva, Switzerland. A forum; B basilica; C Gallo-Roman temple; D Sanctuary with chapels; E Club rooms of the shippers

insulae south-west of the forum to a smaller bathhouse north of it. Whilst none of these is earlier than the later first century, another bathhouse built in the 60s was located outside the western city wall, possibly as part of a guesthouse or *mansio* (**colour plate 5**). Xanten's public baths also filled an *insula*, as did those at Augst and Avenches. Augst boasted another large bath and nymphaeum complex on the periphery (Grienmatt). At the *civitas* capital of Rottenburg an exceptionally well preserved public latrine 105 x 16ft (32 x 5m) in size stood on the northern edge of the town's baths. The latrine, accessible from the street, was paved with large sandstone slabs and had a row of timber latrine seats on one side (**15**). The *vicus* at Heerlen, possibly a settlement of the Baetasii, had public baths covering an area of 27,000 sq ft (2500m²), although the settlement itself was only 25-35 acres (10-15ha) in size.

Water was essential for the functioning of bathhouses, but even more so for daily personal use. The supply of fresh water was often guaranteed by the building of an aqueduct from nearby or more distant sources. Cologne had two of them, the earliest aqueduct bringing in fresh water from the hills 6 miles (10km) to the south-west and a later mainly underground aqueduct built after 85 originating in the Eifel mountains some 56 miles (90km) away. In Augst, a source in the hills south of the city was tapped and the water carried a distance of 4 miles (6.5km) to a water tower whence it was channelled into timber or lead pipes under the street. The supply of water from this aqueduct did not extend to the lower quarter of Augst on the bank of the Rhine. Here the inhabitants relied on wells, of which about 50 have been excavated. Avenches had at least six aqueducts, the largest of which supplied water from a distance of 10 miles (17km). Such technical

15 *Public latrine with stone paving at Rottenburg, Germany.* Courtesy Landesdenkmalamt Baden-Württemberg

advancements are extremely rare in smaller towns. Fragments of an aqueduct built in stone are, however, known at Lausanne, where wells were also dug for water. An aqueduct was an expensive public facility which few communities other than the colonies could probably afford, but if the military was covering the costs, as it was at Mainz, civilians could benefit from its construction. At Mainz, the aqueduct was built between 69 and 96 first and foremost to supply the legionary base, but the *canabae* next to the fort and probably the civilian *vicus* also received water from it (**16**). In most small towns and villages, wells will have sufficed.

Theatres have been found at the colonies of Augst and Avenches, at the *civitas* capitals of Mainz, Heddernheim and Ladenburg, and at the *vici* of Mandeure and Lenzburg. All theatres except that at Heddernheim were stone-built, and they ranged in size from 177ft (54m) in diameter at Heddernheim to an exceptional 466ft (142m) at Mandeure. The rows of stone seats in the second-century theatre at Ladenburg bore the inscribed names of members of the community who donated funds towards its construction. In many cases, the theatres were associated with one or more temples, as at Augst and Avenches and also at Lenzburg where the temple is clearly indicated by aerial photography. The combination of cult theatre and temple is well known in Gaul, for example at Ribemont-sur-Ancre and Trier-Irminenwingert, the theatre being used at times of religious festivals and assemblies of the native population. The juxtaposition of theatre and temples at Augst is particularly interesting (**17**). In the 70s or 80s a theatre was built west of the Jupiter temple on the forum. The theatre was replaced around 110 by an amphitheatre, and immediately west of this a sanctuary housing six Gallo-Roman temples of varying sizes was laid out at the same time. In turn, both the Gallo-Roman sanctuary and the amphitheatre were demolished around 150 and replaced by another theatre and a monumental podium temple (Schönbühl temple). There may also have been a cultic connection between the two Gallo-Roman

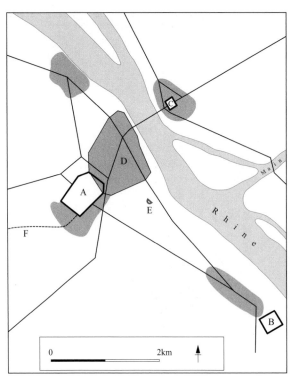

16 *Mainz, Germany.*
   A legionary fort;
   B auxiliary fort at Weisenau;
   C late Roman bridgehead at
   Kastel;
   D civilian town within walls of
   the third century;
   E theatre;
   F aqueduct

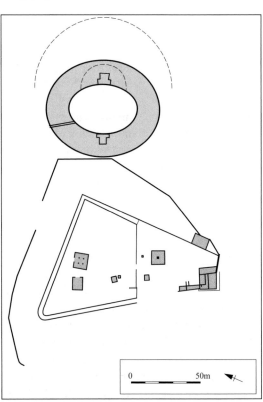

17 *Gallo-Roman temples and theatre*
   (dashed) superseded by an
   amphitheatre at Augst

18 *Avenches, Switzerland.*
  A forum;
  B baths;
  C theatre;
  D Cigognier temple;
  E amphitheatre;
  F canal.
  Crosses = graves

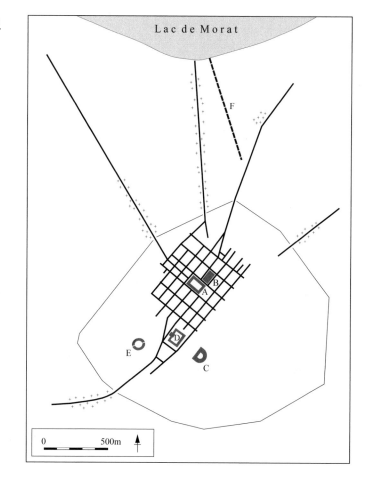

sanctuaries and another amphitheatre in the south-west part of the city. At Avenches, the early second-century 'Cigognier temple' and its large colonnaded forecourt stood directly opposite and facing the theatre 460ft (140m) away (**18**). At both Augst and Avenches the orientation of the temple and the theatre coincide, and they were clearly built to relate to each other. At Mandeure the Flavian theatre on the southern outskirts of the town was axially aligned with the Gallo-Roman sanctuary, and the size of the theatre suggests that it was used for larger gatherings than those expected simply for dramatic festivals (**19**). There is no known temple associated with the theatre at Mainz, but this may be related to the state of research and difficult circumstances for excavations. The theatre there, however, has been interpreted as relating to the stone-built cenotaph of Drusus (Drususstein) who died in 9 BC and in whose memory the legions and the council of the three Gauls (*consilium Galliarum*) held annual festivals.

The amphitheatre could also be the site of cultic assemblies, as it was at the pan-Gallic altar site in Lyon. Both the amphitheatre built near the forum in 110 at Augst and the later amphitheatre erected in the south-west of the city were closely connected with Gallo-Roman temples, suggesting that there was a cultic connection. The existence of this tradition in Germania Superior in the Celtic areas of Switzerland, Burgundy, Alsace and

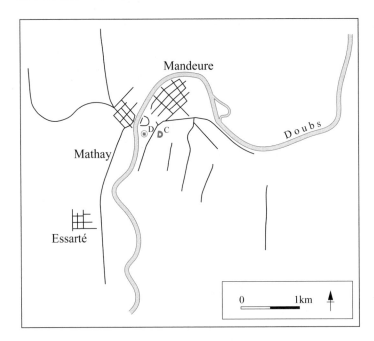

19 *The town of Mandeure and its satellite village Mathay-Essarté, France.*
C theatre;
D temple

Belgium underlines the common religious traditions between them and the rest of Gaul. The Helvetii, Sequani and Lingones continued to send delegates to the great pan-Gallic conferences at the altar of the three Gauls in Lyon, for example, although politically they belonged to the province of Germania Superior after 85. In the towns of Germania Inferior no theatres have yet been found, and amphitheatres are attested at only a few sites. These include Xanten and Cologne, although the amphitheatre at Cologne is known only from inscriptional references to it. The fact that the amphitheatres at Xanten, Augst and Avenches are all roughly the same size (285 x 325ft/87 x 99m; 285 x 328ft/87 x 100m; 285 x 377ft/87 x 115m respectively) may indicate some standardisation in the building of such structures and in the expected number of spectators at these sites. Although these buildings stood in towns of the highest rank, the Flavian amphitheatre at the *civitas* capital at Besançon was larger, measuring 348 x 453ft (106 x 138m). Whether the amphitheatre of the Roman military base at Nijmegen was used by the civilian population is uncertain. It was apparently in use longer than the base itself, but it lies over a mile (2km) distant from the civilian *municipium*. The combination of theatre or amphitheatre and temple is unknown at any of the sanctuaries in Germania Inferior, either in settlements or in the countryside. This may reflect a religious tradition different from that in Celtic areas.

Those areas in the towns not reserved for public buildings were used for domestic housing. The earliest houses in the colonies in the German provinces were timber-framed, either post-built or with timber sleeper beams, and had walls of plastered daub. At Cologne, Augst, Avenches and Nyon these were replaced from about the mid-first century by private dwellings with stone foundations. The simple, rectangular houses of the early period gave way to large peristyle houses with suites of rooms grouped around a central courtyard (**20**). Dimensions of 10,000 sq ft (*c*.1000m²) and more were not uncommon. In the late second and early third centuries some exceptional houses in

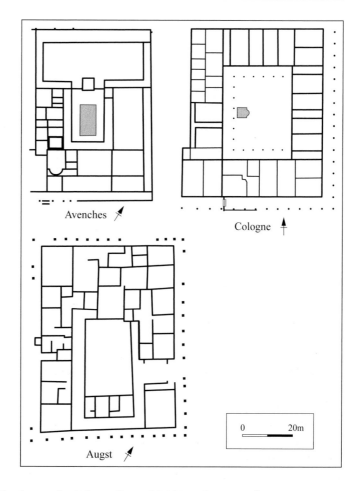

20 Peristyle courtyard houses in Avenches, Cologne and Augst. Grey areas = pools

Avenches

Cologne

Augst

0   20m

Cologne and the Swiss colonies reached sizes of over 32,000 sq ft (3000m²), incorporating the building plots of several older houses into one building. Mosaic floors in principal rooms and elaborate wall paintings were fairly standard by the second century; occasionally private bath suites were added. The courtyard in almost all peristyle houses in Cologne and in some in Augst and Avenches were equipped with fountains and pools, suggesting the presence of a garden. All of these houses were based on Mediterranean prototypes. The introduction of such 'foreign' domestic architecture of internal complexity reflects a different attitude towards inhabited space, and rooms of varying function and status indicate differentiated living. Since these town houses will have been built and lived in by the elite and magisterial classes, be they Italian legionary veterans or the local nobility, an element of social competition is clearly evident. The house was a means by which one's identity as 'Roman' and one's place in a certain level of society could be consciously expressed.

In the *vici*, housing was generally less extravagant and strip-houses predominated, but here too the change from timber to stone took place. In Ladenburg, the strip-houses contemporaneous with the second fort after 80 were timber-framed with daub walls. All houses had street frontage with cellared shops (**21**) in the front part and the private rooms

21 *Stone-built cellar in building 19 in the* vicus *at Walheim, Germany.* Courtesy Landesdenkmalamt Baden-Württemberg

of the owner in the back. The property boundaries were retained after the *vicus* became the *civitas* capital, but the houses were rebuilt in the later second century in stone. Of the many second-century strip-houses in the *vicus* at Walheim, the most remarkable was a two-storeyed commercial building with a sales room, an above-ground storage room for goods and a well preserved storage cellar (**22**). The orthogonal street grid at the *vicus* of Mathay-Essarté on the Doubs river bears a superficial resemblance to the regular planning of the colonies, but not only are the main axes not clearly defined, the housing of the *insulae* at Mathay differs greatly from that of major towns (**23**). The buildings are concentrated on the peripheries of the *insulae*, leaving much space to open courtyards in the centre of the blocks. Most of these buildings were workshops with modest domestic quarters, and there is no hint of houses akin to those of the principal towns which could occupy an entire *insula*. Domestic housing in Rottweil, on the other hand, developed in a manner more closely related to the major towns. Timber houses in the civilian settlement were partially replaced in stone, probably already at the end of the first century. Large complex houses, some with peristyle courtyards, dominated the northern part of the *vicus*. Rottweil remains an exception in this regard. The architectural development of this *vicus* may be connected with the emperor Domitian and his family, the Flavians. The Latin name of the town, *Arae Flaviae*, indicates not only a Flavian foundation, but also an altar and sanctuary at which the imperial family was honoured. Imperial patronage of some kind and the possible attraction of Roman officials may account for the more Romanised character of domestic housing.

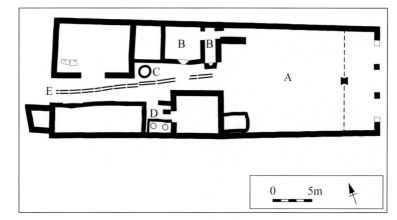

22 Striphouse (building 19) in the vicus at Walheim. The salesroom (A) could be closed off (dotted line).
B cellars;
C well;
D ovens;
E drain

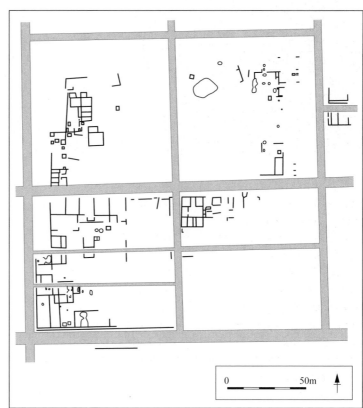

23 Regular street grid with houses and workshops at Mathay-Essarté

Urban cemeteries

Cemeteries laid out along the roads leading into and out of settlements were filled with tombs that kept the *memoria* of the deceased alive. Not only the grave epitaphs, but also portraits and relief depictions were chosen by the deceased and their families and designed to commemorate the dead, their lives and their social status within society. The funerary practice of stone grave monuments, however, was unknown in the pre-Roman Germanic

57

24 *Early first-century gravestone of P. Clodius of the first legion.* Courtesy Rheinisches Landesmuseum Bonn

and Celtic North-West. The first stone funerary monuments erected in the newly conquered German provinces were those of Roman military personnel, both active and retired, as well as Roman merchants from various parts of the Empire (**24**). In the Roman West, the custom of erecting stone tombs of various types spread in the first century AD from northern Italy and the Romanised province of Gallia Narbonensis. The general adoption of this Roman funerary practice by the native population can be understood as the result of an emulative process of expressing status. On the middle and upper Rhine, the native Celtic population adopted the custom fairly early in the first century AD, as a number of tombs and funerary statues around Mainz indicates (**25**), but, on the lower Rhine, it was not until the second century that the local population embraced the custom. Apparently they did not erect permanent grave markers before this time.

The most sumptuous of the monuments, so-called tower tombs, were designed to display status and social standing of leading families in a conspicuous manner. These include the tomb of the aristocratic Iulii in Glanum, that of the merchant *nouveau riche* Secundinii at Igel near Trier, and the tomb of the wealthy legionary veteran Lucius Poblicius and his family (**colour plate 6**) in pre-colonial Cologne. Two of the earliest tomb monuments of the first decades of the first century AD north-east of Avenches at the 'en Chaplix' site were heavily decorated with sculptures of figures out of the pages of Graeco-Roman mythology, such as Bacchus, nereids and tritons, and with portrait statues of the deceased. The possession of Roman citizenship was an honour and distinction that is often highlighted in these monuments. Not only the socially prominent, but also craftsmen, traders, teachers and slaves preserved their memories in the form of built tombs or carved grave markers. Benefaction and generosity were often publicised by the wealthy who purchased a burial plot and a carved grave stone for valued slaves who had died in their possession. The name of the dead slave, for example Severina, the wet-nurse, in Cologne (**colour plate 7**) or the ten-year-old Peregrinus in Speyer, and that of the benefactor appeared in the grave epitaph. Civic identity, professional achievement, public and private careers were expressed in a variety of ways. The tombs reveal to us the attitudes, aspirations and ideologies of a considerable body of citizens and non-citizens in Roman towns. The cemeteries in this sense represent a visual cross-section through a collective of inhabitants who already possessed or came to internalise Roman urban, social and cultural values.

The cemeteries as part of the urban fabric also reveal changes in economic and social structures. Where the cemeteries are well researched, it is apparent that there was a shift in location from the early to late Roman periods. The earliest cemeteries south, west and north of

25 Gravestone of the shipper Blussus and his wife Menimane from Mainz-Weisenau, c.AD 50. Courtesy Landesmuseum Mainz

Cologne were laid out at a distance of between *c*.320 and 430 yards (300-400m) from the city wall. In the suburbs closest to the city were residential districts and industrial zones. By the late third century, however, these had been abandoned and the land was redeveloped as burial sites so that the cemeteries had a more immediate relationship to the city. At most cemeteries outside Roman towns the burials offer a genuine cross-section through many levels of society, with the most ostentatious monuments directly fronting the streets. At some sites, however, there are indications that certain cemeteries were the preferred burial sites of the wealthy and influential. This appears to have been the case at Avenches where, in the cemetery outside the west gate, primarily the city's magistrates, merchants and bankers found their last place of rest. Likewise, one of the four known cemeteries at Besançon, that at the Chamars site, was richer than the others and it included chamber tombs with opulent grave goods and a circular monument over 300ft (91m) in diameter which may have been funerary in function. By the same token, the south-east cemetery at Langres had a relatively high proportion of inscribed gravestones of slaves and freedmen as well as monuments to oriental gods frequently venerated by this sector of society. This particular cemetery may have been a communal burial ground, but probably not exclusively for this group of people.

The urban ideal: acceptance or rejection?

Cities and towns were essential for the operation of the Roman Empire in the political, ideological and economic sense. In those areas in which pre-Roman urban or proto-urban settlements existed, the transformation to a Roman urbanised society proceeded rapidly and without much difficulty. A key element in this regard was the support of the native elite in acting as agents of the Roman state, whereby the leading members of society served as magistrates in the local administration and, thus, identified with the town in which the administration was centred. The wealth of the elite was based on land ownership and they continued to live in the country, but it was also necessary to maintain a residence in the town. The town became the focus of a competitive display of wealth and power, manifesting itself in Roman-style private dwellings and the financing of public building projects. Public benefaction included such donations as an arch and porticoes at Mainz in the third century, paid for by a *decurio* of the *civitas Taunensium*, Dativius Victor (**colour plate 8**), and the refurbishment of the public baths at Heerlen, financed by M. Sattonius Iucundus, a *decurio* of the colony at Xanten in the second century. This worked well in southern and central Gaul and in parts of northern Gaul. But not everywhere was the elite receptive to the urban ideal. This is the case particularly for the lower Rhine zone in those regions where peoples such as the Menapii, Cananefates and Batavi, and to some degree the Cugerni and Baetasii, lived. In the Dutch and German Rhine zone, pre-Roman societies were not based on a developed socio-political hierarchy, nor were they accustomed to living in anything approaching an urban environment. Attracting them to participate in Roman-style government and embrace urban values proved to be difficult, and perhaps they actually resisted this.

The urban development of the capital of the Batavi, the *oppidum Batavorum*/Nijmegen, was slow, and there is little to indicate that the native elite was much interested in the town. During the revolt of 69 when Batavians, other German groups and some Gallic tribes joined forces in armed resistance against the Roman occupation, the Batavians set fire to their capital, viewing the town as a symbol of Roman domination. Since the town seems to have been artificially created by the Roman administration and chiefly populated with people from the Gallic hinterland, the Batavi may have had every reason not to feel any link with it. The capital of the Cananefates, *Forum Hadriani*/Voorburg-Arentsburg, was a very small town (37 acres; 15ha) and never developed beyond the stage of a simple *vicus*. Voorburg and the rebuilt Nijmegen were granted municipal status in the second century, a measure of the Roman government's attempts to foster urban development. Both towns, however, were abandoned by the later third century. As for the Batavian nobility, the foci of their social competition were religious centres not in the towns, but in the countryside, such as those at Empel and Elst, where Gallo-Roman temples, particularly to the Batavian tutelary god Hercules Magusanus, were built and aggrandised. These were the public buildings in which they invested, not those symbolising the Roman state in an urban environment. There is hardly any evidence of urban development at the capital of the Menapii, *Castellum Menapiorum*/Cassel, and it is no coincidence that the capital of the Frisiavones has not even been located archaeologically. None of these groups seemed to have felt any great commitment towards reshaping their settlement pattern to conform with Roman urban ideals. The settlement of the Cugerni/Baetasii at Xanten did have a regular street grid in the first century, but there is no evidence that Roman-style stone-built houses or public buildings existed prior to its elevation to a veteran colony, *Colonia Ulpia Traiana*, around 100 under Trajan. Only then, with Roman state support, did the town develop into a truly urban centre, although the western half of the town was still empty until around 120.

The Ubii and Roman Cologne, on the other hand, are a success story from the Roman point of view. There was nothing village-like about the pre-colonial settlement, rather the *oppidum Ubiorum* directly underlying the later colony was planned as an urban centre from the beginning (see chapter 8). Admittedly this was done with a great deal of Roman state support, particularly since the residence of the Julio-Claudian prince and commander-in-chief, Germanicus, and a sanctuary of the Imperial cult was located within the town, but the Ubii were receptive to the Roman urban ideal. Of all the *civitas* capitals in Germania Inferior, Cologne was the only one to be continually inhabited as an urban centre after the collapse of Roman authority in the fifth century and throughout the Medieval period.

Social competition amongst the elite was not only restricted to displays of private wealth and public benefaction within the closer community. Civic pride could be collectively expressed to the point that cities competed with each other for distinction. Aelius Aristides in his panegyric *To Rome* (97) referred to the competition between cities to 'appear as beautiful and attractive as possible', the result of which was that 'every place is full of gymnasia, fountains, gateways, temples, shops and schools'. Such rivalry between Vienne and Lyon is known from literary sources, and in the second century Augst as the capital of the Rauraci and Avenches as the capital of the Helvetii seem to have been trying to outdo each other in the duplication of a number of monumental public and religious buildings paid for by wealthy families and businessmen. The triumphal arch known as the Porte Noire or Porte de Mars erected around AD 172 at Besançon was highly decorated with relief scenes from Graeco-Roman mythology, and its reliefs allude to Marcus Aurelius as the invincible emperor who restored order by defeating the Marcomanni. The arch is of political significance and stands as a symbol of the town's affirmation of loyalty to Rome. Had at least the elite inhabitants of any of these towns not felt a sense of political allegiance or civic identity and had they not absorbed Roman urban values, the development and embellishment of the community's physical appearance would never have happened.

Despite the creation of many new towns and the expansion of existing ones, the majority of the population in the Roman period lived in the countryside. The density of settlement, the types of rural sites and the role of the countryside in the economy are explored in the next chapter.

4 Farms and villages

A German is not so easily prevailed upon to plough the land and wait patiently for harvest as to challenge a foe and earn wounds for his reward. He thinks it tame and spiritless to accumulate slowly by the sweat of his brow what can be got quickly by the loss of a little blood (Tacitus, *Germania* 14).

Of all pursuits by which men gain their livelihood none is better than agriculture. Farming is the most pleasant livelihood, the most fruitful and the one most worthy of a free man (Cicero, *De Officiis* 1.42.151).

Settlement factors and density

Tacitus, in the above quote, typically oversimplified in a negative way the role of agriculture in Germanic society. In pre-Roman northern Gaul and Germany, societies were primarily based on crop-raising and animal husbandry, although one or the other might dominate, depending on the landscape and the soils. As outlined in chapter 1, the Romans did not find heavily forested landscapes inhabited by nomads, but encountered an already intensively worked agricultural landscape which they proceeded to alter in the intensification of certain areas of agrarian production and the preference for particular crops. In direct contrast to Tacitus' remarks about the negligible role of agriculture in Germanic society, Pliny, in fact, singles out one of these Germanic groups, the Ubii, as being particularly good farmers who successfully practised mineral manuring to enhance the fertility of the soil (*Historia Naturalis* 17.4.47). The presence of granaries in unfortified and fortified pre-Roman settlements in northern Gaul and the lower Rhine also tangibly indicates crop-production, and almost certainly surplus production, of which Caesar himself took advantage in having various tribes pay tributes of cereals to feed his army. However if, for whatever reason, there was a food shortage, raids in neighbouring territories in search of cereals and cattle were certainly undertaken in the pre-Roman Iron Age (*De Bello Gallico* 4.9, 6.10).

In the Roman period, the quality of soils, availability of water and the existence of natural resources were some of the factors determining the nature and density of rural settlement. Whatever was produced had to be transported to markets, so that roads and rivers also played an important role in the Roman economy. Secondary and tertiary roads, often little more than bumpy lanes, connected farms to each other and to markets. Distribution maps in various parts of the German provinces indicate that rural settlement was particularly dense in river valleys. In the Swiss part of Germania Superior, for example, settlements are closely distributed throughout the Aare valley and along the Alpine tributaries. Another high concentration of settlements can be found on either side of the Neckar valley (**colour plate 2**). Loess regions such as those in the Wetterau, but especially those to the west of the Cologne basin, were particularly densely populated due to the high quality of fertile soils suitable for cereal cultivation. The location of farms on land which combined dry and moist ecotypes allowed both cultivation of field crops on arable land and pasturage of animals in meadows. The size of the farms depended, among other things, on geological factors, a greater area being necessary for farms on poorer soils to be able to compete with smaller farms on excellent soils. Farms on less fertile soils could not survive on cultivation alone, and some made use, for example, of the proximity of mineral resources as a supplementary economic basis. In upland and wooded areas cattle, sheep and horse breeding dominated, and where the climate was suitable, for example on the Moselle and Neckar, viticulture was practised. In the sandy regions and Holocene peat and clay landscapes in the Rhine-Maas-Schelde delta the soils were of limited potential for arable intensification. High quality pastureland, however, was ideal for livestock farming, in particular cattle-breeding, and this formed the economic basis of the region.

In Germania Inferior between Bonn in the south and Neuss in the north, the areas where the loess deposits are thicker and annual rainfall higher were settled first, already rather densely in the second half of the first century AD. These soils were well suited to the growing of grain, the prime cash product. Not until the second century did settlement expand into marginal areas on the edge of the Eifel and to the clay and sandy soils between Neuss and Xanten. The exploitation of both core and peripheral lands reflects economic expansion, as well as an attempt to achieve a degree of economic independence so that long-distance import of foodstuffs did not have to be too heavily relied upon. Germania Inferior prior to the second century relied heavily on supplies from the interior of Gaul, particularly Gallia Belgica, to feed the army and the civilian population in the frontier zone. Economic independence may have been achieved through a population increase in the second century, if we interpret the spread of rural sites even to marginal land as an indication of this. New settlers will undoubtedly have been attracted by new opportunities. However, the Roman intensification of agricultural production was achieved by the establishment of a network of working farms, and it is possible that larger family or kin-groups native to the region who had lived in small agrarian villages in pre-Roman times now dispersed to work plots of land in individual ownership or tenancy. This would result in a greater number of farms and a broader distribution of them. Moreover, through increasing diversification (farming, livestock breeding, mining) the existing population might have been sufficient to exploit the land to a maximum. Possibly due in part to climatic changes, from warm and dry to cooler and wetter, and the depletion of overworked soils, an abandonment of rural settlements began after 200, particularly in the areas of poorer soils which could no longer sustain intensive cultivation. Even in the rich loess zone in the hinterland of the provincial capital of Germania Inferior only a third to a half of the farms of the second century remained occupied in the late third and fourth centuries, for which political and economic instability as well as insecurity due to Frankish incursions were responsible.

In some areas of the German provinces, the complete demographic restructuring outlined in chapter 2 will have brought with it the need to survey the land and establish ownership of it. This is particularly the case for the German and Dutch lower Rhineland. Not only were new native settlers brought to the areas, but also Roman veterans received land allotments. Moreover, some areas were reserved for the Roman state, either forming imperial estates or reserves for a state monopoly on certain natural resources. A system of centuriation was put in place after surveying, whereby the portions of land were divided up into regular units.

There is ample evidence for the redrawing of property boundaries according to this regimented plan in Gallia Narbonensis (Orange, Valences, Béziers) and for a less regular centuriation in the *Tres Galliae* (Tongeren, Reims). There are also indications that a form of centuriation was carried out in the German and Dutch lower Rhine and in Switzerland. The farms in the loess zone west of Cologne, for example, seem to have been located at regular intervals and had an overall size of 123 acres (50ha) which corresponds to a Roman unit of measurement of 200 *iugera*. Remains of Roman field systems have survived east of the Meuse near Sittard. Traces of land divisions are preserved in Germania Superior along Lake Geneva and around Avenches and Augst. In these Swiss cases, however, several overlapping systems of centuriation have been detected, suggesting that the land was surveyed and resurveyed more than once. At the moment, these cannot be dated accurately or attributed to particular historical or political events. The fairly regular spacing of *civitas* capitals and *vici* in the *Agri Decumates* might also indicate official surveying and land distribution under Trajan. In other areas where no trace of centuriation has been found there may simply have been a tidying-up and regulation of an older field system. This might be what happened to the pre-Roman parcelling system in the Rhine delta where the land lots in the second century are regular, rectangular parcels and larger than those which had already existed since the late Iron Age. This still leaves open the general question of expropriation and confiscation of existing property by the Romans after the conquest. There is no evidence, however, that legionary veterans were involved in ruthless land-grabbing from the native population as they were at Colchester in Britain.

There is variation in the types of rural settlements (**26**). Some of them are difficult to define, and terminology is not always used consistently by archaeologists. For the sake of the following discussion, these settlements are divided into farmsteads, agrarian hamlets and villas. Farmstead defines a non-Roman or scarcely Romanised native farmhouse with subsidiary agricultural buildings. Agrarian hamlets are clusters of such farmhouses, sometimes within an enclosure and with central stores for the community. A villa refers to a Romanised dwelling, most often with stone foundations, that was the centre of an economic unit comprising both a dwelling and subsidiary buildings in a farmyard and the estate lands. Although the term villa today has connotations of luxury and opulence, many Roman villas were never more than simple but comfortable working farms. A villa could be built on the site of an earlier farmstead, suggesting continuity of ownership and the owner's adoption of a Romanised lifestyle, as we shall see below.

1   The Rhine river flowing north past Mainz on the west bank. Author

2   The Neckar river valley with the Roman villa at Lauffen am Neckar on the east bank.
Courtesy Landesbildstelle Württemberg

3 The second-century auxiliary fort at the Saalburg with its reconstructed circuit walls and gate of the late nineteenth century. Author

4 Stone tower, ditch and palisade of the upper German limes *near the fort at Zugmantel (from* Der römische Limes in Deutschland, *Konrad Theiss Verlag, Stuttgart 1992, fig. 93)*

5 *Excavated remains of a Neronian bath building with its underfloor heating on Benesisstraße west of the Roman city wall at Cologne.* Author

6 *Tower tomb of the legionary veteran Lucius Poblicius in Cologne, c.AD 40.* Courtesy Römisch-Germanisches Museum

7 *Third-century gravestone of the slave and wet-nurse Severina in Cologne.*
Courtesy Römisch-Germanisches Museum

8   Third-century arch donated by Dativius Victor to the city of Mainz. Author

9 Collapsed walls of a stone-built ancillary building at Oberndorf-Bochingen.
Courtesy Landesdenkmalamt Baden-Württemberg

10 Excavated and reconstructed mansio *and baths of the second century in Xanten.* Author

11 Red-painted face jars of the fourth century from Worms. Courtesy Museum der Stadt Worms

12 Handmade Germanic, Belgic and Frisian pottery of the first and second centuries from the fleet base at Cologne-Alteburg. Author

13 Military tilery at the legionary base at Dormagen. Courtesy Rheinisches Amt für
Bodendenkmalpflege

*14 Roman colour-coated beaker (left) and Germanic handmade copy (right) from the fort at
Zugmantel.* Courtesy Saalburgmuseum

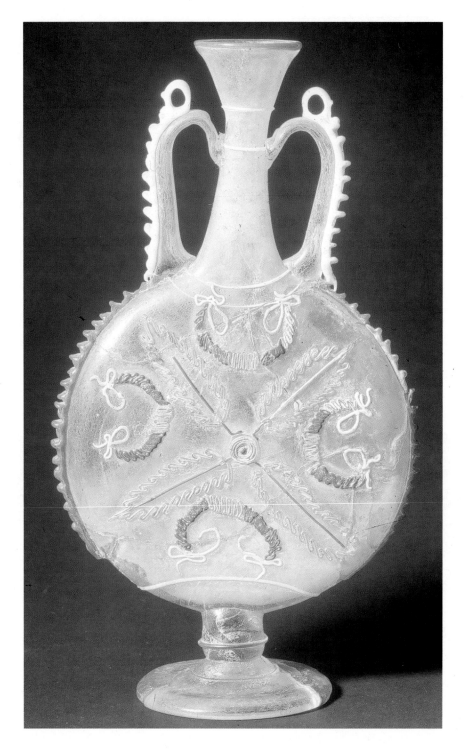

15 Snake-trailed glass flask from Cologne. Courtesy Römisch-Germanisches Museum,
   Photo Mario Corrieri

16 *Personal names and symbols incised in terra sigillata vessels from the fleet base at Cologne-Alteburg.* Author

17 *Statue of Lucius Poblicius clad in a toga as a sign of citizenship, Cologne.* Author

18 *Bronze belt fittings from a grave of the late fourth century at Krefeld-Gellep.*
Courtesy Museum Burg Linn

19 *Excavated pottery kiln of the early first century belonging to the* Oppidum Ubiorum
(Cologne). Large storage jars (dolia) were fired in the kiln. Author

20 *Excavations in 1995/96 of first-century timber barracks at the fort at Cologne-Alteburg.*
Author

21 *First-century gravestone of Fronto, son of Dregenius, who died as a cavalryman in Mainz. His tribal affiliation is recorded as* nature Ubius. *Author*

22 Fourth-century gravestone of Viatorinus, killed by a Frank on the east bank of the Rhine near Divitia-Deutz, Cologne. Author

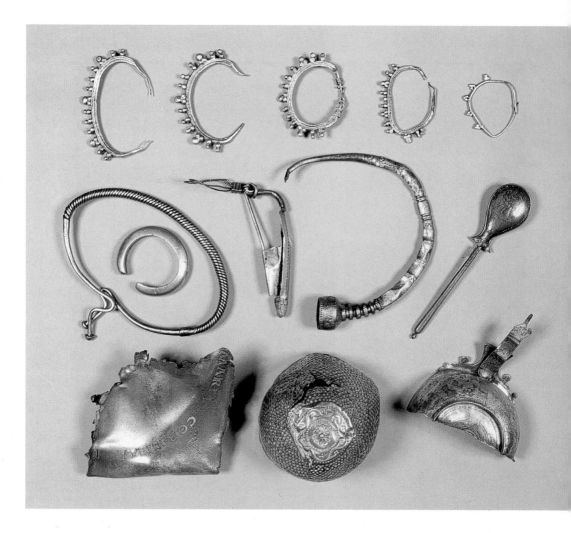

23 Silver from a third-century metal hoard found at Hagenbach on the Rhine. Courtesy
Prähistorische Staatssammlung. Photo Römisch-Germanisches Zentralmuseum

24 Aerial view of the third-century burgus *(dark square) next to a Roman road (light stripe) visible as crop marks, Euskirchen-Palmersheim.* Courtesy Rheinisches Amt für Bodendenkmalpflege. Photo G. Amtmann

25 *Mosaic masonry of a Roman tower on the city wall at Cologne.* Author

26 *Outer wall of the so-called* cryptoporticus *in the forum at Cologne, partially robbed out around AD 1000 and incorporated into later buildings.* Author

Farmsteads and agrarian hamlets

One type of settlement encountered by Caesar was the isolated farmstead or *aedificium*, another the small agrarian settlement (*vicus*) consisting of a cluster of farmhouses within an enclosure. An open-air sanctuary was often associated with the latter settlements. These hamlets continued throughout the Roman period, especially in the northern part of Germania Inferior in the *civitates* of the Batavi, Cananefates, Frisiavones and Menapii. The native house-building tradition persisted, and Romanised architecture is rarely to be found. The houses were rectangular structures, most often timber-built, with internal roof-supports dividing the interior space into aisles (*Hallenhaus*) or with a living section at one end and a byre at the other (*Wohnstallhaus*). The entrances to the houses are on either long side of the building, but those in which livestock were kept have an additional entrance on the short end leading into the stable. These native houses of the first and second centuries AD can be found in isolation or within a small compound of houses. Such settlements are known at Hoogeloon and Rijswijk, the latter settlement having its origins in the early first century AD as a single farmstead. Occasionally Roman influences can be found in the addition of a wooden porticus as at Druten and Oosterhout in the second century or in the use of stone foundations rather than timber, as at Houten in the late second century and Rijswijk in the early third century. Nevertheless, the houses were still constructed according to native principles. The Romanised dwellings within these agrarian hamlets generally represent the houses of the elite, and they remained an integral part of the native settlement. Only very rarely in the northernmost *civitates* are stone-built residences found that resemble those of the villas further south. One such stone-built dwelling of complex plan at Hoogeloon was constructed in the second century within a compound of native farmhouses (**27**). The villa owner was of local origin and possibly had served in the Roman army, judging by the find of a fragmentary military diploma on the site. After AD 200, this Romanised dwelling was replaced by a house of native type with a byre at one end.

Corn production in these regions was not the main economic basis, although the presence of granaries, some with large storage capacities, indicate that arable farming was practised. The soils did not lend themselves to cereal cultivation on a large scale, and there is no question of the region having been able to compete with the fertile grain-growing loess zone to the south. Instead, livestock farming was the principle component of the economy in the Roman period, particularly cattle-breeding and horse-breeding. The *civitates* of the Cananefates, Frisiavones and Menapii paid at least part of their taxes in pastoral products, as did the Frisii in the Dutch coastal area beyond the Rhine who were taxed in cowhides. The Batavi were primarily taxed in manpower, and they were obliged to supply large numbers of auxiliary troops to the Roman army. Batavian horse-breeding was geared towards the Roman military market, and the Batavi supplied their own horses for their cavalry units. Farmsteads like that at Houten only 2 miles (3km) from the Roman military base at Vechten were integrated elements of the Roman surplus economy. In return for supplies to the Roman market not only items of daily use from Gaul and the Rhineland such as pottery, glass, metal and basalt millstones were received, but also building supplies. Timber not native to the Netherlands (silver fir, pine), roof tiles, box-tiles (*tubuli*) and tufa

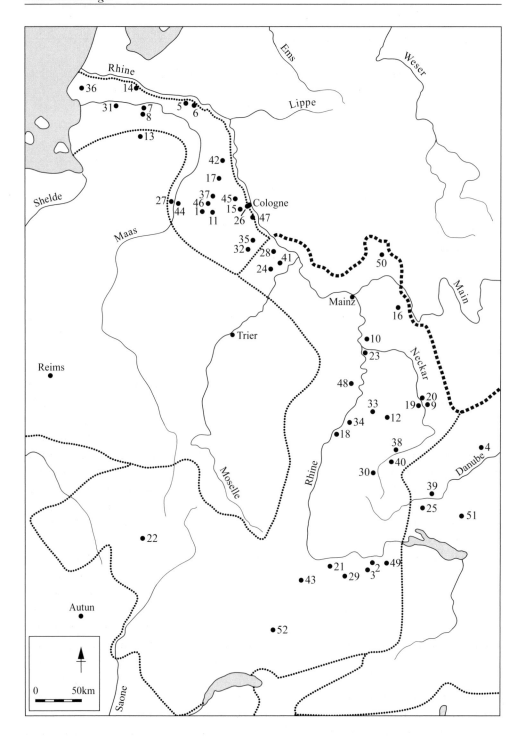

26 (opposite) Map showing villas, farmsteads, hamlets and other rural sites in the German provinces.

1 Aldenhoven-Langweiler; 2 Buchs; 3 Dietikon; 4 Dornstadt-Tomerdingen; 5 Druten; 6 Elst; 7 Empel; 8 Esch; 9 Gemmrigheim; 10 Großsachsen; 11 Hambach; 12 Hemmingen; 13 Hoogeloon; 14 Houten; 15 Hürth-Efferen; 16 Hummetroth; 17 Jüchen; 18 Kehl-Auenheim; 19 Kirchheim am Neckar; 20 Lauffen am Neckar; 21 Liestal; 22 Lux; 23 Mannheim-Wallstadt; 24 Mayen; 25 Meßkirch; 26 Müngersdorf; 27 Neerharen-Rekem; 28 Nickenich; 29 Oberentfelden; 30 Oberndorf-Bochingen; 31 Oosterhout; 32 Pesch; 33 Pforzheim-Hagenschieß; 34 Rheinau-Diersheim; 35 Rheinbach-Flerzheim; 36 Rijswijk; 37 Rödingen; 38 Rottenburg-Hailfingen; 39 Sigmaringen; 40 Starzach-Bierlingen; 41 Thür; 42 Tönisvorst-Vorst; 43 Vicques; 44 Voerendaal; 45 Weiden; 46 Welldorf; 47 Wesseling; 48 Westheim; 49 Winkel-Seeb; 50 Wölfersheim; 51 Wolpertswende-Mochenwangen; 52 Yvonand

stone for the foundations used in construction at Houten were all 'imported'.

Native house-building traditions survived in other parts of the German provinces as well, although they nowhere dominated rural architecture as they did on the northern periphery of Germania Inferior. The timber longhouse with lateral entrances, typical of northern Germany and the northernmost part of Gaul, is found in isolated examples in the loess zone west of Cologne. One of these at Welldorf had timber roof-supports dividing the interior into four aisles. The farmstead dates to the late first century BC/early first century AD and was presumably operated by a non-Roman owner. Native Germanic pottery found at the site may support this. At any rate, it is unlikely that a Roman settler or veteran from Italy or southern Gaul would have built a farmstead in a tradition completely foreign to him. Nearby at Aldenhoven-Langweiler a mid-first-century AD hamlet consisted of at least two Germanic longhouses and a post-built granary. The population was using both native handmade pottery and the ubiquitous wheel-made Gallo-Belgic wares. Neither longhouse was superseded by a stone-built villa, but at Aldenhoven-Langweiler a more Romanised timber house with internal rooms was built around 100 to replace the older longhouse. A similar phenomenon can be observed at a farmstead near Jüchen north-west of Cologne where a Germanic longhouse and two granaries of the early first century AD were replaced by an entirely timber-built residential building and several granaries and outbuildings within an enclosure ditch some time thereafter, with occupation continuing into the third century (**28**). The layout of the residential building with an internal courtyard reflects Roman architectural influence, yet the structural details are based on a native tradition of post-built houses. There are doubtless many more such farmsteads awaiting discovery in the Rhineland loess zone, not least because excavations have focused thus far on more tangible and easily recognisable remains of stone-built villas.

In the *Agri Decumates* Germanic agrarian settlements are also known, but not yet in any detail. Some of them, such as that at Kehl-Auenheim and Mannheim-Wallstadt on the right bank of the upper Rhine, might reflect Suebian or other east Germanic settlers who were allowed to live here under Augustus. One of the houses at Kehl is entirely timber

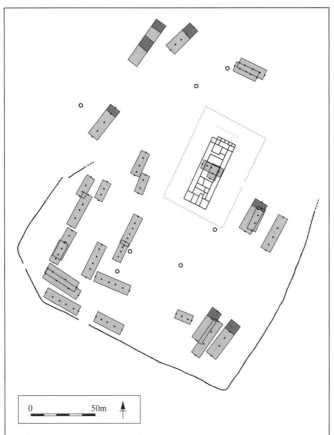

27 *Agrarian hamlet at Hoogeloon in the Netherlands with Germanic longhouses (dark grey = byre) and a stone-built villa which replaced an earlier longhouse*

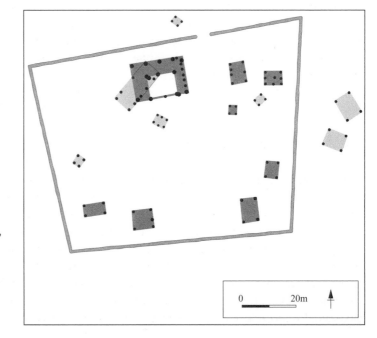

28 *Timber-built farmstead at Jüchen, Germany. Light grey = early first century AD; dark grey = second century*

built with corner posts and walls on sill beams. It was superseded by a poorly preserved structure with shallow stone foundations. This settlement, like the Suebian cemetery 4 miles (6km) further north at Rheinau-Diersheim, was abandoned in the second half of the third century. The settlement at Mannheim-Wallstadt consisted of twenty sunken-floored buildings or *Grubenhäuser*. Further north in the Wetterau, an area assumed to have been a villa zone, small but valuable traces of Germanic settlements of the second and third centuries have been retrieved, largely through field-walking. At Rockenberg-Oppershofen a Germanic settlement of the first half of the second century existed, of which only a *Grubenhaus* has been excavated thus far. At this site Germanic pottery rather than Roman ceramics dominated. In the *Agri Decumates*, as elsewhere, Roman settlers and a Germanic population existed simultaneously, the latter continuing to draw on their native building traditions.

Villas

Villas came in all shapes and sizes, were built at different times and developed in different ways. The principal dwelling, however, was generally one of four basic types: the simple cottage house with a large central room; the winged corridor house which had a portico and two projecting wings on the front; the courtyard house which consisted of three wings between which was a courtyard; and the peristyle house in which rooms on four sides surrounded an internal courtyard (**29**). By the second century most dwellings had stone foundations, but the walls were half-timbered with daub between the timbers. Plastered and painted walls, window glass and tiled roofs were standard fare. Subsidiary farm buildings were often timber-built or were half-timber structures on stone foundations, but rare examples of ancillary buildings built entirely of stone are known, most completely at Oberndorf-Bochingen on the Neckar river where collapsed walls indicate a stone building 36ft (11m) in height (**colour plate 9**). A villa farmyard was enclosed either by a stone wall, a ditch, a hedge or a row of trees to demarcate it from the surrounding countryside and to keep animals out (**30**). The shape of the farmyard enclosure varied and could be square, rectangular, trapezoidal or somewhat more irregular. Some villas were built from the beginning as a fully Romanised complex of buildings, others developed slowly from pre-Roman or early Roman farmsteads. It is these that I would like to look at first.

Classic examples of late Iron Age farmsteads which grew into Roman villas are those at Neerharen-Rekem, Voerendaal and Mayen in Germania Inferior. At Neerharen-Rekem a late Iron Age agrarian hamlet with several Germanic longhouses and granaries was converted in the first century AD to a modest villa with a main residential building, a granary and a stable, only the residential building having stone foundations (**31**). In this first phase of its existence as a Romanised villa, at least one native building, a *Grubenhaus*, existed. In the course of the later first and second centuries, the residential building was enlarged and equipped with an apsidal dining room and a bath suite. In the second century two timber buildings in the farmyard were rebuilt with stone foundations and appear to have served as secondary dwellings, suggesting that the original core family had expanded

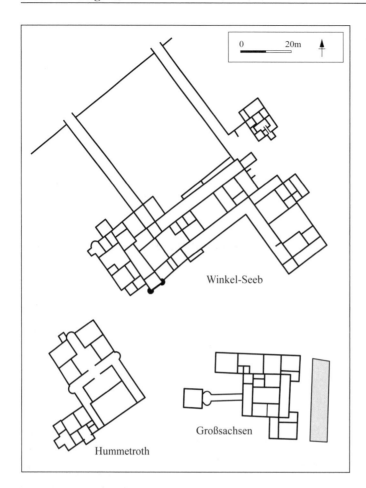

29 Common types of residential buildings of Roman villas at Winkel-Seeb (Switzerland), Hummetroth and Großsachsen (Germany). Grey area = pool

Winkel-Seeb

Großsachsen

Hummetroth

to an extended one or had gained dependants. The types of excavated agricultural buildings indicate that cereal cultivation and stock-farming formed the economic basis. The site at Voerendaal was occupied from the mid-first century BC, apparently as an agrarian hamlet with several timber-built structures. In the second half of the first century AD, a Romanised house with stone foundations and ancillary timber buildings were erected. From the early second century the residential building was enlarged and agricultural buildings with stone foundations constructed. These included a building for the processing of grain and a large stone-built granary with a storage capacity of up to 1400 cubic ft (400m³). The land worked from the farm is estimated to have been an estate of roughly 500 acres (200ha), but this can only be a rough estimate. The villa located in the fertile loess zone east of the Maas owed its wealth to its main cash crop, namely grain. At Mayen, the original late Iron Age farmhouse was a one-room post-built structure with a central hearth, but possibly in the Augustan period this was replaced by a one-room cottage house with stone foundations. The excavator claimed to have distinguished eight different building phases in which a corridor along the front with two projecting wings as well as rooms with a bath and hypocaust heating were added to the core building. Common to Neerharen-Rekem, Voerendaal and Mayen is the relatively rapid

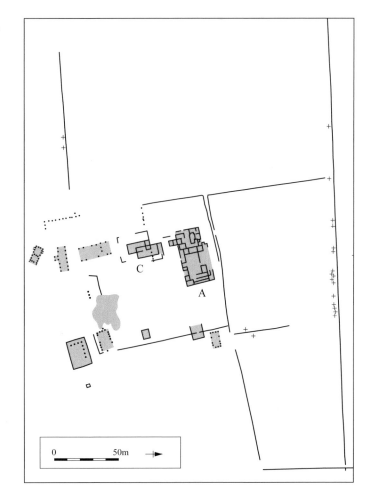

30 Farmstead enclosed by hedges and fences at Hambach 59, Germany.
A main house;
C secondary house.
Crosses = graves

transformation of a native settlement to a Romanised villa, and the repeated improvements to the main residence and the working buildings of the farm indicate an accumulation of wealth that was invested in the villa to make living on the farm more comfortable and the running of it more efficient. The integration of these villas in the Roman socio-economic structure and the market-orientated production of an agricultural surplus made this possible.

The clear continuity of occupation, including the construction of a Romanised farmhouse on the same site as the preceding dwellings, raises questions of ownership and social ties. In the past, it was convenient to interpret the rise of the villa to the allocation of land to Roman legionary veterans, implying that all these villas were owned and run by retired soldiers. Villas with roof tiles manufactured and stamped by the military, like that at Laufenburg on the upper Rhine with tiles of the 21st and 11th Legion from Vindonissa, might be seen in this light. Whilst it is certain that some of the farms were veteran estates, most of them were probably run by native farmers who adapted to the Roman market oriented farming system. The presence of handmade Germanic pottery in small quantities at the first-century AD villa at Müngersdorf west of Cologne led the excavator to conclude

71

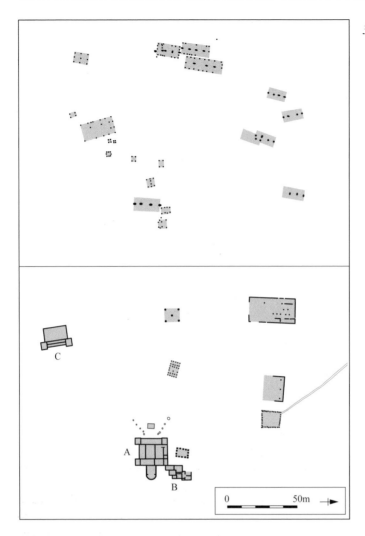

31 *Agrarian hamlet with timber longhouses of the late Iron Age (top) and later stone-built residence with ancillary buildings of the first and second centuries AD (bottom) at Neerharen-Rekem, Netherlands.*
A main house;
B bathhouse;
C secondary house

0   50m

that the villa owner was of local origin rather than a veteran (**32**). Two prerequisites for participation in local government at the *civitas* level were land ownership and sufficient wealth. The magistrates of these towns had their places of residence in the country with an additional one in the towns. Perhaps the native farmers who became villa owners belonged to this sector of the population. Their adoption of a Romanised lifestyle, at any rate, indicates a receptiveness to participation in the Roman socio-economic system. There are, however, differences in the size of villas and the amount of wealth their estates generated. It is not difficult to imagine the owner of the villa at Voerendaal being a member of the local elite, but what of the more modest villas at Neerharen-Rekem and Mayen? Since small and medium-sized villas like these dominate the landscape in both German provinces, we may assume that wealth was fairly evenly distributed. The owners of these villas will surely have had positions of standing within their communities, be it *vicus* or *civitas* capital, even if they were not fabulously wealthy landlords.

Another question is what processes were involved in the transformation of a hamlet in

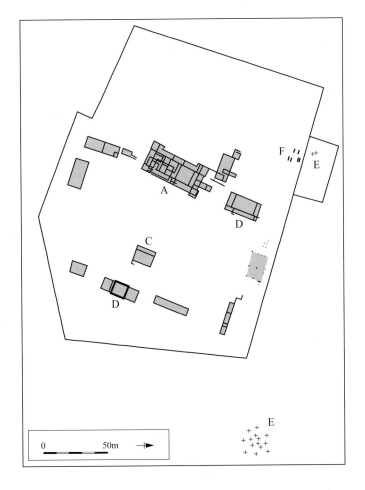

32 Villa at Cologne-Müngersdorf, Germany.
A main house;
C secondary house;
D granaries;
E cremation burials;
F sarcophagi

which several families lived to a villa owned by a single family? If several families lived in the hamlet at Neerharen-Rekem in the late Iron Age, which one of them stayed on to become the villa owner and where did the others go? Characteristic of the native hamlets of the late Iron Age and Roman period in the northern *civitates* is the homogeneity of the settlement. Indications of high-status living and social differentiation within the settlement are lacking. In the peripheral northern zone of Germania Inferior native villages and communal living remained the norm in the Roman period. This was not the case in the southern part of the province. Perhaps here the move away from communal living in the first century AD meant that larger family groups split up, some establishing villas and others working the land from native farmsteads such as those at Welldorf, Aldenhoven-Langweiler and Jüchen discussed above. A closer examination of villas, and in particular the domestic buildings, has revealed that many villa residences were probably not inhabited by one single family, but possibly by two families of relatively equal status. Joint ownership and working of such villas may have been more common than previously assumed. Moreover, the presence of more than one domestic building within a villa compound also suggests that single ownership was not always the case. A secondary dwelling on a farm, separated from the main residence and perhaps equipped with less comforts, may indicate some difference in the status of the families living there, although we have no way of knowing exactly what their personal relationship to each other was. Some kind of kinship, however, is likely.

In the southern loess zone of Germania Inferior a dense network of farms was established as part of a systematic development of the land. Modest but productive Roman villas in close proximity to one another appeared in the second half of the first century and increased in number in the second century (30). The actual enclosed farmyard never exceeded much more than two hectares. Whilst mixed farming was carried out at all of them, the main cash crop appears to have been grain, for which the soils are ideal. These villas were clearly production units established to feed the army and the civilian population on the Rhine, and they may have developed in part due to government encouragement and incentives. The only villa here that stands out in complexity and size is that at Müngersdorf which grew out of a modest farm of the Claudian period to include a stone-built winged corridor house in the midst of eleven ancillary buildings including stables, barns and two granaries in the second and third centuries. Centralised planning may also have been involved in the establishment of *civitas* capitals, small market settlements at fairly regular intervals and a series of compact farms nearby in the *Agri Decumates* and just beyond in the province of Raetia. Consistently small villas at Dornstadt-Tomerdingen, Pforzheim-Hagenschieß, Gemmrigheim, Kirchheim am Neckar, Lauffen am Neckar, Hemmingen, Sigmaringen and Starzach-Bierlingen have a farmyard of between 2.5 and 5 acres (1-2ha) of slightly trapezoidal shape enclosed by a stone wall (33). Internal buildings are a house, a small bath building, stables/barns and, in some cases, a small tower-like granary. We have no information on the overall size of the estates. These villas are located near *civitas* capitals (from Pforzheim-Hagenschieß to Pforzheim 1 mile/2km) or near *vici* as market towns (from Kirchheim am Neckar to Walheim under 2 miles/3km) or in areas between *civitas* capitals and *vici*. All of them were established after the mid-second century as agricultural support units for the civilian population and the military on the *limes*. The economic basis of the villas was mixed farming, and at those on the slopes of the Neckar river evidence for viticulture has also been retrieved. In the northern part of the *Agri Decumates* near the *civitas* capital of Wiesbaden, a number of very small villas with an enclosed farmyard less than one hectare in size were established on the southern slopes of the Taunus mountains. On these farms located up to 980ft (300m) above sea level, it is likely that livestock farming rather than crop cultivation took place, probably to supply the capital with meat and milk. Larger more complex villas like those at Hummetroth (farmyard 9 acres/3.5ha) and Meßkirch (farmyard *c*.20 acres/8ha) are extremely rare in the *Agri Decumates*.

In all of the villas described above there was no firm rule for the placing of the principal dwelling in relation to the subsidiary buildings. Most often, the stables, barns and granaries were scattered around the farmyard, and there was no strict division between the private residential part and the service part of the farmyard. To a large degree, this has to do with the limited size of the farmyard enclosure. At the other end of the scale, however, were the large estates of impressive size and complexity of which we find examples in Germania Superior, particularly Switzerland. The principal dwelling was usually situated at the top or near the top of a long, rectangular farmyard lined with

33 Small villas at Kirchheim, Dornstadt-Tomerdingen, Gemmrigheim, and Pforzheim-Hagenschieß in the Agri Decumates, Germany.
A main house;
B bathhouse;
C secondary house

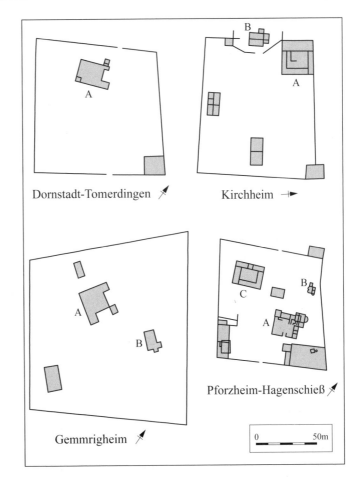

Dornstadt-Tomerdingen

Kirchheim

Gemmrigheim

Pforzheim-Hagenschieß

0   50m

subsidiary buildings. The entire yard ranging from between *c*.12-30 acres (5-12ha) was enclosed by a wall, and the main residential building was separated from the rest of the yard by a perimeter wall. The high-status living quarters (*pars urbana*) are thus distinct from the service area (*pars rustica*). Well-known examples are Oberentfelden (**34**), Dietikon, Buchs, Yvonand and Liestal in Switzerland, Lux west of the Sâone and Thür on the southern edge of the Eifel. Slight variations on this layout can be found at Winkel-Seeb and Vicques in Switzerland. The principal dwelling of these villas is always a complex building, and the same ground plan never appears twice. More than one family could easily have resided here. The villas may have had gardens or parks in the *pars urbana*, although clear archaeological evidence for them has been recovered only at Dietikon where bedding trenches of a formal garden in front of the main residence survived (**35**). Such gardens were a display of status and wealth and they heightened the representative character of the residence. Mosaic floors and marble incrustation as interior decoration are not uncommon, but one has the impression of comfortable rather than luxurious living.

The *pars rustica* at Dietikon has 12 subsidiary buildings 33 x 33ft (10 x 10m) in size along either side of the enclosure wall, that at Oberentfelden nine on either side. It is often impossible to determine the function of many of these buildings with any great certainty,

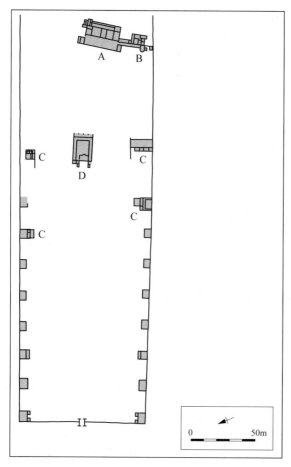

34 Villa at Oberentfelden, Switzerland. A main house; B bathhouse; C secondary houses; D nymphaeum

but the presence of hearths or kilns in those at Dietikon indicate that some of them were domestic units or agricultural buildings. One or more small temples (Dietikon, Vicques, Yvonand) stood within the *pars rustica* or just outside it; at Winkel-Seeb a well-house was centrally placed at the head of this part of the yard.

This type of villa is also well documented in the Somme valley (Estrées-sur-Noye) and in Treveran (Echternach, Fließem) and Tungrian (Anthée) territory, indicating that the type was not peculiar to one region. The principal dwelling at all sites was rebuilt and enlarged several times. The residence at Winkel-Seeb, for example, was rebuilt six times between AD 20 and the mid-second century (*see* **29**). The evidence is not precise enough, however, to tell whether the *pars rustica* was laid out with so many subsidiary buildings from the outset or if these are later additions to an expanding villa. On analogy with an Augustan timber-built villa at Verneuil-en-Halatte in Picardie, which from the beginning had a high-status residential compound and two ranges of domestic units along the limits of the farmyard enclosure, it is possible that the original plan of the Swiss villas included the residence of the local landowner as well as several dependent dwellings. The large number of secondary living quarters probably reflects Celtic social structures (the villa type is not found in the Germanic lower Rhine region) in accordance with which the wealthy landowner retained a retinue of dependants, either kin or clients, at least seasonally. We have no sure way of knowing how large the lands of the estate were, nor is there usually enough evidence from the surroundings to judge whether these large villas may have been situated in a cluster of smaller villas perhaps run by dependants or relatives of the large landowners. An exception is the well-studied eastern Aare valley around Solothurn where villas with farmyards of more than 12 acres (5ha) are fairly regularly spaced at 12-25 miles (5-10km) on either side of the river on the valley floor whilst smaller villa enclosures of 5-10 acres (2-4ha) are located between the large villas or somewhat higher up the valley

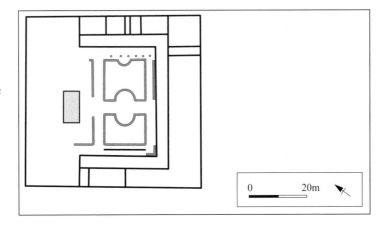

35 Villa residence at Dietikon, Switzerland, with planting trenches for a formal garden in the courtyard. Grey area = pool

0   20m

slopes. Very small villa enclosures of just over 2 acres (1ha) at most are situated on the Jura slopes above these at heights of 1640ft (500m) above sea level or more. This latter group probably belonged to the large landowners and were operated by dependent farmers or hired farmhands who might have lived in the *vicus* at Solothurn.

Rural cemeteries

The inhabitants of farmsteads, villas and hamlets in the countryside maintained communal cemeteries. In Treveran territory one of the most conspicuous types of funerary monuments was the burial mound or *tumulus*. This pre-Roman tradition continued in the Treveran *civitas* well into the second century, and also in the riverside areas of Treveran lands which were detached from Gallia Belgica and reorganised in AD 85 as Germania Superior. Family *tumuli* on or near the grounds of villas include those from Nickenich with funerary statues of family members and dedicatory inscriptions of mid-first-century date. The *tumuli* associated with a second-century farm near Wölfersheim in the *Agri Decumates* might provide some confirmation of Tacitus' claim that many settlers originally came from Gaul (*Germania* 29). But *tumuli* are also occasionally found on Germanic sites in Germania Inferior, particularly on the northern lower Rhine. These are associated with rural hamlets, where the cemeteries are located at a distance from the settlement. The cemetery served by the inhabitants at Hoogeloon lay 1300ft (400m) north-east of the settlement. In the first century this cemetery was characterised by large burial enclosures, with the addition of a *tumulus* in the late second or early third century. One octagonal and two square burial mounds dominated the rural cemetery at Esch.

In the hinterland of the provincial capital of Germania Inferior, no *tumuli* have been found on or near villas. The villas were connected to the main roads leading from the countryside to the city, and the family funerary monuments were built adjacent to these roads as ostentatious forms of display. These include chamber tombs to the west of Cologne at Weiden (**36**) and Hürth-Efferen, and relief-decorated tower tombs within a walled enclosure or so-called grave garden to the south and north of the city at Ossendorf and Wesseling. An enclosed family cemetery in use in the late first and early second

36 *Chamber tomb with sarcophagi and burial niches in Cologne-Weiden, Germany.* Courtesy Rheinisches Bildarchiv

century is known on the estate of a villa owner at Wolpertswende-Mochenwangen north of the Bodensee (**37**). The wealth and status of the family is expressed in the richness of grave finds deposited with cremation burials in four tombs, the largest measuring 21 x 26ft (6.5 x 8m) in size and adorned with a marble funerary inscription. These funerary monuments functioned no less than those of similar type in suburban areas as memorials to the deceased and advertisements of their social status.

Not only the villa owner, but also hired personnel and perhaps slaves lived and worked on villa estates. Whether or not they were all buried together is difficult to determine, and only possible if the actual burials, and not just the tomb buildings or fragments of them, are examined. The chances of relating the identity and status of the deceased to the inhabitants of the villa estates are also increased if the cemeteries are located in the immediate surroundings of the residential sector of villas. At Rottenburg-Hailfingen the completely excavated cemetery included 37 cremation burials from the early second to early third century. These included cremation burials in urns with few grave goods and cremations with whole sets of crockery in larger rectangular pits. One or two richer burials were grouped with several poorer burials in three distinct concentrations, leading the excavator to suggest that each of the groups represents a generation of villa owners buried with their farm personnel. At the farm known as Hambach 516 west of Cologne the earliest cemetery of the first century contained burials of four individuals who may have belonged to the same family, presumably of the first settlers. At Cologne-Müngersdorf cremation burials of the first and second centuries were situated in two locations: in an unwalled area to the north-east of the farm buildings (59 burials) and in a walled cemetery immediately outside the boundary wall of the complex (*see* **32**). This spatial division, which may represent some sort of segregation between the villa's inhabitants, is not fully understood. Possibly the cremation burials belonged to the farm

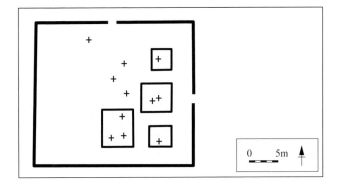

37 Grave complex on the villa estate at Wolpertswende-Mochenwangen, Germany. Crosses = cremation burials

personnel whilst the graves of the villa proprietors were laid out at an unknown site close to the road leading to the villa. In the late third and fourth centuries six inhumation burials in stone sarcophagi were interred in one small area inside the boundary wall, and at least in this phase these probably represent the villa owner's family. The inclusion of sarcophagus burials within the confines of the farm complex may reflect the desire to protect the family burial site from intruders or marauders at a time of social unrest and insecurity, a phenomenon also witnessed after the middle of the third century at Rheinbach-Flerzheim (**38**). Whether or not the farm workers were interred somewhere else in less expensive containers is unknown.

Rural cemeteries occasionally allow insight into population groups which may have shifted in dominance over time. One such example is the cemetery at Tönisvorst-Vorst between Cologne and Xanten. The earliest, Tiberian burials are cremation burials in urns, accompanied by pottery and metal objects identified as Elbe-Germanic in character. In the second half of the first century, this original core of settlers from east of the Rhine may have been joined by a substantial group of newcomers from northern Gaul who buried their dead in a manner characteristic of their homeland, namely in square enclosures. Each enclosure contained at least one cremation burial. Although the settlement to which the cemetery belonged has not yet been located, the burials allow a reconstruction of the size of the settlement and the number of households in it. Only about 30 settlers lived here in the early first century, increasing to between 80 to 200 (12-30 households) in the early second century.

Roadside villages and staging posts

Roadside villages functioned as markets to which produce and goods from the countryside could be taken and sold. Some of them also grew up around an inn (*praetorium* or *mansio*) established for couriers and the transport service of the imperial post system, the *cursus publicus*. Officials and soldiers travelling throughout the Empire on government business were authorised to use the *mansiones* where they could find a room and have a bath for the night, be fed and obtain vehicles or animals for the next leg of their journey. Official government inns are known within some colonies, *civitas* capitals and *vici* in the German provinces, such as Augst, Heddernheim, Rottweil (**39**) and Kembs. Where associated with

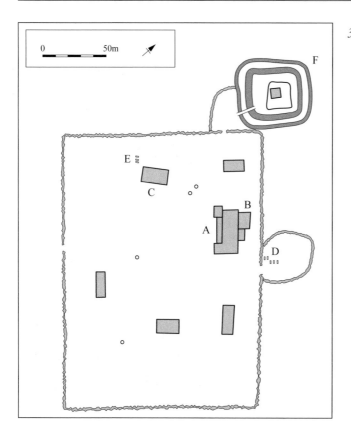

38 Villa at Rheinbach-Flerzheim, Germany.
A main house;
B bath;
C secondary house;
D burials late second/early third century;
E later third-century sarcophagi;
F burgus

civilian settlements, *mansiones* are generally located on the periphery of the town and set back from the street. Whether the inn on a street corner just inside the walls at Xanten was an official one or a large private hotel remains unclear (**colour plate 10**). *Mansiones* are fairly easy to recognise due to the layout of the buildings and their component parts. They include a main accommodation building arranged around a courtyard, a bathhouse and stables as well as other ancillary buildings for the staff who ran the establishment. *Mansiones* are also known outside Roman forts, for example at Vindonissa and the Saalburg. Accommodations and facilities for travellers, however, can also be found on the main Roman roads in the countryside and in more difficult terrain such as the Alps. At these sites, small service villages grew up around the *mansiones*, and it is to them that we turn our attention.

The government established *mansiones* in areas where there had been no provision for the *cursus publicus*, and directives for this have survived. In an inscription from Philoppopolis in Thrace the governor in 61/62 was ordered to build *tabernas et praetoria*, i.e. shops/guesthouses and official inns, on the military roads. An archaeologically known example of such a settlement may be the small roadside *vicus* at Dampierre in Lingonian territory (**40**). The buildings at this site appear to have been built contemporaneously in one organised plan. They front on the main overland route to Langres, and many of them are characterised by their uniform plan as courtyard buildings with a portico on three sides. These have been interpreted as inns associated with the *cursus publicus*, whilst the

39 Inn (mansio) (A) and bath (B) at Rottweil, Germany

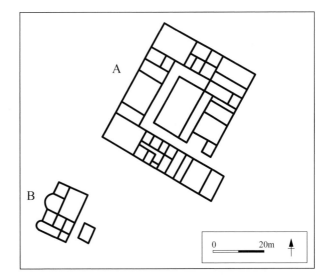

40 Roadside settlement with inns and taverns at Dampierre, France

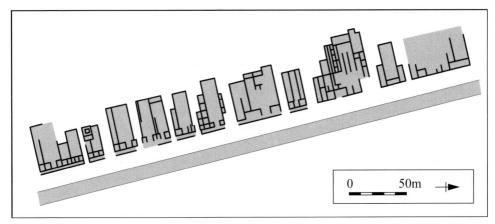

other buildings in the northern part of the *vicus* may have been service buildings and shops. In another text from Pizos in Thrace, dating to the year AD 202, the governor decreed that at both existing and new market settlements *praetoria* and baths should be built for the *cursus publicus*. Pizos itself was set up as a market settlement and settled by 'respectable men' from surrounding villages to care for and maintain the government's staging post. Such settlements, according to the Pizos inscription, had a local administration. Both inscriptions indicate that *mansiones* were linked with market settlements and could be created together.

Latin place names sometimes reflect the existence of inns and guesthouses, for example *Tres Tabernae* on the Via Appia or *Praetorium Agrippinae* at Valkenburg in the Rhine delta. A well-equipped inn would have provided staff such as porters, veterinarians, cartwrights, drivers, grooms, cooks, cleaning personnel, stokers and caretakers for the bathhouse, all of whom lived in the village in which the *mansio* was located. Food, animals and wagons were also procured locally. The upkeep of a *mansio* had to be paid for by the community, although occasionally subsidies from the emperor helped to defray some of

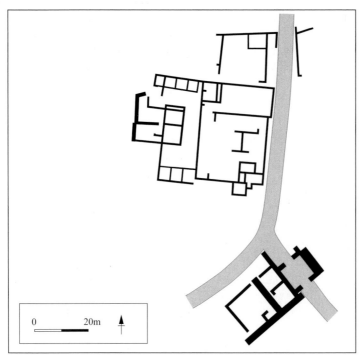

41 Mansio *on the west side of the road leading through the village of Studen/*Petinesca, *Switzerland*

the costs. Although only those with an official pass from the government were allowed to use *mansio* facilities free of charge, private travellers will have also used the inns as paying customers. Traders, merchants and owners of small businesses could earn a livelihood by catering to the needs of traffic and travellers passing through. The non-official traveller, of course, could also stay in any private hostel, guesthouse or tavern, of which there were many everywhere.

Two Roman road-books have survived which contain information for travellers. The Antonine Itinerary of the early third century was an official document recording travel routes and the facilities for lodging and transport along these. Later additions brought the Itinerary up to date, recording routes where new *mansiones* had been built. The Bordeaux Itinerary was written for a private traveller making a pilgrimage from Bordeaux to Jerusalem in 333. Both itineraries name places at which travellers could stay: *mansio, mutatio, civitas, vicus. Civitas* denotes a settlement where one could stop and spend the night; *mansio* means a purpose-built inn; *mutatio* (or *stabulum*) is a hostel where transport/animals could be changed and hired and a basic room and meal could be had; *vicus* is a settlement where there was no purpose-built accommodation. The absence of *mansiones* in the Antonine Itinerary for the routes between Reims and Trier and between Trier and Cologne suggests that there were no purpose-built installations of this kind on these roads. Instead, the traveller made stops at *vici* and *civitates* where the inhabitants were obliged to provide officials with lodgings (in their homes) and transport, although it is archaeologically impossible to tell which of the houses in these towns and villages were requisitioned and used by members of the *cursus publicus* from time to time.

Small villages with a *mansio* or *mutatio*, on the other hand, can be recognised in the

Swiss and Italian Alps. The village of Studen/*Petinesca* lay on the eastern edge of the Jensberg overlooking the overland Aare valley route between Avenches and Vindonissa. Opposite the houses of the *vicus* on the main street lay a complex of buildings comprising a *mansio,* stable facilities, a shop or kitchen and a bathhouse (**41**). The village lay not only on an important road, but may also have been a site of regional religious importance, judging by the two cult complexes on the slope above the *vicus*, one of which contained six Gallo-Roman temples. Winterthur on the road from Bregenz to Augst began probably as a staging post very soon after the first Augustan campaigns into Germany in 15 BC. Timber buildings dated by dendrochronology to 7 BC were erected on either side of the main road in a developing *vicus* in which craft production and tanning took place. A large building identified as a *mansio* stood at the eastern end of the *vicus*.

Staging posts on the mountain passes were not associated with a *vicus*, but a hamlet inhabited by the staff operating such a lonely and exposed post must have existed. On the Great St Bernard pass (*mons Poeninus*) at Bourg-St-Pierre lay a small settlement composed of a *mutatio* compound and temple dedicated to Jupiter Poeninus. Nearby were other buildings of which only a scatter of tile and a milestone have survived. A stone-built courtyard building, subsidiary buildings and a temple have been identified as a *mansio* on the Little St Bernard pass. The *mutatio* named in the Antonine Itinerary as *Murus* might possibly be identified in the staging post at Bondo at the ascent to the Julier and Septimer pass. The excavated buildings include a hostel, a bath and another fragmentarily preserved structure. The Roman road below Riom-Parsonz also led to the Julier pass. On this road was a compound of buildings identified as a *mansio* or *mutatio* with several other structures including the remains of timber buildings. Similar staging posts are known at various other Alpine sites such as Alpnach, Innertkirchen, Zillis and Zernez. The importance of changing animals at regular intervals on such gruelling mountain routes and, therefore, the necessity of available *mutationes* is clear. The limited choice of terrain suitable for stretches of road in these mountainous regions in antiquity or today is aptly illustrated at Péry near Petinesca where the Roman road, the post-Roman road, the modern motorway and the railway are situated in almost exactly the same position.

The roads connecting road stations, ports and towns with each other were essential for the transportation of goods from urban centres and the countryside. The sea, lakes and rivers were also an important part of the transport network. What goods were produced, how trade was organised and how exchange with the transfrontier zones was linked to the Roman economy are explored in the next chapter.

5 Commerce and trade

Commerce should be considered vulgar if it is a rather small affair. If it is extensive and well-financed, importing many products from all over the world and distributing them to many customers honestly, one should not criticise it severely (Cicero, *De Officiis* 1.42.151).

In Upper Germany, Lucius Antistius Vetus, planned to build a Saône-Moselle canal. Goods arriving from the Mediterranean up the Rhône and Saône would thus pass via the Moselle into the Rhine, and so to the North Sea. Such a waterway, joining the western Mediterranean to the northern seaboard, would eliminate the difficulties of land transport (Tacitus, *Annales* 13.53).

Crafts and artisans

Every town had production facilities in which all manner of goods were manufactured. Not all of the manufactured items, particularly the perishable ones such as those made of wood, textile, leather or basketry, to name a few, can be identified in the archaeological record. Nor is it always clear exactly what items were produced in workshops. Metalworking may be indicated by ovens and metal slag, for example, but without the finished or half-finished pieces in these contexts, it remains uncertain what was being manufactured. A bronzesmith's workshop in Augst in which half-finished and discarded pieces of spoons and statuettes were found furnishes rare evidence for manufactured goods. The open-work knife sheaths bearing the name of the bronzesmith Gemellianus and the place of manufacture, *Aquae Helveticae*/Baden, are equally a rarity, however these are attested only as imported items at various sites outside Baden. We are in a much better position with commodities such as pottery, tile, brick and glass which are often found discarded as breakage or as wasters in kilns which can be identified as specifically built for these products.

In the early phase of Roman expansion and occupation in the German provinces, the military employed its own artisans to satisfy its need for pottery and equipment if local supplies were not available. In addition, supplies were transported over great distances to the troops in the north. In particular, amphorae containing foodstuffs such as olive oil and wine were shipped from the Mediterranean and up the Rhône, Rhine and other inland rivers. Fine table wares such as terra sigillata, the glossy red Roman table ware, as well as thin-walled drinking cups from Italy, Spain and southern Gaul were also transported together with edible commodities along these river networks to the army camps. Analysis of the terra sigillata vessels excavated at the Augustan legionary fort at Haltern on the Lippe has shown that this pottery originated in Lyon in Gaul and in Pisa and Arezzo in northern Italy. For its daily, more basic needs of cooking pots and storage vessels, the military depended on its own production at the camp and also made use of local, non-Roman pottery in conquered areas where civilians contributed to the supplies, either by choice or coercion. Pottery kilns have been found at all the earliest Augustan forts along the Rhine, including Dangstetten, Neuss and Xanten, as well as deep in German territory on the Lippe at sites such as Oberaden and Haltern.

In response to the increasing needs of the military and the growing number of civilian Roman settlers in annexed territories, native Gallic potters adapted their repertoire of ceramics to suit Roman tastes and uses. Glossy black terra nigra, fired in kilns in a reducing atmosphere as pre-Roman Gallic pottery was, often imitated terra sigillata shapes, particularly open shapes such as plates and shallow bowls. Both terra nigra and terra rubra, fired in an oxidising atmosphere for a red colour more like terra sigillata, were produced throughout the first century AD. Civilian potters from the interior of Gaul were attracted to the settlements on the Rhine frontier, and potters formerly employed by the military likely also established workshops in these new towns. The pottery industry of early Cologne, for example, supplied the civilian population with a variety of ceramics including terra nigra plates and beakers, white-ware flagons, red earthenware bowls, rough walled cooking pots, bowls and beakers, globular storage jars or *dolia*, large earthenware grinding bowls (*mortaria*) and oil lamps. Based on some of the vessel shapes and moulds, it is probable that Italian and Gaulish potters were involved in Cologne's pottery industry. Many of the wares manufactured in Cologne were produced at other first-century towns along the Rhine, and the repertoire of fabrics and shapes is fairly standard for the time. Rare artefactual confirmation of Gallic potters working in the Rhineland in the late first or early second century comes from a fragmentary *dolium* found at a farmstead near Oberzier west of Cologne. The kiln owner, Auvicco (a local Germanic name) employed a potter, Attaco, whose name is common in western Gaulish regions. Both names were inscribed in the wet clay of the vessel before it was fired.

In areas in which Roman pottery production is indicated, evidence exists for regional differences and localised product specialisation. Colour-coated fine wares, mainly beakers and flagons, were a speciality of the Cologne and Trier workshops in the second and third centuries, and they were exported widely. White pipeclay figurines, often bearing the stamp of the potters Servandus and Fabricius, were both a local speciality in Cologne and an export item, their place of manufacture 'CCAA' being stamped or inscribed on the back and roughly equivalent to 'made in Cologne' (**42**). In the late second and third centuries at Soller very large *mortaria* with a diameter of over 2ft (70cm) were produced and shipped as far afield as Britain. A large number of *mortaria* made by the potter Verecundus from Soller have been found in Silchester. At Nijmegen a particular type of pottery of reddish colour was manufactured in shapes imitating terra sigillata, glass and metal vessels. This pottery, known as Holdeurn ware, was made in the later first century under the supervision of the 10th Legion, both on legionary property and in the civilian settlement near the fort, and it was distributed locally. Another ceramic speciality possibly associated with military production is the so-called Wetterau ware manufactured in civilian potteries

42 *(left and opposite)*
Pipe clay statuette
of the Matronae
manufactured by
Fabricius in
Cologne
(CCAA).
Courtesy
Rheinisches
Bildarchiv

at Frankfurt-Heddernheim and Frankfurt-Nied in the late first and early second centuries. This red-painted fine ware with figural scenes or with handles bearing relief decoration often imitated metal vessels of Mediterranean origin. A ceramic speciality of at least one potter in Worms on the upper Rhine around 300 were the red earthenware flagons, the necks of which were decorated with a female face in relief (**colour plate 11**). A general popularity of red or red and white painted wares in fourth-century pottery in the Rhineland is indicated by production sites of these ceramics in Worms, Trier and Cologne.

Terra sigillata was another regional product with a wide distribution. Essential for its manufacture was a very fine iron-rich clay. This was not available everywhere so that the location of terra sigillata kilns was determined by the appropriate clay reserves. In the first century AD the largest manufactories for terra sigillata were located in southern Gaul, particularly at La Graufesenque, and from the turn of the first to second centuries in central Gaul, most notably at Lezoux. By the early second century other sigillata centres further north in eastern Gaul were established which were located closer to the markets in the German Rhineland and beyond to the Danube and Britain. One of these was located on the east bank of the Moselle river in Trier where terra sigillata was manufactured from the first half of the second century until about 275. The largest and most extensively excavated east Gaulish sigillata centre is that at Rheinzabern (*vicus Tabernae*) on the upper Rhine near the *civitas* capital of Speyer. Military tile production took

place here initially. The first sigillata potters to set up shop at Rheinzabern in the mid-second century came from eastern Gaul where they had worked at Heiligenberg in Alsace. Plain, undecorated sigillata made up about 90% of the manufactured pottery, whilst bowls with moulded decoration comprised roughly 10%. More than 300 different personal names at Rheinzabern are known from pottery stamps, indicating that production there was organised along the lines of small workshops or collectives comprising potters, mould-makers, specialists and workshop owners. Based on fragmentarily preserved tallies of kiln loads, it is estimated that the annual output lay between 500,000 and one million vessels, but even this appears modest in comparison to the southern Gaulish site at La Graufesenque where in a communal firing nearly 30,000 vessels were loaded into just one kiln.

Attempts to establish terra sigillata workshops even further north in the province of Germania Inferior were unsuccessful and short-lived. At Aachen-Schönforst on the western fringe of the province terra sigillata was produced at the beginning of the second century, but the available clay was not entirely suitable for it and production soon ceased. Around the middle of the second century terra sigillata began to be manufactured at Sinzig on the southern edge of Germania Inferior where before that military tileries operated. The potters appear to have worked at Trier and La Madeleine before they settled in Sinzig to make plain and decorated ceramics. Production lasted only 50 years at the most, probably largely due to unsatisfactory raw material. Small workshops such as that at Sinzig most likely were also not able to compete economically with the larger east Gaulish centres.

Rheinzabern terra sigillata was exported as far north as the Antonine Wall in Scotland and the Black Sea in the east, although its main markets were in Germania Superior and the adjacent provinces of Raetia, Noricum and Pannonia. Although these markets were lost after 260 due to the destruction of Roman settlements east of the Rhine in Roman civil wars and Alamannic incursions, the kilns continued to manufacture sigillata until the mid-fourth century, albeit in more modest quantities and with a modified repertoire of vessels. Just as Rheinzabern products were exported to the Danube provinces, Rheinzabern workshops generated artisans with the necessary expertise who migrated to Danubian regions to set up branch workshops. In the last decades of the second century potters from Rheinzabern settled in Westerndorf and Schwabmünchen-Schwabegg in Bavaria (Raetia), bringing their wares even closer to the forts on the Danube *limes* in Noricum and Pannonia. Based on the name stamps on terra sigillata manufactured in Baden on the Swiss upper Rhine, it is assumed that potters had migrated from Westerndorf. An advantage to setting up branches of a central manufactory in other provinces was that the wares could be sold without having to be transported long distances and without being subject to provincial tax or customs when crossing provincial boundaries.

Finally, a regional peculiarity connected with the production of terra sigillata is the so-called Helvetian imitation terra sigillata. This pottery, exclusively made in the Swiss part of Germania Superior, is known from kiln sites at Lausanne, Augst, Vindonissa and Ägerten near Bern. At Lausanne Helvetian imitation terra sigillata was manufactured in the second half of the first century along with 'true' terra sigillata which raises the question of why the two were produced at the same time and whether one really is an imitation of the other. Both ceramics employed the same clay, and the firing temperature was identical; the shapes of the vessels, the quality of the surface slip and the method of firing of the Helvetian ware, however, differ from terra sigillata. Perhaps the Helvetian ware was produced for a regional market in which the vessel shapes conformed more closely to local taste or dining habits. Since many of the bowls and plates are noticeably larger than terra sigillata examples it is possible that the users often shared table vessels for communal dining, rather than assigning themselves individual place-settings which was the Roman practice. Alternatively, Helvetian imitation sigillata might have been cheaper to buy than terra sigillata and appealed to more cost conscious customers. At any rate, the distribution of this pottery is largely limited to the Aare valley and it is rarely found north of the Jura mountains. Ultimately it was entirely replaced by imported terra sigillata or terra sigillata made more locally.

Pottery manufacture of another kind and on a different level was the largely localised production of handmade wares (**colour plate 12**). By and large, the pottery was limited to coarse wares and cooking vessels, and it was used along with wheel-made Roman pottery. Unlike the latter which was produced in large quantities and transported over considerable distances, the handmade wares did not travel beyond the regions in which they were made. Localised production of handmade pottery is attested at Rottweil,

Vindonissa and Solothurn, as well as in the Ardennes in the Namur area, to name only a few sites. Some of the tableware imitates Roman vessel types and shapes. Roman wheel-made pottery production does not seem to have made a great impact in the Dutch Rhineland or the delta area. In Frisian, Cananefatian and Batavian territory handmade pre-Roman pottery continued to be produced well into the late Roman period. It suited the needs of the population and, although Roman imports such as terra sigillata and other wares are not uncommon, traditional kitchen wares, storage vessels and dinner services remained in use.

Clay was also the raw material for tile and brick production. The industry was either managed by the military or by private brickmakers supplying the military and civilian settlements. The military tileries were located on property owned by the army, even if it was not immediately adjacent to a fort (**colour plate 13**). The 5th Legion stationed in Xanten from the early first century to 69 operated a tilery about 56 miles (90km) south of their base in Feldkassel, and Legio XI not only produced tiles at their base in Vindonissa, but also at a local tilery in Rottweil where troops were garrisoned under the command of the legion. Tiles produced in army tileries were stamped with the name of the legion, and they are thus easily attributable to the units responsible for their manufacture. The distribution of stamped tiles sheds light on the activities and movements of the military which could supply this material for building projects not only locally but also at some distance. First and foremost these tiles were made for military building projects, but the army assisted in the construction of major public buildings in the towns as well. Private tile producers operated in all parts of the German provinces. They, too, stamped their products with their names or short forms thereof. Some of them had government contracts to supply tile and brick for public and military building projects. Adiutex and Capio, for example, produced tile for the construction of the Constantinian basilica in Trier and the contemporaneous fort in Cologne-Deutz. M. Valerius Sano based in Krefeld-Gellep worked for both military and civilian clients in the second century.

The skill and expertise of artisans is nowhere better illustrated than in the art of glassmaking. The major centre for this craft was Cologne, and at the moment there appears to have been no other town in the western provinces to have rivalled it. The main raw material for glass, diluvial quartzite sand, was available in ample quantities west of the city. Glass production began here in the first century, but the output and quality of glass manufacture reached its peak in the second and third centuries. During this period, one of the specialities of Cologne's workshops were the so-called snake-trailed vessels. The body of the vessels consisted of colourless glass, and on the surface were applied trails of colourless, white or coloured glass (**colour plate 14**). Shapes included flasks, bottles, jugs and fanciful forms such as glass slippers. Glass beakers or goblets could also be decorated with applied motifs such as dolphins, fish or shells in various colours. Perfume flasks of colourless glass were blown in the shapes of human heads, dolphins, piglets or fish and decorated in the snake-trail manner. Coloured glass in emerald green, cobalt blue and ruby red was made by adding metal oxides, and gold glass was sometimes mixed into the matrix to give a golden, marbled effect. It is often suggested that the rise in the production of luxury glass in the second century was due to the influx of Syrian glassmakers brought to Cologne, but there is no clear evidence to support this. In addition to luxury glass, the workshops in Cologne produced vast quantities of plain wares such as perfume and oil flasks, square bottles and globular urns. Products of the city's glassmakers were exported throughout the western Empire and as far as Egypt, and they are also found in areas outside the Empire such as Jutland on the North Sea and Gotland in the Baltic Sea.

In the fourth century Cologne's glassmakers changed their repertoire to produce bowls, beakers and plates with incised figural scenes such as circus races or Adam and Eve being driven out of the garden of Eden. The finest and most delicate of these late glass products are the so-called cage cups or *diatreta* glasses. This involved making a colourless glass cup and dipping it into liquid glass of various colours and then grinding or cutting the outer layers into patterns or inscriptions. Kilns for the production of these vessels have not yet been found in the city. In the countryside south of the Cologne-Bavay road near Jülich, however, six glass production sites of the second half of the fourth century recently have been excavated at a number of farmsteads located in close proximity to each other. Barrel-shaped glass jugs appear to have been the primary product of 15 kilns at the site at Hambach 132. Vessels stamped with ECVA by the manufacturer were made at two Hambach sites, either contemporaneously or in succession, and they are found distributed around Cologne, Bonn, Krefeld and Jülich. The location and date of these kilns suggest that glass production in the late Roman period partially may have been moved from the city closer to the source of the raw materials, an hypothesis supported by the analysis of the glass which indicates that local sand was used.

With the arrival of the Roman army in the Rhineland, the custom of erecting stone tombs and carving stone gravemarkers bearing likenesses or simple inscriptions spread to the frontier (*see* **24**). Since the pre-Roman population was unfamiliar with this tradition, immigrant stonemasons and sculptors were needed to satisfy the demand. The earliest sculptors appear to have come from northern Italy and from Gallia Narbonensis. Already in the first half of the first century AD, the Romanised native population in some areas began to adopt the funerary practice of commemoration in stone (**43**). At this time, sculptors' workshops were established which catered either to the needs of the civilian population or those of the military. One of these workshops working for the military, to which a whole group of grave reliefs can be attributed, was located in Mainz in the 60s and 70s. This group of reliefs depicting the deceased as a mounted rider defeating a barbarian foe is known as the Romanius-group, named after the gravestone of Gaius Romanius Capito from Celeia (Slovenia) who served in the Ala Noricorum (**44**). A group of reliefs depicting civilians in Celtic and Roman dress, among them that of the shipper Blussus and his wife Menimane, on the other hand, can be attributed to another sculptor's workshop which catered to the local population around Mainz (*see* **25**). In pre-colonial Cologne, a similar division between sculptors working for different clientele is apparent. Two of the earliest gravestones with a bust of the deceased were made from the same stone block by the same sculptor for two soldiers of Legio I and Legio XX in the early first century. Both come from the same cemetery. The type was soon copied for civilian gravestones. For a civilian family of Viromandui four identical stone slabs were cut in the same workshop, two per stone block, and erected in the western cemetery outside Cologne. A study of the popular so-called funerary banquet reliefs of the later first and second centuries in Cologne indicates that several contemporaneous workshops were manufacturing these gravestones and that the products of these various workshops can be associated with particular cemeteries (**45**). Presumably each of the workshops, from which the family chose the funerary monuments, was located next to a suburban cemetery to reduce the effort of transporting the stones to their destination. Although the names of the sculptors are unknown, it is likely that at least by the second century locally trained craftsmen had replaced the original immigrant sculptors.

At Avenches in Switzerland, a site much less heavily influenced by the military, several ateliers of sculptors have been recognised. Here, however, there seems to have been specialisation of another sort. Two of the ateliers focused on the manufacture of gravestones, whilst others specialised in the production of votive monuments of various sizes and colossal religious sculptures.

Industrial settlements

The industrial activity involved in making high quality glass, pottery and metal objects was messy, smelly and dangerous. Kilns were a fire hazard, and the smoke and fumes emanating from them polluted the air. For this reason zones for pottery kilns, glass kilns and metalworking establishments were usually located outside the limits of the town, although there was no hard and fast rule for this. The small settlement at Mathay-Essarté on the west bank of the Doubs may have been a satellite of the *vicus* Mandeure less than a mile (1.5km) to the north, and it appears to

43 Early first-century gravestone of Bella of the Remi tribe, Cologne.
Courtesy Rheinisches Bildarchiv

44 Gravestone of the cavalry trooper
Romanius from Celeia in Slovenia,
first century AD.
Courtesy Landesmuseum
Mainz

have functioned as an industrial dependant of Mandeure, particularly for the production of pottery (**19**). In the suburban areas of towns there was more room to expand, and workshops would have had more space for storage of supplies and raw materials. Moreover, delivery of materials such as clay, ore and timber from the countryside to the workshops would have been facilitated by their location outside town near access roads. There were, however, settlements beyond the urban areas in which industrial production was the main activity.

Pottery production was the means of livelihood and the reason for the existence of settlements such as Rheinzabern and Sinzig. The *vicus* of Rheinzabern consisted of strip-houses, workshops, storage sheds, pottery and tile kilns, clay refinery pits and wells, and over 300 terra sigillata potters are known to have worked in the settlement. The density of pottery kilns and associated buildings in Waiblingen near the Upper German *limes* and the

45 Gravestone of the Spanish-born veteran M. Valerius Celerinus who retired in Cologne in the late first century AD.
Courtesy Rheinisches Bildarchiv

confluence of the Rems and Neckar rivers suggests that this settlement was also established to produce and supply the civilian and military population on the frontier with ceramics, both terra sigillata and a wide variety of household wares. Buildings with street frontage had a double function with living and working quarters, and the manufactured pottery was stored in them awaiting sale. Excavations in 1967 uncovered 300 finished vessels stacked on wooden shelves in a cellar which collapsed when the building was destroyed by fire.

An industrial settlement of another type is the *vicus* of Eisenberg on the overland route from Metz to Worms. Deposits of iron slag up to 16ft (5m) thick and numerous furnaces in the settlement indicate that iron-smelting was the main activity in the *vicus*. Near Eisenberg Roman quarry shafts in an extensive area have been discovered from which the ores for refinement in the *vicus* were brought. Another industrial settlement of iron-

46 *Excavated and surveyed buildings in the iron-smelting village at Bad Neuenahr-Ahrweiler, Germany*

0   50m

smelters is known at Bad Neuenahr-Ahrweiler on the southern periphery of Germania Inferior. A wall enclosed a roughly rectangular settlement of a little more than 2.5 acres (1ha) containing at least 25 half-timbered buildings on stone foundations (**46**). Although excavations were limited, slag heaps spread throughout the enclosed area and a furnace associated with a building in the south-west corner of the settlement indicate the primary industry. There is no evidence of any public buildings or administrative infrastructure. The settlement most likely was purely industrial and under the jurisdiction of another small town or the military.

The military was certainly in charge of industrial settlements on the Erft river in which lime was burnt, an essential element needed for making mortar and, therefore, important for military building projects. The extent of the settlements is unknown, but banks of lime kilns have been detected in several spots along the dolomite cliffs. The site best known through excavations is at Iversheim where, in a building over 100ft (30m) in length, a battery of six kilns was uncovered, one of which was still filled with 500 cu ft (15m³) of burnt lime. A unit of 50 men drawn mainly from Legio XXX at *Vetera*/Xanten was housed near the kilns, as indicated by the inscriptions on votive dedications. Analysis of mortar in buildings in the colony (*Colonia Ulpia Traiana*) at Xanten, and in those in Bonn and Neuss, reveal that this material was supplied from Iversheim. We may assume that many other centres in Germania Inferior made use of lime from the site until the kilns were abandoned in the fourth century.

Merchants and shippers

Roman merchants (*negotiatores*) were active everywhere within the Empire, even in marginal areas and in zones of potential unrest. They could be the victims of violence, as they were in Trier during the revolt of Iulius Florus and Iulius Sacrovir in AD 21, being, as it seemed to conquered peoples, symbols of Roman expansion and exploitation. Once peaceful conditions prevailed, however, the merchants played a vital role in the economic life of the provinces. In the first century Italian merchants were strongly represented in the future German provinces, but Gallic traders were also active there. Such Gallic merchants from the tribes of the Lingones, Remi and Viromandui of central and northern Gaul operated in first-century Xanten and Cologne. By the second century the Italian traders had been replaced by those from Gaul who were actively involved in the economic development of their own regions and profited considerably from long-distance trade. Merchants and businessmen in Treveran territory, for example, might rise in status and power in the early second century to become magistrates in their community and heads of trade guilds, and men from the same social class in Nijmegen also held magisterial offices in local government. Other businessmen involved in the actual transport of merchandise were the shippers and overland transporters. Merchants travelled some distances and had offices outside their communities enabling them to buy up commodities of many sorts, then contracting transport companies to bring the goods to market destinations. In some cases, merchants themselves ran their own transport businesses.

The activities of the merchants and their physical mobility is attested above all in inscriptions. Lyon, a major port on the confluence of the Saône and Rhône rivers whence goods from the south were redistributed to the north, is rich in epigraphic references to merchants from Gaul and the Rhineland. The named origin of merchants indicates that in the southern part of Germania Superior the economic ties with central Gaul (Lyon, Vienne) were strongest, whilst those in Germania Inferior were connected with northern Gallia Belgica. In between these two areas the Treveri, Sequani and Mediomatrici acted as middlemen in trade with the middle Rhine and the *limes* zone to the east. The Treveri, in particular, used their geographic position to develop their role as traders and transporters. They are commonly found not only in central Gaul in Lyon, but also on the middle and lower Rhine in Cologne and Mainz, both capitals of their province, important markets in their own right and ports for redistribution of goods further north and east. The Sequanian Philus who died in Cirencester in Britain in the first century may have been a trader in goods between the Rhineland and Britain.

Merchants involved in North Sea and cross-channel trade are attested in numerous votive inscriptions on second- and third-century altars found in the Nehalennia sanctuary at coastal Colijnsplaat and Domburg in the Rhine-Schelde delta (**47**). These include merchants mainly from Trier, Cologne and Nijmegen, but also men from Boulogne and the Rouen and Besançon areas. These and other inscriptions reveal that merchants specialised in selling particular commodities such as salt, wine, fish sauce, pickled vegetables, grain, pottery and textiles. Some merchants, however, dealt in more than one commodity, for example wine and pottery together. Very long distance trade connections are apparent in the importation of exotic goods such as Chinese silk, a piece of which was

47 *Late second-century*
votive altar from
Colijnsplaat
(Netherlands) to
Nehalennia, dedicated by
the salt merchant M.
Exgingius Agricola who
was based in Cologne.
Courtesy
Rijksmuseum van
Oudheden Leiden

used to wrap the cremated remains of a woman who died around 200 and was buried on the family's rural estate in Wehringen near Augsburg in Bavaria.

Merchants set up businesses for civilian markets, but they often also had contracts to provide the military with supplies, particularly in the Rhineland where troop contingents were stationed. Military ties with salt merchants in the *civitates* of the Menapii and Morini are attested by an inscription from Rimini which records a centurion from Neuss who was in charge of the transactions. The fertile loess zones of the Nervii in Belgica supplied the civilian and military population on the lower Rhine with grain. On board a grain barge found at the Roman fort at Woerden on the lower Rhine were wheat and pottery from Flanders, the homeland of the Nervii. It is also no coincidence that both a grain merchant in Nijmegen and a flour merchant in Cologne were Nervians. Colleges of boatmen and shippers could fulfil the role of transporters of state supplies, particularly from inland sources, but the transport of these supplies between forts on the Rhine frontier will often have been the responsibility of the Roman fleet itself. Civilian merchants with military contracts were in the particularly favourable situation of being able to procure goods for the military without paying customs at the borders of provinces, cities and forts, whilst bringing merchandise for the civilian markets in the same shipments. The profit made on civilian goods was higher if customs taxes were waived.

Shippers (*nautae*, *navicularii*) operated on the navigable rivers, carrying cargoes to many destinations. The Rhine was one of the main arteries for river transport, and the activities of the shippers there are attested already in the first century. The shipper Blussus based in Mainz in the mid-first century is depicted on his gravestone, the reverse side of which carries an inscription referring to his profession as well as a depiction of a river-going vessel (**48**). Shippers are recorded in many inscriptions at sites on Lake Geneva as well as on the Saône and Aare rivers.

Inscriptions indicate that there was a close relationship between merchants and shippers. Treveran wine merchants in Lyon, for example, were often also Saône shippers. Epigraphic records also show that in many cases there was a close connection between shippers and overland transporters (*utriclarii*). The latter chiefly transported wine and are well represented in southern and central Gaul, particularly in Lyon in the later second and early third centuries. From Lyon, where numerous wine merchants were based, wine from southern Gaul was shipped in barrels to more northerly markets in Gaul and the Rhineland. Much of this was brought overland in large carts. One of the routes used by the *utriclarii* led from Lyon via Langres, Metz and Trier to Cologne. Again, the Treveri are particularly active in this branch of the wine trade until the mid-third century when viticulture on the Moselle was established and the area became self-sufficient in wine production.

Merchants, shippers and transporters were grouped together in clubs and guilds. The wine merchants and Saône shippers in Lyon formed such a guild (*corpus*) which represented their interests, as did those on the Swiss rivers and lakes. The headquarters and nearby temples of the merchants and shippers at Lausanne on Lake Geneva were located in the commercial and religious centre of the *vicus* next to the forum (**14**). The merchants involved in trade on both sides of the Alps also formed a guild (*corpus cisalpinorum et transalpinorum*) in major trade centres such as Lyon, Avenches, Budapest and Milan.

Cross-frontier exchange

Merchants were also active beyond the frontier. In 69 *negotiatores*, presumably with military contracts, were active in the territory of the Frisii according to Tacitus (*Historiae* 4.15). Roman contractors licensed fishing rights in the same area in the later second or third century, and their activity is recorded on a votive inscription found at Beetgum. In procuring supplies for the army, a military purchaser accompanied by two centurions from Legio I and V ventured in the first century AD into Frisian lands to buy cattle. Their purchase was recorded on a wax tablet found in Tolsum in Friesland. The Frisii were

48 Reverse side of the gravestone of Blussus and Menimane from Mainz-Weisenau with a depiction of a river-going vessel. Courtesy Landesmuseum Mainz

known in general as suppliers of cattle, hides, fish and dairy products, and, although they lived immediately beyond the frontier, their economy was in part geared towards the production of surpluses for Roman markets, even after they were no longer forced to pay tribute in oxhides to the Roman government after the mid-first century. Roman traders had established themselves at the court of the Marcomannian king Maroboduus (Tacitus, *Annales* 2.62). There is also evidence for German traders operating on a much smaller scale within the borders of the Empire. The Tencteri on the east bank of the Rhine, for example, voiced complaints about having to pay customs and duties on trade with Cologne, as well as being under police supervision when entering the city (Tacitus, *Historiae* 4.64-65). According to Tacitus (*Germania* 41), however, there was only one Germanic tribe that was permitted to trade not only in the trading posts on the frontier, but also deep within the Empire in the first and early second centuries, and this was the Hermunduri on the borders of Raetia.

Goods, people and ideas crossed the frontier for various reasons and under varying circumstances. Trade between the Roman provinces and the peoples beyond the frontier was one kind of economic exchange, but Roman artefacts outside Roman territory can also be the result of raids, payment of bonuses to tribes to keep the peace and discharge settlements to non-Roman mercenaries, although the latter two probably involved gold, silver and metal prestige items rather than utilitarian items such as pottery. East of the Main *limes*, Roman imports at native settlements such as Gaukönigshofen in Franconia and Sülzdorf in Thuringia comprise Roman *fibulae* and pottery from the late second and third centuries, including terra sigillata. North of this stretch of the *limes* in the native settlement at Naunheim on the Lahn river the same range of Roman imports are to be found. About 20% of the total ceramic and metal assemblage found in the Germanic cemetery at Gießen on the upper Lahn river to the north-west of the *limes* consisted of Roman imports dating to the period 150-250. These include terra sigillata, terra nigra, coarse wares, weapons, brooches and jewellery and a few coins. The native Germanic pottery included rather clumsy imitations of Roman vessel shapes, similar examples of which are also found in the material assemblage of the fort and civilian settlement at Zugmantel on the *limes* (**colour plate 15**). Further north of Gießen to the west of the Fulda and Weser rivers, Roman pottery, metal and glass imports have been found at a Germanic settlement of the Chatti at Fritzlar-Geismar. In addition to these objects, basalt millstones from the Rhineland and substantial amounts of Roman bronze coinage, but not gold or silver coins, occur in the material assemblage, leading the excavators to suggest that this low denomination Roman coinage was used in part as currency in some form of rudimentary monetary economy.

One of the trade routes from the *limes* into transfrontier Germany led through the Gießen basin to the tributaries of the Weser river, and it is apparent that the native population at Gießen profited from trade in both directions. Another access route led through the Tauber valley in which sites such as Tauberbischofsheim-Distelhausen 15 miles (25km) east of the frontier have mixed second-century assemblages of Rhine-Weser Germanic pottery and Roman imports. Roman forts controlled the few openings in the *limes* which gave access to these routes. These include Butzbach overseeing the Gießen route, Osterburken and Jagsthausen with *limes* gates leading into the Tauber and Jagst valley, as well as Reinau-Dalkingen with a monumental gate opening onto the Jagst.

Roman imports such as terra sigillata, oil lamps and coins are also found at several first-century sites in Frisia. Even after the Rhine frontier was established and Frisia excluded from the Empire in AD 47, Roman imports reached native sites. Most of these second- and third-century sites are located along the coast or near water, a factor that is related to transport. An analysis of the terra sigillata vessel forms present at these sites indicates that one particular kind of bowl (form Dragendorff 37) is prevalent. This type of vessel within the assemblage of imported wares must either have been used more commonly than others in dining or this particular vessel type had some meaning or status we cannot grasp. What is interesting to compare is the terra sigillata assemblage at Hatsum in Frisia with that at Rijswijk just south of the Rhine in the territory of the Cananefates. At both sites there is a very similar percentage of vessel forms which may indicate that both sites had similar economic contacts with the Romans, although one was outside and the other inside the Empire. These imports were probably exchanged for cattle raised for Roman markets.

A transfer of technology and ideas from the Roman provinces to the Germanic lands is also clearly in evidence. Not only was Roman pottery imported and copied, but also potters trained in the techniques of building kilns and manufacturing Roman pottery were employed beyond the upper German *limes*. Surprising evidence for this comes from the Germanic settlement in the territory of the Hermunduri at Haarhausen south of Erfurt (Thuringia) where pottery kilns of Roman type were built after the fall of the *limes* in the second half of the third century. The wheel-made pottery from the site over 62 miles (100km) east of the former *limes* includes Roman vessel shapes such as jugs, beakers, bowls, plates and, above all, *mortaria*. The kilns produced pottery for a regional market in the Thuringian basin, an estimated 70,000-80,000 vessels annually. Wares from Haarhausen have been found on about 170 sites in this region. Either Germanic potters trained within the Empire worked at Haarhausen or Roman potters were employed there by choice or coercion. The capture of Roman prisoners by Germanic groups is recorded in historical and textual sources, as is the desertion of some Roman provincials to the Germanic side (Tacitus, *Historiae* 4.23.3). Some of these prisoners or deserters could well have been Roman craftsmen and technicians (Cassius Dio, *Historia Romana* 67.7.4). Since the Hermunduri seem to have had special treaty agreements with Rome, perhaps Roman personnel with the necessary technological know-how collaborated with them.

What role Roman imports in general played in native society is uncertain. Even if Roman ceramic and metal vessels may have been used as tableware, it is fairly certain that they were also considered objects of status and prestige. Such objects may have been exchanged again within Germanic society as sought-after gifts, thereby contributing to social differentiation and reproduction of status within that society. So-called princely graves beyond the frontier as far away as Poland and Denmark are recognisably those of the elite not only because of the rich grave goods of native production, but also in the inclusion of Roman metal, weapons and glass which must have been symbols of elevated social status. Social and economic relationships between Romans and transfrontier peoples were probably far more profound than the meagre archaeological record allows us to recognise. Trade with the Roman provinces and service in the Roman military allowed the acquisition of Roman prestige items which surely contributed to wealth and status of the individuals involved. The fact that Roman pottery was produced in large quantities for regional distribution in Germanic Thuringia suggests at least a partial adoption of Roman cultural customs, even if the pottery was utilised chiefly because of its value as an object of social status. The manufacture of *mortaria* at Haarhausen, vessels essential for the preparation of food in Roman cuisine, suggests that Roman dining habits may have been adopted to some degree. Drinking from Roman cups and beakers, rather than dining with Roman cooking pots or plates, appears to have been more popular with the Germanic population at Gaukönigshofen, since most of the imported Roman pottery there consists of drinking vessels. Even certain Roman funerary customs such as the placing of a coin in the mouth of the dead were occasionally adopted, most notably in the third-century Germanic cemetery at Haßleben north of Erfurt. These graves are commonly referred to as princely graves and attributed to the tribal elite, mainly because the dead were buried in timber-lined chambers and the grave goods include gold and silver jewellery and imported Roman objects such as gold coins and bronze vessels. The graves also include wheel-made pottery from Haarhausen and Germanic handmade wares. All of this suggests close ties between a regional population group in Thuringia, or at least the elite of this group, and Roman provincial territory. The use of Roman objects and the adoption of selected social and cultural customs, even if largely superficial, were perhaps a means by which status in this Germanic society could be consolidated and displayed.

Technology transfer also took place in animal husbandry. In north Hessen and Thuringia, the homelands of the Chatti and Hermunduri, analysis of animal bones has shown that, in addition to small Germanic cattle, cattle considerably larger than the Germanic animals and more akin to the Roman breeds were raised. This can be explained by contact and exchange with the Roman Empire, within the boundaries of which new stock from the Mediterranean had been brought already in the early first century AD. The Hermunduri, who had trading privileges within the Empire, almost certainly imported Roman cattle for breeding purposes. Beyond the frontier at the native settlement at Heeten in the Netherlands, large breeds of Roman oxen were used in the first half of the fourth century, probably to transport iron ore for processing at the settlement. Presumably these were 'imported' or were bred at Heeten using Roman stock, demonstrating again the economic links between transfrontier zones and Rome.

In this and the preceding chapters, reference has been made to the role of the military in many aspects of provincial life. The 'military', however, was not an anonymous, faceless entity. The next chapter is devoted to the soldiers who were recruited in all parts of the Empire, absolved a fixed period of service, married, begat children and, if they survived army life, settled down to civilian life in the provinces.

6 Soldiers and civilians

(The Batavi) are not subjected to the indignity of tribute or ground down by the tax-gatherer. Free from burdens and special levies, and reserved for employment in battle, they are like weapons and armour — 'only to be used in war' (Tacitus, *Germania* 29).

On the day (the recruits) join the army, they lost their original city, but from the very same day become fellow citizens of your city and its defenders (Aelius Aristides, *To Rome* 75).

Recruitment

Following Caesar's Gallic campaigns, men native to northern Gaul and the Rhineland were recruited into army service, but neither the recruitment policy exercised by the Romans nor the quota of recruits was consistent throughout the German provinces. In the late first century BC and well into the next century, irregular units of soldiers were employed by the Roman military which operated as groups, so-called 'ethnic units'. These were acquired in times of trouble on the basis of treaties between Rome and client tribes who were considered part of the Empire. The Batavi fought under their own native leader, Chariovalda, with Germanicus in AD 16, for example, and the Chauci, Frisii and Nervii also supplied units of fighting men at this time. During the Batavian revolt of 69/70 on the lower Rhine, such *ad hoc* native contingents were still being used to reinforce the regular Roman troops. We know of a *tumultuaria manus* composed of Baetasii, Tungri and Nervii and *tumultuariae Belgarum cohortes* who were sent to fight against the Batavi. The sources do not always distinguish clearly between the non-Roman soldiers who were formally recruited by conscription (*auxiliariae cohortes*) and troops of allied native groups (*sociae cohortes*) who were loosely attached to the Roman army, and it appears that both types of armed forces could co-exist. The use of irregular forces ceased, however, after the Batavian revolt was put down by Vespasian. Conscription of regular auxiliary troops, employed as aids to the legions, became an essential element of Roman military policy.

The conscripted non-Roman auxiliary troops (*auxiliariae cohortes*) fought as ethnic units of those *civitates* which were obliged to supply military manpower as part of their tax obligations. Both cavalry and infantry were levied from many parts of Gaul. These include cavalry units such as the Ala Longiniana Gallorum with men from the Remi, Aedui and Bituriges and infantry units such as the Cohors Aresacum with recruits from the *civitas* of the Aresaces near Mainz. *Civitates* in the upper Rhine region supplying soldiers were the Aresaces, Helvetii, Lingones, Mattiaci, Sequani, Rauraci and Vangiones; those on the lower Rhine were the Baetasii, Batavi, Cananefates, Cugerni, Sugambri, Ubii and Sunuci.

It was the responsibility of the elite leaders of the individual *civitates* in Gaul to ensure that enough recruits were provided in their region to meet the quota prescribed by the Roman government. There was no prescribed age for recruits, and ages of soldiers upon entering military service could range from between 20 and 28. This policy did not apply to those areas, however, in which continued unrest and resistance to Rome prevailed. In northern Gaul after the Batavian revolt, and in Pannonia and Thrace immediately after the conquest, for example, there appears to have been government dictates regarding the age of the recruits. Here the policy appears to have been to find conscripts who were on average 20 years of age to remove as many young men as possible as potential troublemakers from the area, and harness their energies in a controlled environment.

The Batavian revolt acted as a lesson that ethnic units, drawn from men in their own *civitas* and stationed within it, could be unreliable. The Batavi had not been obliged as an allied *civitas* to pay tribute to Rome in the early first century, but by treaty negotiations they supplied a large number of troops to man the frontier. Their society had developed into one with a pronounced martial ideology, and their military potential was interwoven with Roman frontier policies. In comparison to other frontier tribes such as the Menapii, Morini and Baetasii, the Batavi supplied the largest contingent of military manpower on the lower Rhine, approximately 5000 men. Both the Batavi and the Ubii supplied men who served in the highly regarded imperial bodyguard in Rome. Tacitus (*Germania* 29) referred to the Batavi as fighting machines for the Roman army, and they were held in high esteem by the Romans for their bravery and tactical skills. However, the fact that this ethnic unit under the command of its own aristocratic leaders changed sides when one of their own Roman-trained nobles, Iulius Civilis, declared war on Rome, indicates that their allegiance to their own people was stronger than that to Rome. We have seen in chapter 3 that the Batavians had not been particularly receptive to Roman urban ideals, and may even have actively resisted Roman-style urbanisation. Clearly, their relationship was a slightly uncomfortable one which may have been easily upset by circumstances. One of these circumstances was that Vitellius, a candidate for the office of emperor after the murder of Nero in 68, introduced conscription to enlarge his fighting forces in his conflict with Vespasian, his rival contender. In 69 eight cohorts and one cavalry unit of Batavian auxiliary troops were assigned to the 14th Legion. By resorting to this measure, Vitellius broke with the tradition of an allied federation between Rome and the Batavi. One of Civilis' accusations against the Romans was that this prescriptive recruitment was a breach of the Batavian treaty with Rome. After Vespasian successfully put down the revolt and assumed imperial power in 70, his military reforms led to the restructuring of recruitment and deployment of native troops. Ethnic units everywhere played a greatly reduced role thereafter, nor were they left as garrisons in their own *civitates*, but were sent to other parts of the Empire to remove them from their family and social ties. The Batavi, for example, were subsequently sent to Britain, Pannonia and Dacia. Moreover, additional security was given by replacing native commanders with officers from Italy. Finally, the military units on the Rhine were now strengthened with numerous recruits from Thrace and the Danube, so that the former ethnic units were transformed into a colourful mixture of men from a variety of regions.

Multicultural diversity in the military

In the first century AD the Rhine was heavily garrisoned by legionary soldiers drawn from Roman citizens from Italy and Gallia Narbonensis, and to a lesser extent from Spain. In the excellent collection of inscribed gravestones in the Landesmuseum in Mainz one encounters a strikingly large number of monuments to Italian legionaries from places such as Milan, Turin, Piacenza, Cremona, Verona and Brescia, and to southern Gaulish legionaires from Béziers, Narbonne, Fréjus and Aix-en-Provence. Many of these men upon retirement after 20 years of service chose to remain near the place where they were last stationed, marrying and establishing families there. Veterans such as Lucius Baebius from Veleia in northern Italy and Lucius Poblicius from Campania (**colour plate 6**) settled in Cologne where they died around AD 30 and 40 respectively. Baebius had served with Legio XX in Ubian territory south of Cologne, and Poblicius had been stationed in *Vetera*/Xanten with Legio V. The Spanish-born Marcus Valerius Celerinus served with Legio X in Spain and Germania Inferior (Nijmegen) before retiring in Cologne and marrying Marcia Procula in the late first century (**45**). By the second and third centuries, the Mediterranean legionaries had become a small minority, and local Rhenish, Gallic and Danubian men were much more strongly represented.

The thousands of active legionaries on the Rhine who had not yet settled into civilian life also made an impact on local society. These men during active service were not only posted at the forts, but were also seconded to administrative duties in the provincial capitals of Cologne and Mainz and to policing duties as *beneficiarii* in many locations outside the towns and villages. They were also often involved in procuring military supplies in close contact with civilian merchants and traders, and would have been a familiar sight on the streets and in the public places and taverns everywhere. Contacts between the legionaries and the local population are well illustrated by the surviving letters on discarded wooden tablets at Vindonissa. These include correspondence between a local woman named Vindoinsa and a legionary soldier, Annius Lucianus; a letter to Bellicca, a native female employee (or landlady) of a tavern; and another letter inviting a soldier to come to a raucous party at a tavern (possibly written by the landlady herself). The address of the taverns is given as 'opposite the baths' or 'House number 12', and they were located within the fort, not in the civilian settlement outside it. Also located within the fort were the shops of a wine merchant (house number 13), a shield maker (house number 8) and a smith (house number 30). The letters leave no doubt that contacts between military personnel and civilians were frequent.

In addition to the legionaries, tens of thousands of auxiliary soldiers made their presence felt in many levels of society. In first-century Mainz, for example, auxiliaries from Spain, Gaul, the Rhineland, Dalmatia, Thrace and Syria were stationed alongside the legions. Each of them will have contributed to a multicultural environment in the city. One can easily imagine the many dialects, including the local Celtic, the official Latin and heavily accented Latin of many non-native speakers, which must have been encountered on numerous occasions. For many, if not most, of the auxiliary soldiers, Latin was the language in which they conversed with other comrades who had a different mother tongue. The letters from Vindonissa are often written in a form of Latin in which words and names are spelled as they are pronounced in the spoken language, sometimes with evidence of imperfect skills and with the resulting spelling mistakes. Latin graffiti is often found incised on pottery vessels once in possession of individual soldiers, including those men who served in auxiliary units whose first language may not have been Latin (**colour plate 16**). Although the soldiers had to speak Latin to understand each other, the spoken, and perhaps written, native language of any soldier was almost certainly not forgotten. The Syrian auxiliary recruit Barsemius (or Barsemis), stationed at Krefeld-Gellep in the late first century, for example, scratched his name in Aramaic on a terra sigillata bowl in his possession.

The names and origins of military personnel recorded on funerary inscriptions, votive dedications, letters and in graffiti reveal that the influx of people from other parts of the Empire contributed to a diverse multiethnic mixture on the frontier. Modern references to 'the Romans' or 'Roman soldiers' are oversimplified and out of place, because they do not take this diversity into consideration.

Marriage and children

Marriage during active service was neither officially recognised nor sanctioned, although it was tolerated. Legionary soldiers were no more allowed to marry than the auxiliaries, although an exception was made for officers. It was not until 197 that the ban on soldier marriages was lifted by the emperor Septimius Severus. Despite the official ban in the first and second centuries, most soldiers did marry and have children. Upon honourable discharge, liaisons with women, out of which children had been born during active service, were officially recognised and became legal. There was a great deal of concern on the part of auxiliary soldiers and their 'wives' to make sure that the children born before discharge from the army were legally recognised as their offspring so that these children would be the legal heirs to their fathers. In the second century, soldier fathers could draw up a will providing for their families in the event of their death during military service. The emperor Hadrian in 119 decreed that it should be possible for children born of soldiers during military service to claim possession of their father's property, although the parents had acted contrary to military discipline.

The non-Roman auxiliaries were granted Roman citizenship only upon discharge. With the prospect of citizenship at the end of the 25-year period of service, a powerful incentive was provided for native men to join the army. These veterans received the right to contract a legal Roman marriage, although in most cases this meant the legitimisation of a long-standing relationship maintained during active service. Discharge also meant that the children of such unions were officially recognised as legal heirs. The discharge diplomas guarantee the veteran and 'his children and descendants' Roman citizenship, but only the offspring of the officially recognised wife. This policy was adhered to until 140 when it was decided to grant citizenship only to the veteran and his children born after discharge as a result of a legalised marriage, but no longer retrospectively to his offspring born when he was in the army. Children born during active service of the father, according to the new regulation, received the grant only if they enlisted in the legions. This resulted in the growth of military families, with military service becoming a hereditary profession. The number of legionaries serving with the garrisons at *Vetera*/Xanten, Bonn, Strasbourg and Mainz, who were born on the frontier zone and who probably were offspring of military families, increased substantially from the early second century under Trajan. With Caracalla's universal grant of citizenship to all inhabitants of the Empire in 212, it was no longer necessary to join the army to acquire Roman status, although army families still continued to flourish. According to the *Historia Augusta* (58.4), hereditary military service was institutionalised when the emperor Severus Alexander in the early 230s decreed that grants of land on the borders should be given to veterans and remain in their possession only if their heirs entered into military service.

The careers of military families can be followed in funerary inscriptions. A father and son are jointly commemorated on one grave relief of the early second century in Wiesbaden. Gaius Iulius Clemens was a 60-year-old veteran originally from *Forum Iulii*/Fréjus; his son, Gaius Iulius Sabinus, was a 25-year-old centurion in active duty with Cohors II Raetorum when he died in Wiesbaden (**49**). Clemens had settled as a veteran on the upper German frontier, and at least one of his sons followed him in a military career. In another case, a military family of the third century is recorded on inscriptions in Lyon. Lucius Septimius Mucianus, recruited around 215 in Philippopolis in Thrace, was a veteran of Legio XXX from *Vetera*/Xanten. He predeceased his son, Lucius Septimius Peregrinus, who served in the same legion, by 10 years in 250. Mucianus' wife, Secundinia Iusta, probably was also the offspring of a military family. Her cousin, buried with them in Lyon, was a centurion in the Cohors I Germanica in Germania Inferior. It is not unlikely that Secundinia was born on the frontier in Germania Inferior, and that it was here that she and Mucianus met and married. The family moved to *Lugdunum*/Lyon when vexillations of all four German legions were sent to garrison the city. The history of this family illustrates that soldiers could not only be posted from the interior to the frontier, but also from the frontier to the interior. Also siblings often chose a military career. Two brothers from Milan, Marcus Cassius, a veteran of the 14th Legion, and his brother, Gaius Cassius, who served in the same legion, were both posted to Mainz before AD 43. Two other brothers from Veleia in northern Italy, Gnaeus Mussius and Marcus Mussius, also served in this legion in Mainz as a standard bearer and centurion respectively.

Reference to the military careers and the mobility of soldiers and their families is normally limited to the soldiers themselves and their sons; however, some information on wives, daughters, mothers and sisters can also be gleaned by studying texts and inscriptions. Whilst a non-citizen auxiliary and his children received Roman citizenship upon discharge, his non-Roman wife was excluded from this privilege. If a citizen legionary married a citizen woman while he was in the army, the children were illegitimate, but, nonetheless, Roman citizens. If he married a non-Roman woman during duty, his children would have the non-Roman status of the mother. In any case, the daughters of legionaries and of veteran auxiliaries were Roman citizens, and probably highly desirable 'items' on the marriage market, particularly for citizen men looking for citizen wives on distant frontiers. After Caracalla's blanket grant of Roman citizenship in 212, the distinction in status of women was no longer relevant.

Veterans' wives are often commemorated in funerary inscriptions, but unless the

49 Early second-century gravestone of the auxiliary soldier Gaius Iulius Sabinus and his veteran father Gaius Iulius Clemens.
Courtesy Museum Wiesbaden

origin of the wife is recorded or her name is recognisably native to a particular area it is impossible to determine whether the wife was born locally or elsewhere in the Empire. Lucius Poblicius, the veteran of Legio V who died in Cologne around AD 40, had a family which included a wife, a son and a daughter, all of whom are represented as statues on the family's funerary monument (**colour plate 6**). His daughter's name, Paulla, survives on the dedicatory inscription, but the wife's name does not, so that is impossible to tell whether she, like Lucius Poblicius, came from Italy or from another region. An unnamed, probably Italian, veteran officer whose tomb is fragmentarily preserved in Wesseling south of Cologne had a wife, Perrnia Paulla, whose inscribed name suggests that she came from Chiusi in Italy. Aurelius Paulus, a centurion of Legio I Minervia in Bonn, buried his Syrian wife from Sidon, Aurelia Gaiana, in Cologne in the later second or early third century. The couple possibly had met when her husband's legion took part in the eastern campaigns of Lucius Verus or Severus Alexander against Parthia. That she followed him to Germania Inferior suggests that women, too, enjoyed a great deal of mobility, even if, perhaps, within the confines of a marriage or promised marriage. Polla Matidia, the wife of legionary veteran Lucius Iulius Fal.... who had served with Legio II, was somewhat surprisingly a professional dancer known under the name of Olympia. Her husband commemorated her around AD 20 with a gravestone in *Asciburgium*/Moers-Asberg on the lower Rhine (**50**). If a soldier died while he was still actively serving, the wife does not appear at all in the grave epitaph. It is as if she never existed, and neither the wife nor the children could be the legal heirs of the deceased. Instead, grave monuments were set up by army comrades of the deceased who inherited whatever the soldier left behind. Also mothers and fathers set up gravestones to their deceased soldier sons, as Agilla Amusa and Calvisius Mons did in Cologne to commemorate their son, Lucius Calvisius, actively serving in Legio XXII. In rare cases, a sister is named as the beneficiary of a deceased soldier. Togia Faventina, for example, commemorated her brother, Togus Statutus, who served as a scout on the frontier in the Numerus Explorates Divitienses and died in Mainz in the early third century.

Soldiers who already had wives and families living near them must have found transfers to other parts of the Empire very disruptive to their personal lives, and in many cases not only the wives, but also entire families were taken with the men when they were posted elsewhere. The family of Mucianus and Secundinia, who moved from *Vetera*/Xanten to Lyon, is a good example of even extended families who were mobile.

Life after active service

Although some legionary veterans settled outside the area of their last posting, sometimes returning to their homes, most did not. Evidence for this is provided not only by inscriptions, but also by Tacitus (*Annales* 14.27) who says that most veterans scattered themselves in the provinces where they had completed their military service. Studies of the military diplomas issued to discharged auxiliaries indicate different patterns of veteran settlement in different parts of the Empire. Some auxiliary veterans valued family and kinship ties enough to return to their homelands. This seems particularly to be the case with many Thracian veterans who, based on the find-spot of discharge diplomas, settled in their homeland. Other auxiliaries retired to the tribal areas of their wives which were often identical with the province or region in which the soldiers were last stationed. After long postings in one area, new family ties and a familiarity with the surroundings certainly played a major role in the veteran's decision to remain where he was. Twenty-five years was a long time to be away from one's original home, and circumstances could have changed dramatically to make a homecoming not a viable option. Furthermore, if solders were born on the frontier and had served there, as their families may have done before, there was little incentive to move elsewhere after retirement. Increasingly, the more sedentary soldiers in the later Roman period may have felt greater allegiance to the region they defended, their homes and family groups than they did to the central Roman government.

Legionary soldiers were either given sums of money or land grants upon retirement.

50 *Early first-century*
gravestone of Polla
Matidia
(Olympia), wife
of a legionary
veteran, from
Moers-Asberg,
Germany.
Courtesy
Rheinisches
Landesmuseum
Bonn

These land grants could be in a region completely different from the last posting. The allotments, however, could be sold and the veteran was free to move to the area of his choice. According to Tacitus' accounts (*Annales* 1.17), veterans did not react favourably to being forced to settle in unfamiliar or remote underpopulated areas to which the government sent them. Many of the veterans of the fleet at Misenum sent to Paestum in the government's attempt to repopulate parts of Italy in AD 71 did not stay there, but moved to other parts of Italy or to the provinces.

The post-military careers of veterans can be followed in some cases. After retirement one Italian-born legionary veteran from Ostia settled in the early colony at Cologne and became a *duovir* in the city's administration. The unknown Italian(?) veteran, whose monumental tomb was found in Wesseling, probably established a farming estate there, either bought with his retirement bonus or as a development of his land grant. At least one Batavian auxiliary veteran certainly returned to his native village at Hoogeloon where he built a Romanised villa in the early second century (**27**). A fragmentary discharge diploma was found on the site. Judging by the amount of military equipment found in sanctuaries of Hercules Magusanus on the northern Rhine, many Batavians returned home after being discharged, commemorating their release from military duty by dedicating no longer needed equipment to the tutelary god of the tribe. Other veterans may have been active in the commercial sector of civilian life. One of them, a former *beneficiarius*, became a merchant involved in North Sea trade and dedicated an altar to Nehalennia at Colijnsplaat in the late second or early third century. Q. Attilius Primus was an interpreter and centurion with Legio XV before he retired in the first century and went into business as a *negotiator* in Germanic territory north of the Danube. His knowledge of the area and of the languages spoken there will have been of enormous benefit to him as a private merchant in cross-frontier trade.

Not only did military service secure a regular salary before retirement, but the bonuses and citizenship received upon retirement paved the way for advancement in society in a number of ways. A military career was surely viewed as a positive step towards social mobility. The legionary veteran could be certain of an elevated position within society, especially if he retired on the frontier where men like him were a cut above the native population. Assuming a magisterial post in local government or investing his accumulated wealth to excel in the commercial sector may have been far more possible in the provinces than in his homeland. The auxiliary veteran left the army a Roman citizen, had seen the world, learned many skills and become fluent in Latin, all of which opened doors for him in society. In praise of the possibilities Rome opened to non-Romans, Aelius Aristides in his ode *To Rome* (74) wrote that in an Empire-wide policy of army recruitment no one was classed as an alien and anyone could be accepted for any employment and do well. As to be expected in a panegyric flagging the thoroughly positive aspects of the Roman Empire, this comment cannot be taken at face value, yet there is more than a grain of truth to the claim that ethnic origin and non-Roman status did not hinder a career. This applied to the highest office of emperor, no less than to the common man rising through the ranks of the military. What impact the retiring auxiliary soldier had in the long run on his native community is difficult to assess. His status in his native society was surely positively influenced, and he returned with a familiarity with Roman culture. The retired soldier who went back to his rural community at Hoogeloon in the early second century visibly expressed this familiarity and status in the building of a Romanised house that stood out from all the others. But he appears to have given only a limited Roman 'flair' to the village as far as we can tell by the physical remains at the site. None of the other houses was rebuilt along these lines, and by AD 200 the veteran's house had been abandoned and replaced by a more modest one of native type.

Germans in the late Roman army

The emperor Probus (276-82) is recorded in the *Historia Augusta* (14.7) as having taken German recruits, 16,000 in all, 'whom he scattered through the various provinces, incorporating bodies of 50 or 60 in the detachments or among the soldiers along the frontier, for he said that the aid the Romans received from barbarian auxiliaries must be felt but not seen'. These German recruits were different from the first- and second-century auxiliaries since they did not come from conquered territories within the Empire, but were drawn from the regions beyond the frontiers. Recruiting contingents of troops from non-Roman, and often repeatedly hostile, peoples increased in the fourth century, particularly under Valentinian I (364-75) and Gratian (367-83). At that time the western Empire was continually under pressure from Germanic peoples such as the Alamanni, Franks and Saxons, and the frontiers were heavily fortified and manned, a development which required increased numbers of soldiers (see chapter 9). Numbers were swelled by settling conquered peoples within the Empire and pressing them into military service in return for land. Not only large groups of such 'prisoners', but also tribal units under the command of their own elite leaders, were integrated into the army. In the fourth century many Germanic names appear in the written sources recording non-Roman men who were given command posts, for example Balchobaudes who became a tribune in 365/6, Fullofaudes who was a general in 367/8 and Frigeridus, a general of Gratian in 377. Mallobaudes was a commander of Frankish troops and, at the same time, a Frankish king in 378. Fraomarius was king of the Bucinobantes, a subtribe of the Alamanni, who served as a tribune in 372 and participated in the defence of Britain. Other Alamannic chiefs, such as Bitheridus and Hortarius, also held commands over Roman troops. Nobles such as the Frank Arbogast (388-92) and the Vandal Stilicho (395-408) moreover could rise in rank and power to become supreme commander of the army (*magister militum*) in all of Gaul.

The attraction for non-Roman recruits from beyond the frontier, particularly for the Germanic nobles, was the immediate integration into Roman society and the possibility of achieving positions of power and wealth within the military in a very short period of time. The benefits of acquiring land and possessions on Roman soil was a further enticement. The heavy recruitment of Germanic peoples in the late Roman army meant an increased Germanic element in the military forces, and since they often brought their families with them to their postings new Germanic population groups were introduced to Roman settlements, slowly changing the fabric of Roman society. Those holding Roman land and defending Rome's north-west frontiers acted as protection against other external Germanic and non-Germanic peoples seeking their fortunes within the Empire.

Clearly, the Roman army was a melting pot for men and their families from all parts of the Empire. The civilian population also comprised many people with diverse origins. Such a constellation will have meant that people with different identities came into contact with each other, identities which were multiple and often negotiable. The next chapter examines these ethnic and cultural identities.

7 Ethnic and cultural identities

Now although the geographer should tell of all the physical and ethnic distinctions which have been made, whenever they are worth recording, yet, as for the diversified political divisions which are made by the rules (for they suit their government to the particular times), it is sufficient if one state them merely in a summary way (Strabo, *Geographia* 4.1.1).

The people who dwell in the interior above Massalia, those on the slopes of the Alps and those on this side of the Pyrenees mountains are called Celts, whereas the peoples who are established above this land of Celtica in the parts which stretch to the north . . . as far as Scythia, are known as Gauls; the Romans, however, include all these nations together under a single name, calling them one and all Gauls (Diodorus Siculus, *Bibliotheke Historike* 5.32).

Self-identification and identification by others

How native peoples identified or thought of themselves could differ from the way in which they were identified by the Romans. Ethnic identity is only one of many levels of identity, but it is one which is explored here. Although Caesar and Tacitus clearly simplified the ethnographic situation by recognising only Celts/Gauls and Germans in north-west Europe, there was some confusion on the part of the Romans as to who was purely Celtic and who was purely Germanic. Nor did the Rhine really seem to separate Gauls in the west from Germans in the east. The transrhenine Germans according to Tacitus (*Germania* 4) had 'never contaminated themselves by intermarriage with foreigners but remained of pure blood, distinct and unlike any other nation'. Remarks such as this influenced archaeological studies in Germany at a much later date and were ideologically appealing to German nationalists of the early twentieth century. The fact that not only Germanic, but also Celtic peoples lived east of the Rhine, however, had to be acknowledged in Roman historiography, and Tacitus' explanation for this was that there had been migrations of Celts eastwards into Germany (*Germania* 28). The west-bank Treveri claimed to be of Germanic descent, but their material culture has greater similarities with Celtic peoples (*Germania* 28). Caesar grouped the Ubii with the other transrhenine Germanic tribes, but considered them more civilised because they had been in contact with Gallic and Roman traders (*De Bello Gallico* 1.1).

Tacitus' blanket term *Germani* referred to the Treveri, Nervii, Ubii, Vangiones, Triboci, Nemetes, Batavi, Chatti, Usipetes, Tencteri, Bructeri, Frisii, Chauci, Cherusci and Cimbri.

But is there any indication that all these tribes really thought of themselves as a German nation? All evidence suggests that this national identity did not exist in the minds of Germanic peoples. A few examples will help to illustrate this. From the time of Augustus to Nero, the imperial bodyguard in Rome consisted of men who were responsible for the personal safety of the Emperor. The bodyguard included recruits from the lower Rhine, including the Baetasii, Frisii, Batavi and Ubii. For the Romans, they were the homogeneous German bodyguard, the *Germani corporis custodes*. All members of the bodyguard were buried together in a communal cemetery, and their gravestones of similar design did indeed signify a strong group identity. The additional information on the nationality of the deceased, possibly supplied by their comrades, however, differentiated the individual men within that group. The men are named, for example, as *natione Ubius* or *natione Batavus*, and thus this information identified those members of the Imperial bodyguard as ethnic Germans of a *particular* people. This reflects the way these men perceived their ethnicity, as members of a specific native group, even if joined by external Roman agency to a larger national group. It cannot be demonstrated that one of the main attributes of ethnic community, a collective proper name, was used by the Germanic peoples. Inscriptions recording the origin of Germanic groups throughout the Empire consistently cite the tribal affiliation of the persons in question. One of the *equites singulares* in Rome in the second century is recorded as a member of the Triboci (*cives Tribocus*), a merchant who dedicated an altar to Nehalennia on the North Sea coast is identified as a Treveran (*cives Treveri*), and a flour merchant residing in Cologne is named as a Nervian (*cives Nervius*). These are only a few examples of many tribal affiliations recorded in the sources.

The consolidation of ethnic units in a German nation (*Germani*) seems to be a Roman political and ideological construct, and as far as we know only the Romans used the term. Strabo, recording his *Geography* in the Augustan period, wrote that the Germans were very like the Celts, only wilder, taller and blonder, and that for this reason the Romans assigned the name *Germani* to them to indicate that they were genuine Gauls (*Galatae*), 'for in the language of the Romans *germani* means genuine' (7.1.3). Writing in AD 98, Tacitus claimed that the name *Germania* 'is said to have been only recently applied to the country', and what was once the name of one tribe, 'not of the entire race, gradually came into general use in the wider sense' (*Germania* 2). The 'recent' Roman application of the name may not have predated the first century BC when contact between Rome and the Germanic peoples became firmly established. If this is so, the Romans played a role in the ethnogenesis of the Germans by identifying them as a specific group. It could be said, however, that even below this level the Romans played a role in the construction and consolidation of tribal groups. Many of these groups first appear as historic peoples for the first time when they came in contact with Rome, and many of them were a mixture of various, probably unnamed, peoples and clans that were given the name of the dominant or favoured group by the Romans. The Roman, state-driven establishment of discrete tribal territories as *civitates* with definite boundaries further contributed to group identities. As a result, external agency could well have influenced each group's own perception of themselves.

The late second- and early third-century attacks by peoples beyond the frontiers indicate that a significant restructuring of the Germanic world was taking place. Powerful tribes were splintered into smaller groups, old tribes disappeared and new peoples and confederacies, some of them simply warbands, were formed. This fluidity is reflected in the many names of groups which appear for the first time, but which encompassed constantly changing component parts. Such confederate groups include the Alamanni and the Franks. From the early third century a group of tribes and subtribes known to later Roman sources, and to us, as the Alamanni were wreaking havoc between the Danube and the Rhine, and beyond this in Gaul and Italy. The emperors Caracalla in 213 and Gallienus in 259/60 were engaged in war with a group modern scholars call the Alamanni, yet a careful examination of the written records indicates that the actual name *Alamanni* does not appear in Roman sources before 289. The Romans understood, and helped to construct, the name as meaning 'all men' or 'collective contingent'. The Germanic tribes involved in the conflicts with Rome in the third century, however, did not identify themselves as Alamanni. Gallienus drove these Germans back out of Italy across the Alps, but they were not entirely defeated until April 260 near *Augusta Vindelicum*/Augsburg in the province of Raetia. A votive altar at Augsburg commemorating this victory names the Germans as 'Semnones, or, as they are called, Iouthungi' (see chapter 9). Here we have the Suebic/Elbe-Germanic group Tacitus recorded in the first century as the most ancient and noble of the Suebian subtribes (see chapter 1). The myth of the divine descent of the Semnones is perpetuated in the third century by the Semnones themselves: Iouthungi means 'those who have the true descent'. The Iouthungi may have been the leading group behind the incursions into Roman territory, but many other Germanic tribes we cannot identify by name were also involved. By the late third century, the Romans ignored the specific names of the Iouthungi and other groups, lumping them all together as the Alamanni.

Their Germanic contemporaries, the Franks, were likewise a mixed group of Germans joined together under one generic name by the Roman sources. According to Gregory of Tours writing in the sixth century, the Franks consisted of groups of Bructeri, Chamavi, Amsivarii and Chattuarii. Like the Alamanni, who sometimes in Roman sources of the fourth century are confusingly either called Alamanni or Iouthungi or Suebi, the name *Franci* after the mid-fourth century is occasionally interchangeably used with Sicambri (Sugambri). The Salii who joined the Frankish confederation in the mid-fourth century especially used this name. The earliest Frankish law code, the *Pactus Legis Salicae*, does not preserve the name 'Frank' at all, but refers only to the Salii. The Sugambri of the early Empire had once lived east of the Rhine until they were transplanted to the west bank around Xanten by Tiberius in 8 BC where they became known in Roman sources as the Cugerni. Possibly not all the Sugambri were absorbed into the Empire at that time (Strabo, *Geographia* 7.1.3), leaving part of the tribe or subtribes behind who later re-emerged as the Salii. Nevertheless, the name of the Sugambri disappeared from the historic accounts by the late first century BC. Like the Semnones/Iouthungi, the Salii/Sicambri may have been regarded as a tribe of particularly high status, so that this Germanic group in its own self-definition alluded to or constructed a noble and heroic past through the name. In perhaps only ideologically constructing this connection between the Sugambri of the late first century BC and the Salii almost four centuries later this group of the Franks may have drawn on Roman historiography with which they were undoubtedly familiar and which recorded the Sugambri as particularly formidable Germanic enemies.

As far as the Gallic peoples are concerned, an awareness of common language, religion and culture was certainly felt by many of them, and the widespread resistance to Roman domination at the time of Caesar indicates that there was a general desire among the Gauls for independence. However, although polity and ethnicity need not necessarily coincide, a Gallic nation united under one political leadership did not exist. The fragmentation and constant conflict within the peoples of Gaul clearly indicate this. The geographer Strabo (*Geographia* 4.1.14) implied that the first people the Greeks came into contact with in *Massilia*/Marseilles on the Mediterranean coast may have been a tribe with the name *Keltoi*, and that the name stuck as a general term for all barbarian people in the north and west. Certainly, for the earlier Greek ethnographers, the western, non-Greek part of the world was occupied in broad terms by the Celts. But early Greek generalisations about non-Greek peoples surrounding them cannot be regarded as having a factual basis built on exact knowledge of these groups' ethnic characteristics. Indeed, Ephorus of Cyme (405-330 BC) equated compass points in the then-known world with broadly generalised peoples, putting Indians in the east, Ethiopians in the south, Celts in the west and Scythians in the north. Neither do the Roman historians inspire confidence in their knowledge of ethnography when in Britain the Caledonians with their red hair are said to be of German origin and the swarthy-faced and curly-haired Silures immigrants from Iberia/Spain (Tacitus, *Agricola* 10-12). In actual fact, Caesar and other Roman authors localised *Celtae*/*Galli* only in the south of a specific geographic region the Romans called Gaul, whereas the Aquitani lived in the west and the Belgae in the north. The Aquitani, at least, had their own language and cultural traditions which differed from the rest of Gaul. Diodorus Siculus recorded that it was the Romans who included these peoples together under a single name, calling them all Gauls (*Bibliotheke Historike* 5.32). This is similar to the way the Romans used the name *Germani* for a large group of Germanic tribes. The very generalised Roman representation of the ethnography of western Europe must be distinguished from the realities of the situation, however, since the Gauls, like the Germans, identified themselves at a tribal level in terms of nomenclature, and not with the ethnonym *Galli* or *Celtae*. Moreover, both the Gauls and the Germans identified themselves in opposition to each other and both claimed to have, and were known for, different qualities. The Treveri and Nervii, for example, could claim that their German descent rendered them braver and more warlike than the neighbouring Gallic tribes (Tacitus, *Germania* 28). It was the Romans who united the Gallic polities, but not without repeated factional strife and internecine struggles, into the larger unit of the *Galli* and constructed the concept of pan-Gallic unity by establishing a cult centre of Rome and Augustus at Lyon to which delegates from over 60 Gallic *civitates* were sent annually.

Revolts and nationalism

Roman historians recorded three uprisings of Gallic and Germanic peoples in the first century AD: the revolt of Iulius Florus and Iulius Sacrovir in 21, the revolt of Iulius Vindex in 68, and the Batavian revolt of 69/70. All three are often interpreted by modern historians as having been fuelled by nationalistic sentiments and the longing for independence from Rome. But was this really the motivation behind the uprisings, and is there any sense of unity in opposition to Rome?

Tacitus delivered the reasons for the revolt of Florus of the Treveri and Sacrovir of the Aedui: dissatisfaction over tax levies, aristocratic debts to the Roman government and the cruelty and arrogance of Roman governors. Both leaders were nobles of their tribes and Roman citizens, and they each had their retainers (in good Gaulish tradition), but there seem to have been few other nobles or local coalitions involved. The Treveri ultimately rejected Florus, so that his retinue shrank to a mob of debtors and dependants with grievances. Sacrovir, apparently aware of thin support within the aristocracy, took the sons of Gallic nobles in *Augustodunum*/Autun as hostages to force cooperation from this sector of society. Had the revolt succeeded, independence from Rome might have been the consequence, but the motivation for it was resistance to oppressive Roman demands, not Gallic nationalism.

The revolt of Vindex was motivated by disgust and loathing for the extravagances and oppressive behaviour of the emperor Nero and his government. A Roman senator and son of a senator as well as the governor of Gallia Lugdunensis, Vindex was not alone in his desire to remove Nero from power, and he negotiated with Roman leaders in other provinces, including Galba, governor of Spain, to this end. It was left to Galba to bring about an end successfully to Nero's rule in 68, and it was Galba who thereafter minted coins referring to the *Tres Galliae*, rewarding Vindex's followers and punishing the Gauls who had not supported him. There is no evidence that Vindex aimed to establish an independent Gallic state or was a traitor to Rome.

Iulius Civilis, a Batavian noble and Roman citizen, launched a revolt in northern Gaul in 69/70, having first gone through the motions of being in support of Vespasian as his preferred candidate for imperial office. Once Vespasian had defeated his opponent Vitellius, however, Civilis' true aim for political independence became apparent. In his attempt to muster support for his plan, he tried to seduce the Gallic *civitates* into rising against Rome and establishing an *imperium Galliarum*, a Gallic Empire. Nationalistic sentiment on the part of the Gauls, had it existed, should have been fuelled by Civilis' grand plans. The Gauls at a conference at Reims, however, rejected his overtures and decided to side with Rome. Only the Gaulish Lingones could be won as allies. In the end, Civilis succeeded in uniting several Germanic tribes in what was much more a German revolt than a Gallic one. Even then, many of them had to be coerced into joining him, some later changing sides in support of Rome. Civilis did not even have the undivided support of his own tribe. The transrhenine Germans enlisted by Civilis showed little interest in a German cause, and seem to have been primarily attracted to join in by the lure of loot and treasure. Again, dissatisfaction with the Roman government and the policies of military conscription, as well as Civilis' own personal grievances, were the prime motivation for the uprising.

Had either the Germans or the Gauls thought of themselves as nations or one people, political and territorial independence from Rome and the creation of a Gallic or German state may well have been a desirable goal. If one accepts Anthony Smith's definition of a nation, it is apparent that several criteria for nationhood are not fulfilled by Gallic and Germanic society, most notably a mass public culture, a common economy and common legal rights and duties for all members. Any unity amongst the Gauls or Germans may have been perceived by them on a cultural level more than anything else, although even then diversity is apparent. Amongst these larger groups, smaller communities, *civitates*, formed the primary basis of allegiance. Resistance to an outside force such as the Romans occasionally led to supraregional alliances, but they were shortlived and did not lead to the formation of a nation. If Gallic and Germanic nations did not exist, nationalism cannot have been the prime motivation for any of the first-century revolts. Nor did the Gauls or Germans put up a united front, rather the individual interests of each tribal grouping far outweighed any sentiment of national unity. It must be stated, however, that we are informed about their interests only because the Roman sources record the revolts, speeches and other activities of the tribal leaders. That the aristocratic leaders were continually engaged in power struggles and concerned about their own representation in terms of themselves and in comparison to other tribal leaders and to the Romans is clear, but this may leave us somewhat poorly informed as to how the tribal masses defined their own identities. Nevertheless, many of the latter may have not have perceived their identity other than in regional terms or perhaps not even beyond the horizons of their kin-groups.

Kinship structures

It is often difficult archaeologically to isolate something unique in character or culture to individual tribal units. This is due, in part, to the fact that in the late first century BC the Romans carried out a major reorganisation of tribal structures in the newly annexed lands, particularly in northern Gaul and in the Rhineland (see chapter 2). Any of these realigned peoples known to us in the Roman sources are almost certainly a mixture of subgroups of other tribes. Some native groups were redistributed in areas with new boundaries, which may have had little to do with the original spatial and cultural arrangements. Is it possible in this fluctuating situation to recognise any kind of kinship between groups or within groups?

We may discard the claims of brotherhood and kinship between the Aedui and the Romans as anything more than political and ideological constructs of the elite (Strabo *Geographia* 4.3.2; Caesar, *De Bello Gallico* 1.33). The construction of an origin myth linked with that of Rome itself is fairly common in northern Gaul, but it is an invented common ancestry (see chapter 1). On the lower Rhine, however, actual kinship between tribes and within tribes is occasionally detectable, even if only very superficially. Kinship groups existed, for example, within the cult organisation of the Matronae or ancestral mother goddesses in the area between Cologne, Neuss and Aachen (**51**). The Matronae cult had its roots in a pre-Roman ancestor cult, and the native names of the Matronae are often related to names of local communities, population groups and clans. A loose kinship structure is apparent in the Matronae Cantrusteihia, ancestral mothers associated with the Condrusi who, at the time of Caesar, lived in the Condroz-Namur area on the Maas river. Dedications to these goddesses found in the territories of the Tungri, Nervii and Ubii indicate that in the wake of Augustus' demographic reorganisation the Condrusi were absorbed by and possibly had family relations with these three groups. The sanctuary of

51 Votive altar to the three mother goddesses (Matronae). The Matronae are depicted at the top of the stone, a family of worshippers stands below.
Courtesy Rheinisches Landesmuseum Bonn

the Matronae Vacallinehae at Pesch in the Ubian *civitas*, for example, was associated with the clan of the Vacalli who lived in the immediate vicinity. The Matronae Gesahenae were the ancestral goddesses of the Gesationes clan, members of which dedicated votive altars at several sites west and east of Cologne. Family ties are revealed in a dedication by Bassiania from Rödingen. She donated an altar to the Matronae Etrahenae and the Matronae Gesahenae, the first group of Matronae being the cult of her mother's family, the latter group the ancestral cult of her father's family. The same two ancestral Matronae groups received a dedication from M. Iulius Amandus at Bettenhoven in the second century. Family ties may also be reflected in the dedications to specifically local Rhenish Matronae by immigrant Roman soldiers. Many of these men, particularly from northern Italy, were familiar with a matron cult from other parts of the Empire, and they married into local families who worshipped their own ancestral mother goddesses.

The Matronae names of the second and third centuries also reflect both the latest Germanic language influx introduced to the area by the Ubii and the mixed Germanic and

Celtic language which pre-dated the Ubian migration. The survival of both language groups evident in inscriptions indicate that different population groups co-existed and continued to speak their languages.

Ethnic costume

It must be assumed that to wear native dress rather than Roman/Italian garments in the Roman period was a personal choice, and to be displayed on a stone monument wearing it was a statement of the adherence to traditional customs, an assertion of ethnic identity, a mark of status within the community, or all three. At any rate, the retention of national costume cannot simply be classed as mere conservatism. Information on native dress, both Celtic and Germanic, is provided by sculptural depictions of individuals. A group of mid-first-century grave statues and reliefs from Mainz-Weisenau and Nickenich on the middle Rhine and Ingelheim south of the Eifel represent the local Celtic population in both native and Roman dress. The men either wear the short Gallic hooded coat, which by then had become a typical article of Gallo-Roman clothing, or a toga, the symbol of Roman citizenship. The women, however, are consistently dressed in their native costume, complete with heavy Celtic neck torques, double *fibulae* and jewellery. On the grave monument of the shipper Blussus and his wife Menimane from Mainz-Weisenau, both wear native costume (**25**). Depictions of the Celtic costume of this type did not outlive the first century, although thereafter a longer version of the Gallic coat replaced the short hooded one. Nevertheless, at least one characteristic element of Celtic costume, the paired *fibulae* used to pin the garment at the shoulder, is known from grave finds as late as the third century in Alpine valleys and eastern Switzerland, indicating that this type of dress had a greater longevity in more remote and peripheral regions.

Germanic dress, in particular that worn by the Ubii, continued to be depicted well into the third century, although images of Ubian women in purely Roman clothing outnumber those in traditional costume. Stone sculptures and reliefs depicting Ubian women wearing their costume and voluminous headdress are found on funerary and votive monuments in Cologne, Bonn and the Ubian countryside (**51, 52**). The clothing of the Matronae is modelled on that of the local, mortal population. The dress of the Germanic goddess Nehalennia, as depicted on second- and third-century reliefs from the coastal sanctuaries at Domburg and Colijnsplaat, differs somewhat from the Ubian costume in the addition of a shoulder cape and the use of a smaller headdress (**47**). This may represent the traditional costume of the Germanic peoples in the Rhine delta area.

There is no way of knowing to what degree native Celtic or Germanic costume continued to be worn on a daily basis, with the exception of the Gallic coat which was clearly commonly worn in all levels of society. Perhaps the traditional clothing was worn only on festive occasions and in religious contexts, for which there are numerous modern parallels. At any rate, native costume often appears to have been gender specific. It is interesting to compare the traditional costumes of the peoples in Noricum and Pannonia where, again, it is the women, and not the men, who are depicted in national dress.

52 Head of a funerary statue from Cologne of an Ubian woman wearing a voluminous headdress. Courtesy Rheinisches Bildarchiv

Negotiating cultural identity and status

By 'sharing' the benefits of citizenship and civilisation with the peoples of the Empire, Rome 'redivided mankind into Romans and non-Romans', whether their origins lay in Asia or Europe (Aelius Aristides, *To Rome* 59-60, 63). Those allowed to 'share', however, were the 'more cultured, better born and more influential', 'qualified men' and those 'fit for office or a position of trust'. Aelius Aristides, writing in the second century, was echoing the sentiments already expressed by Velleius Paterculus in his *Historia Romana* in the early first century who recorded the extension of citizenship to many peoples in Italy from 390-100 BC and the 'growth of the Roman name through granting to others a share in its privileges' (1.14-15). If being Roman meant having common (Roman) citizenship and had nothing to do with ethnic origins, spoken language or common descent, the resulting implication is that, whilst one may be Roman, there was ample room for defining and expressing other identities related to local associations, wealth and status. Citizens and non-citizens alike could adopt the recognised symbols of the Roman way of life or *Romanitas*, thereby negotiating a more accepted identity in Roman society. Many incentives were offered to adopt Roman culture by choice, not least of which was the prospect of elevated social status and acquisition of power. One of the ways of ensuring the 'civilisation' of native peoples was the provision of a Latin education by which particularly the sons of aristocrats were schooled and educated. The school at Autun was perhaps best known and most frequented by the Gaulish elite, but Suetonius in his *Lives of the Twelve Caesars* seems to suggest that there was also provision of a Latin education for young German men in the Rhine area, although the reference is to a military school which offered rudimentary Latin lessons (*Caligula* 45). The fathers of the boys enrolled at Roman schools may indeed have supported the system and doubtless saw personal gain in sending their offspring to receive an education, as Plutarch (*Lives: Sertorius* 14.2-3) observed in regard to the Spaniards, but the historical sources leave no doubt that the boys were, in fact, hostages and were kept at the schools as pledges of their fathers' loyalty to Rome.

Any number of overlapping identities could be consciously conveyed not only in life, but also in death. Images of individuals, many possibly disguising or distorting reality, reveal a renegotiation of identity in death. For those who chose the motifs for their own grave monuments, or for the families or heirs of the deceased who had the monuments made, imagery and message were important. Auxiliary soldiers who died in active service were often depicted as mounted on rearing horses and giving a defeated, cowering barbarian the last blow (**44**). The native auxiliary soldiers themselves, however, were often recruited from 'barbarian' or barely Romanised areas. The image thus conveys the message that the soldier distanced himself from the barbarian and was one with the civilised Roman world. This makes him an insider as opposed to the barbarian who was clearly an outsider, at least in the imagery chosen. Auxiliary soldiers who died before retirement, and therefore without citizenship, were also often represented as men of leisure and Roman culture, reclining on a dining couch and wearing the toga. Legionary veterans frequently chose to represent themselves wearing a toga, to which they were entitled, and holding a scroll in the pose of a philosopher (**colour plate 17**). This symbolism alluded to the cultivated literary interests of the deceased, whether or not these interests were real. Native women or women of low status could want to be depicted as Roman matrons in the appropriate dress, thereby choosing a visual image of honour, piety and status (**43**). Depictions of the deceased in native costume express another choice. The inscription on the gravestone of Blussus and Menimane (**25**) reveals that it was Menimane who commissioned the carving of the stone for her husband and herself while she was alive, and therefore it was she who chose to have them depicted in Celtic, rather than Roman, finery. The jewellery worn by both — a heavy neck torque, bracelets, rings — the slave in the background and the money pouch held conspicuously in Blussus' hand are intentionally chosen visual evidence of wealth and standing in the community. The attributes depicted in any of these images were selected for their meanings, and they were one way to negotiate an elevated position in society that may not have conformed to reality, but could be claimed in death.

In the later Roman empire, citizenship, ethnic origins or cultural identity played a lesser role than other factors such as group association, class and religion. Hereditary service in the army resulted in a military caste, and many of the men serving in the army, as their fathers and grandfathers had done, may have defined their identity based on this group association. The emergence of relatively standardised uniforms, including the broad belt with chip-carved buckles and metal fittings so commonly found at sites used by the army and in graves, functioned as immediately visible markers of this status (**colour plate 18**). Government officials and bureaucrats wore similar trappings, again marking them as a discrete group in society whose identity could be expressed, among other things, in their appearance. The more sedentary units of the late Roman army and the instalment of frontier militia groups who defended their territories surely also contributed to more local allegiances and group identities. With an increasing Germanic element in the army, the borders between 'Roman' and 'German' blurred, the common denominator being military service (see chapters 6 and 9). In the fourth century, the rich became richer and the poor became poorer, the latter often being tied to the former, especially in the countryside where wealthy landowners controlled huge estates worked by the less fortunate. The privileged *honestiores* and the lowly *humiliores* were clearly distinguished, even formally by name. This class divide is apparent in all of the western Empire at this time, and it transcended ethnic origins.

A combination of factors in the later third century led to the western Empire formally breaking with the central Roman government. From 260-73, the Gallic Empire encompassed the provinces of Spain, Gaul, Germany and Britain (see chapter 9). This was led by western provincial governments with the help of provincial troops and very likely with the support of the elites and merchant classes in reaction to the central government's increasing demands on taxation as well as the perceived inability of Rome to protect those provinces most under threat from barbarian incursions. Does this mean that the peoples of the western Empire, whether Iberians, Gauls, Germans, Britons and the Romanised mixtures thereof, identified themselves as some sort of common western block? Perhaps self-interest and a sense of self-preservation were unifying factors, resulting in a situation in which other cultural, political and social divides were bridged. For late Roman writers such as Salvian, religion was an essential criterion for categorisation of the population. Christian or non-Christian, Orthodox or Arian Catholicism: these were communities of which one was part and within which identity could be defined. Religion could transcend ethnic origins and it did not necessarily relate to class, although many of the Christian clerics and bishops who wielded power were, at the same time, from aristocratic families. Prosper of Aquitaine, writing in the mid-fifth century, remarked that 'Christianity is not content to have the boundaries of Rome as its limits; for it has submitted to the sceptre of Christ's cross many peoples whom Rome could not subject with its arms' (*De Vocatione Omnium Gentium* 2.16).

To illustrate how identity and status could be negotiated on a communal level in the early Roman period, an examination of the behaviour and attitude of the Ubii is useful. The Ubii rapidly internalised Roman culture in the first century AD, leading Tacitus to assert that they had 'earned the right to have their city promoted to a colony' (Tacitus, *Germania* 28). This city, Cologne, will be looked at as a case study in the next chapter.

8 Cultural relations on the frontier: Cologne as a case study

The Romans were holding portions of Germany . . . and soldiers of theirs were wintering there and cities were being founded. The barbarians were adapting themselves to Roman ways, were becoming accustomed to hold markets, and were meeting in peaceful assemblages (Cassius Dio, *Historia Romana* 56.18).

Booty was secured from both districts, but they (Civilis and his Germanic reinforcements) proceeded with greater severity in the case of the Ubii, because, although a tribe of Germanic origin, they had renounced their fatherland and adopted the name of Agrippinenses (Tacitus, *Historiae* 4.28).

The early settlement and modern foundation myths

The Germanic Ubii first appear by name in Caesar's accounts of the Gallic wars. According to him, this group living east of the Rhine were once an extensive and prosperous people, but by 55 BC the Ubii were under constant threat by the much stronger Suebi and were forced to pay tribute to them, leading the Ubii to conclude treaties of protection and mutual assistance with Rome (*De Bello Gallico* 4.3, 4.8, 16). During the last decades of the first century BC they migrated or were intentionally transplanted by Augustus and led by Agrippa to the west bank of the Rhine (Strabo, *Geographia* 4.3.4; Tacitus, *Annales* 12.27, *Germania* 28). A town, the *oppidum Ubiorum* (town of the Ubii), was founded by the Romans as the central focus of Ubian territory, and it was promoted to a veteran colony (*Colonia Claudia Ara Agrippinensium*) in AD 50 by Claudius (**53**). The *oppidum Ubiorum* was long thought in archaeological and historical scholarship to have been established in the second half of the first century BC. This belief was based on an interpretation of Tacitus and Strabo, but scholars could not agree whether the town was built in Agrippa's first period of office in 39/38 or in his second one in 20/19 BC. In AD 14 Legio I and Legio XX had a winter base in Ubian territory (Tacitus, *Annales* 1.39), and it has been suggested that Legio XIX was also stationed there prior to the Varian disaster in AD 9. The need to spatially accommodate both a civilian settlement and a military base in and around Cologne led to various hypotheses and to a dispute whether the pre-colonial remains excavated in various locations in Cologne belonged to the fort or the *oppidum*. The former hypothesis was, and often still is, favoured. Recently excavated evidence and a more sober analysis of the remains, however, suggest that both historical

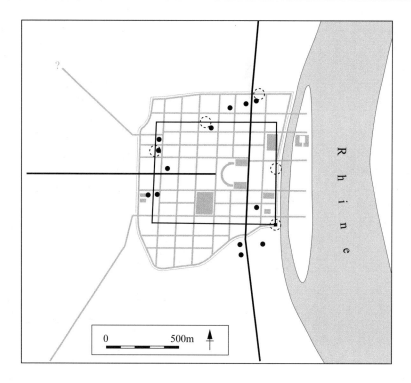

53 Early first-century oppidum Ubiorum *on the site of the later colony (light grey). Excavated remains of ditches and ramparts are in dashed circles. The dots mark the remains of houses, kilns and other features.* Author and S. Schütte

and archaeological sources have been used to create a modern foundation myth.

After many decades of excavations, no artefacts have been found in Cologne that can be dated to the first century BC. Pottery and coins found throughout Cologne are consistently of early first-century AD date, and although coin hoards may contain Republican and Celtic issues, the overall composition of the hoards makes it clear that they were buried in the early first century AD. Remains such as a stone-built tower (*Ubiermonument*) on the river bank, dendrochronologically dated to AD 4/5, the orthogonal street grid of late Augustan/Tiberian date, fragmentarily preserved timber and clay domestic buildings (some with mosaic floors and painted walls), civilian and military burials of the first decades of the first century AD and a contemporary nucleated pottery industry (**colour plate 19**) indicate that the settlement is of early first-century AD date. The settlement was fortified. Scant remains of a pre-colonial earth and timber rampart in the north were excavated in 1948, but south of this further stretches of a possible double ditch were recently observed (but not recorded) on building sites. The existence of two different northern boundaries marked by ditches is puzzling. Another stretch of a timber rampart on the riverfront was built to abut the above mentioned *Ubiermonument* (**54**), the timbers of which have a recalibrated date of AD 9. One is tempted to connect the fortification of the riverbank with the military disaster east of the Rhine in the same year

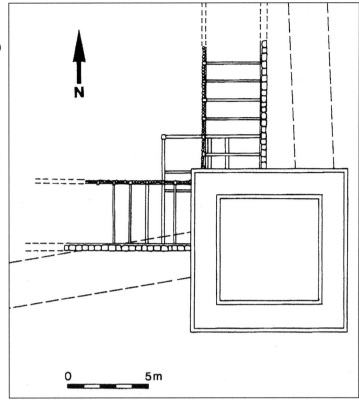

54 Early first-century stone tower (Ubiermonument) at the south-east corner of the Oppidum Ubiorum *with abutting timber rampart on the north (excavated) and west (conjectural).* Courtesy S. Schütte

N

0   5 m

and interpret the action as a response to a very real threat from Germanic tribes, but this can only be hypothetical. Remains of the western defences of the settlement were uncovered in 1992 in the form of a flat-bottomed boundary ditch 16ft (5m) in width which was backfilled around AD 50. No trace of a rampart survived. If one connects the *Ubiermonument* and the riverside fortifications, the most recently excavated ramparts on the north and the boundary ditch on the west, an approximate extent of the settlement can be recognised which is smaller than the later colony founded in 50. Indeed, the western boundary ditch found in 1992 was built over, probably under Vespasian, with a large private house, and this later redevelopment of urban property extended further west to the stone-built wall of the colony. The colony's stone-built wall on the riverbank likewise extended further east and closer to the Rhine than the earlier timber rampart had done. By the first half of the second century, the harbour between the riverbank and the island had silted up and been intentionally backfilled with all manner of dumped material so that the island was thereafter connected to the mainland, leaving the new harbour on the eastern edge of the island (**9**).

The quest for evidence pointing to a foundation of the settlement in the last decades of the first century BC is fruitless if one bases the quest on remarks by Tacitus and Strabo. In actual fact, neither author says that a town was founded for the Ubii under Agrippa, merely that they left the east bank and arrived on the west bank at this time. To claim that the *oppidum Ubiorum* was founded in 39 BC is a careless misinterpretation of the evidence.

If the foundation date is one modern myth, the assertion that a military base preceded the later *colonia* on the same site is another. Even more disturbing is the postulation that an Ubian civilian settlement, in existence since 39 BC, was confiscated by the Roman state as the site for a legionary base in the early first century AD, thereby relegating the displaced civilian population to the southern and western peripheries of the fort. This treatment of the Ubii is completely at odds with the political intentions of the Roman state and with the special status this group enjoyed since the later first century BC. The 'fort theory' was first proposed in the 1960s when a 'ditch' was excavated in sondages in the western part of the city. This was interpreted as the ditch of an Augustan fort, and therefore all remains of that date were classed as military in nature. How precarious such an interpretation can be was made clear in 1992 when large-scale excavations directly south of the 1960s ditch site proved beyond the shadow of a doubt that the 'ditch' was in reality nothing more than a series of re-filled quarry pits on the same alignment as an Augustan street. Despite all previous attempts to make architectural remains fit the picture of a military camp, there is no indication whatever that the Roman army occupied the area on which the colony later stood. None of the buildings bears any resemblance to barracks, nor is the spatial layout of the settlement reminiscent of a fort. The presence of Legio XIX was deduced by a graffito on a single Arretine sherd of dubious provenance and must be severely questioned. Excavations in 1995/96 2 miles (3km) south of Cologne (Alteburg) at the Claudian base of the Rhine fleet (*Classis Germanica*) indicate that there was a late Augustan/Tiberian fort in this location (**colour plate 20**). It was a temporary camp with timber buildings occupied intermittently from year to year. It was certainly in existence in AD 14 when Legio I and Legio XX, or more likely just detachments of them, were stationed for the winter in Ubian territory, and it is the only candidate we have for a military installation near Cologne of this early date. The two legions were permanently stationed in Neuss and Bonn at least since the 30s AD, the Alteburg site remained in the possession of the military, however, and was used as the permanent fleet base from the mid-first century until the late third century AD.

The spatial division between civilian and military in pre-colonial Cologne has become increasingly clear in recent years. The *colonia* was preceded by a civilian town of the early first century AD on the same site, the *oppidum Ubiorum*, while to the south military occupation occurred.

The relatively late date of the establishment of the *oppidum* needs an explanation, especially since Ubian migration to the area pre-dates it. Excavations at sites along the west bank of the Rhine at Neuss, Bonn, Dormagen and Remagen have revealed small, scattered settlements which were established around 30 BC, according to the pottery evidence, on sites where no previous late Iron Age occupation had occurred. At Bonn, sunken-floored buildings and post-built dwellings characterised the settlement. The settlement at Remagen had a timber palisade, one post of which is dendrochronologically dated to 9 BC. Since these settlements appear suddenly and the excavated pottery differs from the late Iron Age ceramics characteristic of the west bank, the evidence may reflect new occupation of the region by groups of Ubii. By 12 BC, at which time a second Gallic census was conducted, the general limitations of the Ubian *civitas* will have been established and, as a result of the German campaigns of Augustus at the same time, the main north-south and east-west roads along the Rhine and to the interior of Gaul completed. Around the turn of the first century BC to the first century AD the decision to consolidate Ubian settlers in a new centre on a hitherto unoccupied site in Cologne must have been made. By this time the territorial infrastructure was stable enough for the Romans to establish an urban centre and the consolidated settlement was imposed on the Ubii and on this un-urbanised region. The *oppidum Ubiorum* was founded as a *civitas* capital and laid out according to a Roman plan which is evident in the spatial organisation of the town. In fact, the layout of the town is highly reminiscent of new Augustan towns in northern Italy such as Turin and Aosta and in Switzerland at Avenches. At Cologne pre-colonial elements such as the central forum and the regular street grid were retained in the *colonia*. Monumental stone architecture pre-dating and underlying the *colonia*-period *praetorium* or governor's palace as well as the establishment of a sanctuary of the Imperial cult of Rome and Augustus (*ara Ubiorum*) in the early years of the first century AD indicate that the town was possibly planned as the capital of a larger German province which would have included the east bank lands up to the Elbe, had the plans for conquest and consolidation not been shattered by the defeat of Varus.

The *oppidum Ubiorum* was established at a time when, as Cassius Dio says, towns were being built under Augustus in Germany (*Historia Romana* 56.18). Dio's remarks have always been regarded as pure rhetoric, but recent discoveries at Haltern and Waldgirmes suggest that there was indeed a concerted effort in the late first century BC and early first century AD to plant the seed of urbanism and establish Roman administration in the 'wilds' of Germany (chapter 2). Completely new towns, built where none had been before, were essential for the administration of areas incorporated into the Empire, and they are particularly common on the lower Rhine. Cologne, Nijmegen (*oppidum Batavorum*) and Xanten (*oppidum Cugernorum*) are all towns created *ex-novo* for population groups who moved or were moved into the area in the context of the Augustan reorganisation of the region. Within this group of northern *civitas* capitals, Cologne was the first to be awarded colony status, followed half a century later by Xanten, and within the hierarchy of towns on the lower Rhine Cologne's status was further elevated in AD 85 by its promotion to provincial capital.

Population

Historical and archaeological sources reveal a mixed population in early Cologne. Tacitus refers to Ubii, Italians and provincials living there (*Historiae* 4.65). This is confirmed by inscriptions on grave monuments and votive dedications, as well as by burial practices. A mixed population is particularly evident in the north-west cemetery where cremations in Roman fashion are found alongside non-Roman inhumations and horse burials. One of these excavated inhumation burials was marked above ground by a gravestone naming the deceased as a Gallic woman of the Remi tribe (**43**). Most of the preserved grave epitaphs of the first century in Cologne record either retired or still active members of the military who, with the exception of fleet personnel from Asia Minor and Egypt, came from Italy or the Alpine region. Epigraphically attested foreign civilians in the *oppidum Ubiorum* include an Italian slave merchant and settlers from Gaul, in particular from the tribes of the Remi, Treveri and Viromandui. These latter groups may well have been engaged in trade or were merchants of some kind, much like the delegations of Lingones and Remi who operated in Xanten and on the lower Rhine in the 60s AD. Although they are not attested in any inscriptions, it is also likely that German traders from the east bank of the Rhine were involved in the economic life of the *oppidum*, even if they may not have lived there on a permanent basis. The Tencteri, at least in AD 69, were obliged to pay customs duties on trade with the colony and were under police supervision when entering the city (Tacitus, *Historiae* 4.64-65).

The other significant group living in Cologne at this time are the Ubii themselves, but they are not attested in early inscriptions in the city. This is related to the fact that the custom of inscribing gravestones or setting up inscribed votive dedications was not native to the area, and it was not until the second century that the local population was competing in this Roman form of social display. Ubii are attested outside Cologne in epigraphic sources as soldiers serving in auxiliary units under Tiberius and they are mentioned as having participated in the struggles during the Batavian revolt (**colour plate 21**). They are also recorded in Rome as members of the imperial bodyguard where their ethnic affiliation as *natione Ubius* is named. We have no idea how many Ubii were relocated to the Cologne area, nor do we know how many other Germanic subtribes may have joined them. Unlike other Germanic groups on the lower Rhine, not a single personal name of any member of the Ubian nobility is preserved in the sources. Had the Ubian nobility been finished off by the Suebi, or had they been absorbed by the latter group? Were the Ubii who migrated to the west-bank only part of a larger band or the retinue of disgruntled leaders who saw better opportunities in a Roman alliance? According to Suetonius (*Tiberius* 9), 40,000 Sugambri (or Sugambri and other subtribes) were transferred to the west bank of the Rhine by Tiberius, if we can rely at all on this number. If a similar number of Ubii were resettled in the new *civitas Ubiorum* covering approximately 4000km² (1500 sq miles), that would amount to only about ten Ubii per square kilometre. Such a low population density is very improbable. It is more likely that many of the Ubii were concentrated nearer the Rhine and the capital whereas other pre-Ubian Germanic groups continued to live in the hinterland. Recognisable Ubian personal names are much more common in the eastern part of the *civitas*, between the Erft and Rhine rivers, whereas personal names reflecting the pre-Ubian *Germani cisrhenani* dominate west of the Erft. At any rate, the Ubii were the dominant group in this restructuring and they had special status due to their long-standing alliance with Rome.

By the end of the first century AD there is no longer any mention of Ubii or the tribal affiliation *natione Ubius*. By the time of the Batavian revolt in 69/70 the inhabitants of Cologne, now a Roman colony, referred to themselves as Agrippinenses after the name of the colony. Other Agrippinenses include a native of Astigi in Spain who retired as a legionary veteran in Cologne in the late first century (**45**). Some of the Agrippinenses who died far away from home simply name 'Ara' or 'Claudia Ara' as their origin. The fact that foreign colonists and Ubii equally could be Agrippinenses indicates that this status could be granted (veteran colonists) or inherited by birth (parents Agrippinenses). Roman citizenship, however, was a requirement, and we can be sure that many Ubii such as the veterans of Ubian cohorts and their families had this citizenship. Moreover, the large number of *Iulii* in Cologne and its territory indicate that Augustus had granted citizenship to parts of the population. Magistrates with Roman citizenship of the second and third century in Cologne who refer to themselves as Agrippinenses often have personal names which suggest that they were of local origin and members of the Ubian elite.

According to Tacitus, the other Germanic groups on the lower Rhine resented the Ubii for having adopted the name of Agrippinenses and having renounced their Germanic origins (*Historiae* 4.28, 4.64). We cannot be sure that this sentiment really was expressed by opposing Germanic peoples, but the inscriptional sources do confirm that this name had become common for citizens of Cologne of Ubian extraction. Although Roman rhetoric must be filtered out of Tacitus' recorded 'speeches' delivered during the Batavian revolt, the reluctance of the native inhabitants of Cologne to give up the 'Romans' to the besiegers because the original Roman settlers were united to them by ties of marriage and blood-lines probably reflects the reality of the existence of a mixed population. Intermarriage with Romans was a significant factor in ideological terms. One of the arguments used by the emperor Claudius in 48 to persuade senators to admit Gauls to the Roman senate was that the Gauls were mingled 'with us . . . in their way of life, in their culture and by intermarriage . . .' (Tacitus, *Annales* 11.24). Intermarriage between the Ubii and the indigenous population who had survived the Gallic wars, the remnants of the *Germani cisrhenani*, presumably also occurred, although naturally in Roman sources only marital unions with Romans are mentioned.

Culture, society and identity

The historical written sources reveal changes in the Roman perception of Ubian identity over a period of 120 years. Caesar in 55 BC considered them to be only slightly more civilised than other Germanic tribes, but by AD 69/70 the Ubii are portrayed as possessing qualities opposite to those of the Germans threatening the Empire. The Ubii had become important allies to the Romans and had 'earned' the right to have their city promoted to a colony. What they had done to be given this privilege is not stated, but it can be inferred that not only their unflagging loyalty to the Roman cause was responsible. They had also successfully adopted the relevant symbols of *Romanitas*. The Ubii had shown themselves to be reliable, and were given a position of responsibility and dominance in their new territory and a multitude of privileges. The initial identification by the Romans of the Ubii as a weakened Germanic tribe seeking protection as suppliants under Caesar gave way to the Agrippinenses' confidant self-definition of themselves. Their self-identification as allied partners of mixed Ubian and Roman ancestry was defined in relation to the temporal and physical juxtaposition of the other groups in the region. This may have manifested itself more distinctly within some levels of Ubian society than in others, and in this regard material culture is informative. The strongest association with Roman material culture and customs can be recognised in the urban capital where, not surprisingly, the elite came into closest contact with the symbols and bearers of Roman life, and where they profited from them as privileged leaders in the new order. In this sense, the identity of the Ubii had been transformed in a context in which individual social agents acted strategically in pursuit of their own interests. It need not be, however, that all members of this ethnic group shared the same interests or experiences. Individual or group perceptions of culture and identity, language and religion, may have differed on other levels of Ubian society depending on class and location. Those who lived in the countryside in rural settlements and villages, for example, may have perceived their identity in a different manner than those in the city, particularly in the context of indigenous Germanic groups to whom ancestry and kinship were of importance.

Unlike the indigenous population, Ubian culture had no roots in the region. The Ubii and the Romans entered the scene together and their futures were inextricably bound to one another. In fact, without the Roman identification of them, the Ubii might have remained unnamed and indefinable in archaeology. The historic Ubii may not have been one homogeneous group of people, but, like the Cugerni and Batavi who first appear as historic groups when they were incorporated into Roman territory, were given one name by external agency. The transplantation of the group known as the Ubii from their ancestral homeland in the late first century BC and the Roman creation of a new political state for them meant that the socially and culturally dislocated newcomers were forced to arrange themselves in an ongoing process with the differing cultural traditions of both their Roman protectors and their new Germanic neighbours west of the Rhine.

The rapid Ubian adoption of Roman material culture may be explained as a conscious emulation of visible Roman ways. It cannot be implied automatically, however, that such emulation expressed Roman identity, or at least not entirely. An element of social competition is evident at almost every level, reflecting a desire to define status within the local hierarchy by means of Roman symbols. How this status was expressed and the meaning behind it, however, surely differed. For the Ubian population outside the capital, the display of status may have expressed itself in the patronage of local sanctuaries, rather than in the building of Roman-style houses. For those in the urban centre, status was expressed in the adoption of a visibly Roman lifestyle (see chapter 3). Native traditions in house building or pottery production, for example, are absent in the *oppidum* from the beginning, and Roman state cults dominated the temple landscape throughout the first century AD. Funerary and religious practices, however, conformed more slowly to Roman models, even in the capital. The adoption of the Roman practice of commemorating the dead with stone monuments did not generally occur until the second century, and the incorporation of native cults into the urban fabric of the town did not pre-date this period. Something that is decidedly not Roman which persisted in Ubian society, at least with the female sex, is costume, implying some adherence to and assertion of traditional values (see chapter 7). The persistence of ethnic traditions is also reflected in the German language of the Ubii (but also of the indigenous population or *Germani cisrhenani*) which continued to be spoken throughout the Roman period. Significantly, this is more recognisably detectable amongst those members of the group who did not live in an urban environment, and it is in the countryside that non-Roman names predominate over Roman names with *tria nomina*. It is also here in Cologne's hinterland that more traditional Germanic timber architecture survived in the context of farmsteads (see chapter 4).

Roman colonists who resided in the *oppidum Ubiorum* and in the *colonia* played a significant role in the transmission of Roman culture in Cologne. They included Italian soldiers and veterans, Italian traders, soldiers from other parts of the Empire, Gallic traders and craftsmen who contributed in their own ways to the creation of a multicultural Roman society in this frontier town. Nevertheless, it would be misguided to interpret the culture of the Rhine frontier as entirely the product of Roman military impetus. The Ubii, at least those involved in the social and political life of the colony, contributed willingly to their own construction as Agrippinenses. This does not mean that once they became Agrippinenses they ceased to be Ubii, even if on the surface they had a Roman lifestyle. In the appropriate circumstances, anyone could become an Agrippinensis, whether a legionary veteran from Spain or an Ubian citizen. In this pluralistic society, ethnicity was not relevant as a criterion for membership in the collective. Common to all members was, on the local level, the city and region in which they lived, and, on the global level, the place of their community in the larger structure of the Roman Empire.

9 Late threats and responses

After these preparations he first of all aimed at the Franks, those namely whom custom calls the Salii, who once had the great assurance to venture to fix their abodes on Roman soil at Toxiandria . . . and they offered peace on these terms, that while they remained quiet, as in their own territories, no one should attack or molest them (Ammianus Marcellinus, *Res Gestae* 17.8.3).

For instance no shows are given now in Mainz, but this is because the city has been destroyed and blotted out; nor at Cologne, for it is overrun by the enemy. They are not being performed in the most noble city of Trier, which has been laid low by a destruction four times repeated, nor finally in many other cities in Gaul and Spain (Salvian, *De gubernatione Dei* 6.39).

The Augsburg victory altar

The third century witnessed repeated civil wars and foreign invasions, both of which are varyingly assessed by historians as to their contributory role in the disintegration of the Roman Empire. Since the murder of Severus Alexander in Mainz in 235, a series of contenders for the imperial office were heaved into position by their supporting armies, and often just as quickly and unceremoniously murdered by them. Armies, out of self-interest and a lack of allegiance to the Empire, made emperors, and the troops increasingly were withdrawn from the frontiers in western Europe to fight against rival imperial candidates, leaving the frontiers inadequately guarded. External pressure in the eastern Empire, for example in Persia, also required troop withdrawal from the west. Already in the later second century, Germanic attacks on the *limes* and incursions of barbarian peoples into Germania Superior, Raetia, Noricum and Pannonia alarmed the Empire. This increased in the third century with attacks and raids by the confederate Germanic groups known later as the Alamanni in 213, 233, 242, 254 and 259/60, and by the Frankish confederacy in 259 and 276.

In 260 Postumus, a governor or high-ranking military official under Gallienus, broke with the central Roman government, establishing a 'Gallic Empire' consisting of Spain, Gaul, the German provinces and Britain. A fascinating inscription from Augsburg, the capital of Raetia, is extremely informative about the climate and circumstances in the year 260 in regard to internal discord and external threat (**55**). The inscription is carved on an altar commemorating the victory in April 260 near Augsburg over the Iouthungi (later known as 'Alamanni') by the provincial army of Raetia, troops from the German provinces as well as units from Raetian *civitates*. The Iouthungi were defeated and driven off, in the process of which thousands of Italian prisoners held by the Iouthungi were freed. Gallienus had seriously weakened the Iouthungi in battle near Milan in the winter of 259/60, but it would appear that they retreated north across the Alps in the spring of 260 taking their spoils and prisoners with them. It is not Gallienus, however, who is named in the inscription as emperor, but Postumus. The altar was set up before 11 September 260 under his rule. That Postumus is named emperor is a clear indication that he had by then split from the central government under Gallienus, and Raetia had clearly also joined Postumus' Gallic Empire. Gallienus recovered Raetia, probably already by 264, but not without military struggles with Postumus. After Raetia was rejoined with the Empire, the names of Postumus, the Raetian army and the Raetian governor were chiselled off the surface of the Augsburg inscription (without being made entirely illegible), a treatment typical for those who had fallen out of favour and whose memory was to be eradicated (*damnatio memoriae*).

55 Altar found in Augsburg, Germany, commemorating the Roman defeat of the Iouthungi in AD 260.
Courtesy E. Schallmayer

Traditionally, coin hoards and evidence of destruction dating to around 260 and the early 260s in Alsace, Burgundy, the Sâone region, the *Agri Decumates* and Switzerland are attributed to trouble with marauding hordes of Alamanni, but they may equally be a result of military confrontations between the forces of Gallienus and Postumus. The remaining Roman troops on the upper German *limes* disappeared in 260, perhaps not because they were all killed by the Alamanni, but because they were withdrawn from the frontier by Postumus and incorporated into his forces. Many of them will have been withdrawn already by Alexander Severus in the early 230s for his campaigns against the Persians. Moreover, both Gallienus and Postumus deliberately involved the Alamanni in their civil war by making heavy use of them as mercenary soldiers. It would not be the last time Roman emperors drew barbarians into internal conflicts as a trump card: Constantius II, when waging civil war against Magnentius, let the Alamanni into upper Germania in 352 to damage Strasbourg, Breisach and Augst, and thereby weaken Magnentius' position. It would seem, then, that civil war within the Empire and pressures from peoples beyond the frontiers could and often did go hand in hand.

56 (opposite) Map showing late Roman German provinces and sites referred to in chapter 9.
  1 Aachen; 2 Ägerten; 3 Altrip; 4 Alzey; 5 Andernach; 6 Arnheim-Meinerswijk; 7 Augst;
  8 Avenches; 9 Basel; 10 Bavay; 11 Besançon; 12 Bingen; 13 Bitburg; 14 Bonn; 15 Boppard;
  16 Brackenheim-Hausen an der Zaber; 17 Bregenz; 18 Breisach; 19 Brühl-Villenhaus;
  20 Cuijk; 21 Deutz; 22 Euskirchen-Palmersheim; 23 Faimingen; 24 Frankfurt;
  25 Froitzheim; 26 Gennep; 27 Hagenbach; 28 Illzach; 29 Jülich; 30 Jünkerath; 31 Kastel;
  32 Kloten; 33 Koblenz; 34 Krefeld; 35 Ladenburg; 36 Langres; 37 Liberchies; 38 Maastricht;
  39 Moers-Asberg; 40 Monheim; 41 Neerharen-Rekem; 42 Neumagen; 43 Neupotz;
  44 Neuss; 45 Qualburg; 46 Rheinbach-Flerzheim; 47 Robur; 48 Solothurn;
  49 Stein am Rhein; 50 Tongeren; 51 Voerendaal; 52 Winterthur; 53 Xanten; 54 Yverdon;
  55 Zürich; 56 Zurzach

Political, military and economic reforms

The strategy of most of the short-lived emperors in the third century was to survive by making sure their armies were well paid, either by pressing cash out of the communities or by plundering the treasuries. More money was in circulation, but it had lost much of its earlier value due to the fact that its silver content had been drastically reduced in order to produce as much coinage as possible to pay the soldiers. Not until Diocletian was reform in many sectors seriously attempted to cure the ills afflicting the Empire.

During Diocletian's reign from 284 to 305 the provincial boundaries in the west were redrawn. Germania Inferior was now called Germania Secunda, and its limits were extended westwards to include former Tungrian territory and the Tungrian capital Tongeren (**56**). The provincial capital remained Cologne. Germania Superior was divided into two provinces: Germania Prima with its capital at Mainz (formerly northern Germania Superior) and Maxima Sequanorum with its capital at Besançon (formerly southern Germania Superior). Towns such as Langres which had belonged politically to Germania Superior now lay within the jurisdiction of the province of Lugdunensis I. The number of provinces everywhere was increased by subdividing the existing ones, and each 'new' province had its own bureaucratic apparatus. Above the provinces were the dioceses, twelve in all, each overseen by a *vicarius*. On a higher level, the Empire was divided into four prefectures: Oriens, Illyricum, Italy and Gaul. Each of these was ruled by a praetorian prefect who represented the emperors. Finally, the Empire at its highest level was split into an eastern and a western Empire, each half ruled by an emperor with a junior emperor or Caesar. The late Roman Empire was a highly bureaucratic state, the efficiency of which was very debatable. Importantly, command of the army was now divorced from the tasks of the civilian officials. On a local level, the increasing financial demands of the government to support the state and its defence rendered the once successful devolution of the *civitates* significantly unattractive. The financial burdens of local magistrates to compensate for shortfalls in tax revenues and their unwillingness to serve in local government is reflected by the potential difficulty in 367 of finding even three *decuriones* in office (as opposed to the earlier 100) in the towns of the western Empire (Ammianus Marcellinus, *Res Gestae* 27.7.3).

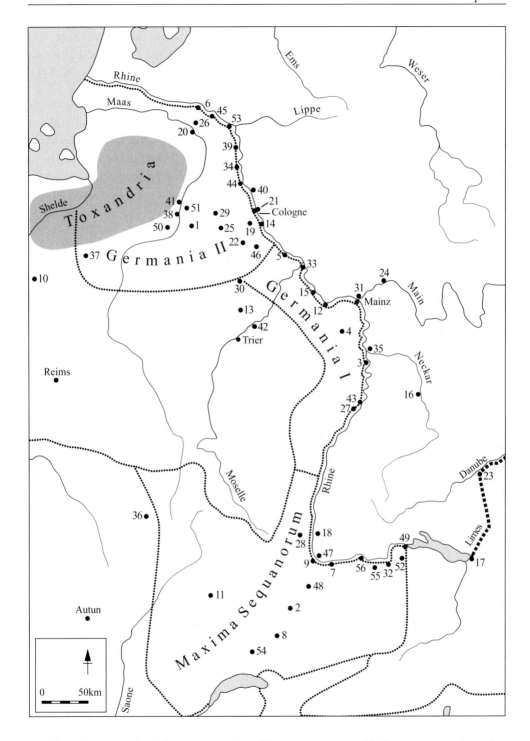

Since Augustus both legionary and auxiliary troops were chiefly concentrated on the frontiers. In case of emergency, troop contingents or vexillations were drawn from the frontier and sent where they were needed, and to the frontier they returned when the job

135

was done. This worked well enough until the third century when it became painfully clear that troops skimmed off the frontier, usually to fight in civil wars or on more distant fronts, opened the doors to many non-Roman peoples eager to take advantage of the weakened borders. Diocletian and his successor Constantine completely reformed the military strategy of the Roman Empire in the late third and early fourth century. Troop command was in the hands of military chiefs (*duces*), one chief per province in Germania Prima, Maxima Sequanorum, Germania Secunda and Belgica Secunda. These were based in Mainz, Besançon, Cologne and somewhere on the Belgian Atlantic coast. Troops were divided into a frontier army (*riparienses,* later known as *limitanei*) and a mobile field army (*comitatenses*). The field army was further subdivided in the later fourth century into the elite class of legionary, cavalry and Germanic auxiliary troops (*palatini*), the *comitatenses* comprising the rest of the legions and cavalry and the pseudo-*comitatenses* who included former *limitanei*. The *limitanei* manned the forts on the frontier, the field units were garrisoned in the interior. However, the field army could and did end up in skirmishes on the border. One of the officers of the cavalry unit *vexillatio comitatensis Stablesiana VI* fell in 320 on the northern Rhine near Deurne where his equipment was recovered in excavations. The legions were reduced in strength from 6000 to 1000 men each, the border units were made up of 500 men or less. Since the beginning of the fourth century Germanic auxiliaries were particularly employed in the mobile field army, and the mounted imperial bodyguard (*scholae palatinae*), in the first-, second- and third-century tradition of this unit (*Germani corporis custodes, equites singulares*), was composed almost exclusively of Germans. A clear Germanic element is also recognisable in the *limitanei* units of the second half of the fourth century.

After the collapse of the western frontier in 406, Germanic federate troops (*foederati*) defended the borders against further barbarian incursions. One example of a late Roman fort and the finds from it must suffice here to illustrate the changing character of late Roman defence. Archaeological excavations and analysis of the finds at the site of the Constantinian bridgehead fortress at *Divitia*/Deutz opposite Cologne have provided evidence for the transition in the composition of personnel defending the frontier. After it was built between 310-15 regular Roman units, including mounted scouts, were stationed at *Divitia*. The fort is named in a grave epitaph of the fourth century recording the death of the soldier Viatorinus at the hands of a Frank in enemy territory (*in barbarico*) (**colour plate 22**). After the Valentinianic restructuring of the Rhine frontier, a different unit of border troops (*limitanei*) of Germanic extraction was garrisoned here. Numerous bone and bronze hairpins, bracelets of bone, glass and bronze, earrings and *fibulae*, all part of Germanic female dress, indicate that the troops shared the fort with their wives, and presumably families. This is a common phenomenon in the late Roman forts and fortified settlements in the Rhineland. The numerous and often confusing array of timber posts within the buildings in Deutz suggest that the barracks were subdivided and internally re-arranged to accommodate the new inhabitants. *Divitia* was still occupied after the collapse of the western frontier in 406, but by Germanic *foederati*. The material assemblage of the first half of the fifth century includes Germanic bone combs, Germanic handmade pottery found at other contemporary sites on the east bank of the Rhine, late Roman pottery such as Argonne ware and red-slipped bowls and bronze *fibulae* types generally identified as

Saxon or Anglo-Saxon. Not until after the mid-fifth century is an intrusive group of settlers detectable in the use of timber-built structures in and through the ruins of the Roman buildings and in the associated purely Germanic finds.

The military restructuring initiated by Diocletian was not the only measure taken by this emperor to tackle problems afflicting the late Empire. He also attempted to come to terms with economic instability. Instability had not been universal in the Empire in the third century, and in fact the Gallic Empire had seen a prosperous economy and a flourishing merchant class in northern Gaul and the Rhineland. After the end of the bitterly contested Gallic Empire in 273, however, the economy in the western provinces was in serious trouble. Diocletian introduced new coinage in bronze, silver and gold and disposed of the completely worthless copper *antoniniani* that had been in circulation. Furthermore, inflation was rampant and extortionately high prices were demanded for goods and services. In 301 Diocletian and his co-emperor Maximian issued an Empire-wide price edict to cap the prices which could be charged for transport costs, commodities and services. Although the price edict seems to have had little effect on the then current practices, it gives us insight into some of the goods available at the time. Of the products from the western provinces, for example, we read of Gallic beer (much cheaper than wine), Menapic hams and woollen cloaks of the Nervii (most expensive variety). In order to safeguard adequate tax revenues in this inflationary economy, taxation in kind rather than in coin was introduced, although the latter was never completely replaced.

Destruction and rebuilding in the third and fourth centuries

There are two main problems in assessing the evidence for destruction and rebuilding in the late Roman period. For one thing, it is often difficult to date damage or destruction of sites precisely and it is also often uncertain who was responsible for it. Most often 'barbarian hordes' are made the culprits, even though it is unlikely that many of the attacks by the Alamanni or Franks involved more than a few hundred or a few thousand at a time. Julian, Caesar under Constantius II, encountered a raiding party of 600 Franks in the countryside near Jülich in 357, for example, and this might have been a typical 'invasion' force of the time (Ammianus Marcellinus, *Res Gestae* 17.2.1). The incursions were frequent, it is true, but they need not have involved the numbers recorded by some of the ancient sources such as Ammianus Marcellinus (*Res Gestae* 16.12.27, 12.63) who talks of 35,000 Alamanni battling against 13,000 Romans (with, of course, 6000 dead Alamanni and only 247 lost on the Roman side). Furthermore, Roman written sources could exaggerate the extent of destruction. After all, the historians of the time were writing for a Roman audience upon whom they wanted to impress the gravity of the situation and the efficacy of the emperor who dealt with threats to the Empire. Ammianus Marcellinus claimed that in 355 in the Rhineland 'no city (is) to be seen and no stronghold, except that at *Confluentes*/Koblenz . . . and a single tower near Cologne' (*Res Gestae* 16.3.1). For such destruction at Cologne, at least, there is not a shred of archaeological evidence. In modern German scholarship the Alamanni are made responsible for just about any destruction on the *limes*, in the *Agri Decumates* and the upper Rhine. Even when no concrete evidence confirms it, the date is often fixed at 259/60 to tie in with one of the biggest attacks by the Alamanni. It is more than likely that some of the destruction and disturbance can indeed be attributed to the Alamanni. A ritually executed Roman family on a farming estate at Harting in Bavaria bears witness to this: the victims were tortured, scalped and their skulls crushed before they were dumped into a well. Ritual defacement and smashing of statues and monuments to Roman gods in *vici* such as Bad Wimpfen and Walheim and at the villa at Brackenheim-Hausen an der Zaber also seem more likely to have been acts of Alamannic vengeance. It was almost certainly Alamannic looters who lost their booty on the west bank of the Rhine at Hagenbach and Neupotz near Speyer before they could cross the river. The collection of silver vessels cut into pieces and silver jewellery at Hagenbach included silver votive plaques robbed from a sanctuary of Mars in Aquitania, altogether 346 pieces (**colour plate 23**). The loot lost at Neupotz (in total over 1000 objects) consisted of weapons, horse-trappings and bronze and silver vessels packed in two large cauldrons, the latest coins in the treasure being issues of Gallienus. Both raiding parties must have been on their way back from the Gallic interior around 260. The possibility that signs of violence in the third and fourth centuries could have been the result of Roman armies engaged in civil wars, however, is rarely considered. In some cases, the Franks, Saxons and Alamanni were encouraged by the feuding emperors to invade the territory of the opponent and cause disruption.

The other problem is that rebuilding at many sites is also difficult to date precisely and, therefore, any such activity is not easily attributable to a particular emperor (which archaeologists are tempted to do). There is a tendency to associate most rebuilding with two emperors: Constantine in the early fourth century and Valentinian around 370. In some cases, this is corroborated by archaeological evidence, in others it is no more than an educated guess.

In some areas in the German provinces, settlements were being abandoned already in the late second or early third century. The civilian settlement outside the fort at Sulz on the Neckar was badly damaged by fire at the end of the second century and not rebuilt. The *vicus* at Solothurn barely survived into the third century. After Alamannic attacks in 233, some of the Roman population east of the *limes* may have fled the area. The *decurio* Dativius Victor and his family from *Nida*/Frankfurt-Heddernheim, who donated a public building with an arch in Mainz on the left bank of the Rhine 25 miles (40km) west of *Nida*, may be representative of many who found refuge in safer communities well behind the *limes* (**colour plate 8**). In northern Gallia Belgica and the Dutch Rhineland, the attacks and incursions of the Chauci between 172-4 caused widespread destruction from the Belgian coast to the Somme. *Civitas* capitals such as *Tarvenna*/Thérouanne, *Bagacum*/Bavay and *Samarobriva*/Amiens lay in ashes. Fortifications in response to the danger from the sea were built along the North Sea coast and around towns.

Most evidence for destruction or severe damage to towns, however, dates to the second half of the third and fourth centuries. Destruction in the 270s in Augst was either a result of Aurelian's attempt to recover the Gallic Empire or of an Alammanic incursion. The latest coin found in the foundation walls of a fortified area (*enceinte réduite*) built in the northern part of Augst dates to 276. This fortified area is only 7 acres (3ha) in size and is a drastic reduction in the extent of the colony. It appears to have been used by the civilian population. The reduction in size of towns and their fortifications is a trend observed everywhere (**57**). According to Ammianus Marcellinus (*Res Gestae* 15.11.12), Avenches in 355 was abandoned and lay in ruins. Somewhat later a fortified settlement was built above the town on the Bois de Châtel. In Basel, a fort on the Münsterhügel was built in the later third century. At Winterthur, a small central part of the *vicus* was encircled by a defensive wall built with state funds from Diocletian and Maximian in 294 which is commemorated in a building inscription. Late third-century fortified Langres shrank in size from 173 to 49 acres (70 to 20ha), and Dijon, Mandeure and Illzach were also fortified to enclose a much smaller area. Around 300 the already reduced urban area at Augst was relocated to the riverside at Kaiseraugst and enclosed in sturdy fortifications (*see* **11**). Speyer was destroyed in the late third century, as witnessed by burnt deposits and human skeletons in these deposits and in well shafts. It was rebuilt on a smaller scale in the early fourth century and further reduced and fortified in the second half of that century. Xanten was badly hit in the 270s. In the early fourth century a fortified settlement known as *Tricensimae* (probably in reference to the 30th legion still stationed at Xanten) was erected in the centre of the old colony, occupying the central nine *insulae* and taking up only 18 acres (16ha) as opposed to the original 180 acres (73ha) (**58**).

The Frankish invasions in the second half of the third century further weakened the most northerly part of Gallia Belgica and Germania Secunda. By this time, a line of small fortified posts (*burgi*) along the Cologne-Bavay-Boulogne road, the so-called *limes Belgicus*, represented *de facto* the limit of Roman territory. The sandy regions north of the *limes Belgicus* between the Maas, Demer and Schelde rivers were largely depopulated, and towns such as Nijmegen abandoned. There was no rebuilding of the towns, but a fort occupied by a military unit (*numerus Ursariensium*) was built at Nijmegen, perhaps under Constantine. In the Eifel, Ardennes, Condroz and Hunsrück numerous fortified posts were built in the later third century on hilltops and slopes as control points and places of refuge in the interior in the case that the Rhine or the *limes Belgicus* was overrun. *Burgi* were also built at private rural estates such as at Brühl-Villenhaus, Froitzheim and Rheinbach-Flerzheim (*see* **38**) in the loess areas near Cologne, and a number of small *burgi* with earth and timber ramparts are known around Zülpich. In some of these a stone built granary was built within the enclosure. Aerial photography in the last 20 years has aided in the detection of numerous *burgi* to the west and south-west of Cologne such as that at Euskirchen-Palmersheim lying next to a Roman road (**colour plate 24**).

South of the Cologne-Boulogne route the pattern of destruction and subsequent rebuilding continued throughout the fourth century. Constantine (306-37) engaged in a series of campaigns against the Franks, and during his reign several *vici* along the roads from Cologne to Trier and from Trier to Mainz were consolidated in size and provided with stout fortifications. They, together with the *burgi* and *castella* such as Liberchies and Maastricht on the Cologne-Boulogne road, added to the security of the roads and the maintenance of communication and supply routes. The fortified *vici* at Aachen, Jülich, Zülpich, Bitburg, Jünkerath and Neumagen were inhabited by the civilian population and contingents of the army. The *vicus* at Yverdon on the road from Avenches to Pontarlier was fortified in 325/6 for which dendrochronological analysis of the timber piles supporting the walls gives a precise date. At the same time, purely military posts were established

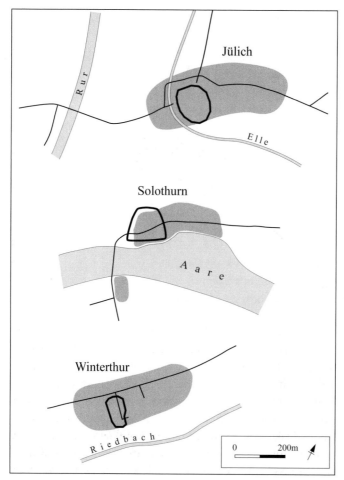

57 *Late Roman fortified towns of smaller size (thick black line) than the earlier* vici *(grey) at Jülich (Germany), Solothurn and Winterthur (Switzerland)*

along the Rhine, for example at Monheim (Haus Bürgel) and Deutz opposite Cologne (*see* **9**), and on the Maas at Maastricht, the latter fort dated dendrochronologically to 333. Models for the fortified bridgehead at Deutz had already been built on the Main river opposite Mainz at Kastel (*see* **16**) under Probus in the late third century and across from Zurzach and Stein am Rhein on the upper Rhine around 300. At many sites built in the later third and fourth centuries recycled worked stone, blocks and reliefs from grave monuments and public buildings were used, an obvious indication that building material was needed quickly. Reused material at Deutz and Neumagen include parts of monuments dating to as late as the mid-third century, but also older material from the first and second centuries. Building activity can also be dated to the sons of Constantine. The bridge across the Maas to a fort at Cuijk was built with timbers dating to 339, and can thus be attributed to Constantine II.

In the middle of the fourth century Frankish and Alammanic incursions as well as infighting between Magnentius and Constantius II caused widespread upheaval in the German provinces. Kaiseraugst, Breisach and Strasbourg were heavily damaged in the 350s, as were the *vici* of Altrip and Alzey. Excavations at Alzey have uncovered layers of

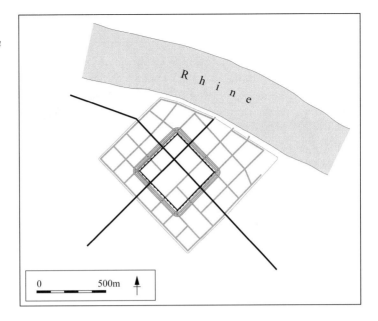

58 The fourth-century fortified settlement on the site of the earlier colony (light grey) at Xanten

burnt debris up to 3ft (1m) thick in the *vicus* area. The *colonia* at Xanten was destroyed in 351/2, and Cologne fell in 355 to remain in Frankish hands for ten months. At Deutz no evidence exists for destruction at this time, but there is a hiatus in the coin series there from 353 to 364. After the mid-fourth century the *burgi* on the Cologne-Boulogne road were only sporadically occupied, and military units that had been stationed at them and other *castella* were probably reunited with the mobile field army under Magnentius. Substantial rebuilding, however, did take place in the second half of the fourth century in many areas. Julian had seven 'cities' (forts?) rebuilt in 359 along the length of the Rhine: Arnheim, Qualburg, *Tricensimae*, Neuss, Bonn, Andernach and Bingen. Many sites have been attributed to Valentinian I (364-75) simply on the basis of the remark of Ammianus Marcellinus (*Res Gestae* 28.2.1) that in 369 this emperor 'fortified the entire Rhine from the beginnings of Raetia as far as the straight of the Ocean with great earthworks, erecting lofty fortresses and castles, and towers at frequent intervals, in suitable and convenient places as far as the whole length of Gaul extends . . .'. Some of Valentinian's activities can be precisely dated by archaeological evidence. Dendrochronology furnished a date of 368/9 for the timbers in the foundations of the fortifications at Ägerten on Lake Biel, and coins from the fortified *vicus* at Solothurn date to 364-94, suggesting a date for its construction during this period. The bridge across the Maas at Cuijk was repaired and old timbers replaced by new ones in 368/9. Upon the ruins of the *vici* at Altrip and Alzey forts were built on a smaller scale than the earlier settlements. Both forts were visited by Valentinian I personally in 369/70. A fort at Robur across the river from Basel was built under Valentinian I in 374, as preserved written sources record his orders for its construction. Valentinian I was also responsible for the construction of watchtowers on the Danube-Iller-Rhine-*limes*, or at least for their construction in stone rather than timber. The forts stretched from Basel to Stein am Rhein along the Rhine, and the most easterly of the forts along the Danube, Faimingen, was connected further south along the *limes* to one at Bregenz. One of the many *burgi* along this *limes* has preserved its building inscription which dates to 371. Many other fortified sites such as Avenches, Olten, Zürich, Ladenburg, Krefeld and the stone watchtower at Moers-Asberg are regarded as the fruits of Valentinian's building programme, but with less clear evidence. Some of the building work in the provinces may date to his successor, Valentinian II (375-92), as coins in the foundations of the *burgus* at Kloten indicate. This *vicus* on the overland route from Vindonissa and Baden to Winterthur was rebuilt and fortified after 378.

In the towns whose occupation areas were reduced in size and enclosed in circuit walls in the late Roman period it is worth noting what exactly was included within the walls. At Xanten only the area of the forum, Capitolium, the public baths and so-called palace remained within the enclosure. At Bavay the new circuit walls of the late third century left only the forum and neighbouring public buildings defended. At Winterthur the enclosure surrounded the public buildings and main temple complex of the *vicus*. At Basel unidentified buildings on stone foundations and a large granary (*horreum*) lay within the walls. Cologne was not reduced in size and remained within its walls. Whether these were of first-century date or were repaired or partially rebuilt as late as the third century, as some evidence seems to suggest, remains unclear (**colour plate 25**). One of the major public buildings, the so-called *cryptoporticus* at the west end of the forum, partly collapsed after 378 (coin dates), but the debris was dumped into the underground rooms, the dumped material covered by very level layers of soil and sand and the superstructure repaired to remain in use for a long time thereafter. The collapse could have been caused by old age or a fire, but deep cracks in the foundations of the building suggest some kind of seismic activity (the latest manifestation of this occurring in 1992). The *praetorium* was rebuilt, possibly under Constantine, and it remained in use until it was destroyed by an earthquake in the eighth century. Evidence on the periphery of Cologne in the residential districts, however, suggests that perhaps not all of the town was occupied in the fourth century. House walls in the western part of the city are sometimes found robbed out, and coins in the backfill of the trenches indicate that building material was being salvaged here some time after 350. This cannot be interpreted as a sign of decay or decline, however, since retrieval of building material means that something else was being built, but we do not know what or where. The central public and religious buildings of the towns were by far the most substantial buildings in the settlement, and occupation continued here, perhaps making use of the buildings in a different way than originally designed, because of their stability. Perhaps also urban housing that had been so important in the early and middle Empire as dwellings of the magistrates who participated in local government had less significance in the late Roman period, so that less private wealth was invested in such status symbols, or the town houses of the landowning class were abandoned in favour of their rural homes. Likewise the maintenance of public and religious buildings may no longer have been subsidised by the wealthy, leaving the sturdy stone buildings in a state of disrepair but still sufficiently intact to be utilised in one way or another. Patronage by the aristocratic landowning class may by this time have been channelled into the Church which offered positions of power and influence. Late Roman churches associated with the burials of Christian martyrs are among the most characteristic buildings which sprang up in the suburbs of towns in the late fourth century, some of them becoming episcopal centres.

A reduction in the size of the towns could reflect a decline in population numbers, and numerous sources reveal that, at least in the fifth century, it was not uncommon for noble members of society to leave the north and re-establish themselves in southern Gaul, especially after the capital was relocated at Arles. Trier and Cologne may have been an exception due to imperial patronage and their continued important status. However, we cannot rule out the possibility that the fortified core of many towns was used as a stronghold for civic and military purposes and that the population may have lived outside it or further afield in the countryside. Neither does it seem unlikely that the walled towns protected government property and that which was due the government, namely the collected taxes in kind (*annona militaris*) comprising grain and foodstuffs for the army. We have seen that in the third and fourth centuries rural estates often had stoutly walled granaries or *burgi* protecting the granaries, indicating that adequate grain storage was essential for the supply system. The towns' governments still had the obligation to collect taxes, and the best place for storing the exacted food supply was within the fortifications. At Basel it is precisely a large granary that was enclosed within the walls. Julian rebuilt fortified settlements enclosing granaries in 359 specifically to store the grain supply from Britain (Ammianus Marcellinus, *Res Gestae* 18.2.3-4). The importance of maintaining and protecting late Roman towns and cities may also be related to religion. The Christian Church had become a major power since the fourth century, and the focus of this power was on the cities where the bishops were based, not on the pagan countryside.

After Valentinian I there was no further systematic attempt to fortify the western frontier, although there was work on some existing circuit walls at the very end of the fourth century. The army of the western Empire was needed to protect the Danube from the Goths and Italy from the Visigoths. Troops were continually withdrawn and the protection of the Rhine weakened. Finally, on the last day in 406 the frozen Rhine was breached by Alani, Vandali and Suebi (also occasionally referred to as Alamanni), and possibly Quadi, Heruli, Saxons and Burgundiones. These were no longer mere raiding parties, but larger groups compelled by the Huns further east to migrate westwards in search of land perceived as immeasurably rich. Although Frankish federate troops managed to hold the frontier on the lower Rhine, the middle and upper Rhine border from Mainz southwards collapsed. Contemporary and later Roman sources typically depict the events as highly dramatic. The regular Roman troops left the frontier and the interior of Gaul and Germany, but the civilian population remained to experience a transformation of their world. Germanic federate troops now defended the frontier of an Empire whose Emperors were far away. But these troops also defended the lands they and the remaining Roman population held as well as that of many Germanic settlers who had put down permanent roots since the late third century.

Germanic settlement and establishment of kingdoms

The sandy regions north of the *limes Belgicus* were depopulated by the last quarter of the third century. Constantius Chlorus after defeating the Franks in 296 settled them in this area between Rhine and Schelde, and references are made from the period of Probus to

Laeti, Germanic captives settled in the interior of Gaul to defend and work the 'deserted lands which they must restore to growth' (*Panegyric to Constantius Chlorus* 9.3). The Salii, one group of the Frankish confederacy, were 'allowed' under Julian to settle in the region known as Toxandria between the Schelde and Maas which, although it was not garrisoned and effectively no longer under Roman control, was still regarded by the Romans as Roman soil. After the mid-fourth century, the Salii expanded their territory to annex the region of Kempen and Brabant and possibly Flanders. The Sarmatae, a non-Germanic group originally from the steppes of the Black Sea, settled in the area between the Moselle and Nahe rivers by the 370s. Ausonius, after accompanying Gratian in 370 on a campaign against the Alamanni, returned to the Hunsrück and Moselle valley, noting on his travels 'the fields which Sarmatian settlers recently have been forced to tend' (*Mosella* 9). In 413 the Burgundiones were planted as *foederati* on the west bank of the upper Rhine around Worms, and in 418 the Visigoths were formally settled in Aquitania. The policy of allowing non-Roman peoples on a formal basis to settle within the Empire reflects a response to a situation which could not be altered, but at least ameliorated. Ever more pressure was put on the Roman western frontier by a variety of Germanic peoples, and continual infiltration since the late third century ended in many of them remaining in areas south and west of the Rhine. Furthermore, the increasing numbers of Germans in the regular Roman army meant that ever more Germans and their families entered the Empire and remained there. Stilicho's decree of *hospitalitas* in 395, in which non-Roman groups were officially given the right to settle, simply made the best of what was already widespread. It was probably more difficult to expel Germanic groups once they had settled than it was to leave them where they were and harness that energy as a stablising military presence. Germanic settlers acted as protectors of the frontiers, and the lands they occupied acted as buffer zones between the Roman interior and the 'barbarians'. Originally, northern Gaul and the lower Rhine were given up to them, but as more and more territory was lost, these buffer zones shifted further south to include the Moselle and the upper Rhine.

The archaeological evidence for Germanic settlement is varied. It generally stems from cemeteries, but excavations are revealing remains of Germanic buildings and associated features in parts of the German provinces. Whether the ethnic identification of individuals is possible by a study of the grave goods is an often debated issue. Graves are particularly common outside forts and *castella* in the fourth and first half of the fifth century which include weapons, belts with chip-carved buckles and bronze fittings, *fibulae* and bronze hair pins. These burials are often attributed to Germanic *limitanei* and *foederati*, and they can be distinguished from other contemporary graves which do not contain these items, particularly weapons. This latter group is generally identified as burials of the Roman population. Both types of burials, however, contain Roman pottery, glass and coins. The military belt with a chip-carved buckle was a standard item of the army uniform, but also of government bureaucrats in the fourth and fifth centuries. It could indicate that the deceased was a soldier or an official, but the chip-carved buckle and belt reveals little about the origin of the individual and whether he was Roman or German (**colour plate 18**). One might anyway ask if there was such the clear dividing line between the two by this late date. Some grave goods, on the other hand, might better indicate population origins.

Trumpet-shaped brooches (so-called *tutulus fibulae*), for example, were part of Germanic female dress, and their distribution suggests that they were particularly common in Saxon regions. If such *fibulae* reflect movement of particular groups, then those found in female graves at Vron north of the Somme may indicate the settlement of Saxons in the North Sea coastal regions. Anthropological analysis of skeletal remains has not helped to identify different population groups, and even in post-Roman Germanic cemeteries the various Germanic peoples cannot be distinguished from each other. It cannot be seriously questioned that Germanic *limitanei* and *foederati*, and perhaps Germanic mercenaries, did military service and settled in regions west of the Rhine, but it is a problem to identify them archaeologically with absolute certainty. Not all Germanic federates would have remained within the Roman frontiers after retiring. The high concentration of late Roman military equipment found in the former *Agri Decumates*, the Weser and Elbe regions and on the Frisian North Sea coast suggests that many must have returned home.

A stronger case for Germanic settlement can be made when not only graves, but settlements as well as cemeteries survive for study. The excavated graves outside the late Roman fort at Krefeld-Gellup on the lower Rhine, for example, suggest that Germanic troops were employed in its defence at the end of the third century. The grave goods have affinities with the material culture characteristic of the region between the Rhine and Weser rivers. Around 400, Elbe-Germanic *foederati* appear to have manned the fort. In both periods, not only the fort was occupied but also the former *vicus* area next to it. Timber-framed houses typical of northern Germany and the area east of the Rhine, both longhouses of the *Wohnstallhaus* type and post-built granaries, were built as quarters for the garrison and their families. The latter phase of occupation continued into the early sixth century. The Roman villa at Neerharen-Rekem on the Maas was abandoned by 250 or slightly later by its owner, and thereafter the ruined site was reoccupied by Germanic settlers who built timber longhouses and at least 25 sunken-floored buildings (*Grubenhäuser*) (**59**). At Voerendaal the Roman villa lay largely in ruins by about 300, but a granary was built into the ruins of the main house and one of the villa's ancillary buildings appears to have remained in use in the fourth century. After the middle of this century these structures were superceded by *Wohnstallhäuser* and *Grubenhäuser*. The late fourth-century settlement at Gennep in the Dutch province of Limburg occupied a site without previous Roman habitation, and it is characterised by Germanic houses and approximately 100 sunken-floored buildings. This and the other late fourth-century villages established on earlier Roman sites presumably reflect the settlement of Frankish newcomers, possibly the Salii who expanded their territory beyond Toxandria.

At a number of sites in the former *Agri Decumates* traces of fourth-century Alamannic occupation, primarily burials and timber structures, have often been detected within the ruins of Roman villas or adjacent to them. Near the cathedral in Frankfurt and on the site of a Roman villa in Frankfurt-Elbelfeld handmade Germanic pottery, late Roman pottery and glass as well as coins of Constantius II (351-61) were found within the context of post-Roman buildings with dry-stone walls and *Grubenhäuser*. A hoard of 77 bronze coins dating to 341-6 found in the remains of a timber building in the ruined Roman civilian settlement at Heidenheim has been interpreted alternatively as an indication of continuing Roman habitation after the fall of the *limes* or as evidence of Alamannic squatters. An

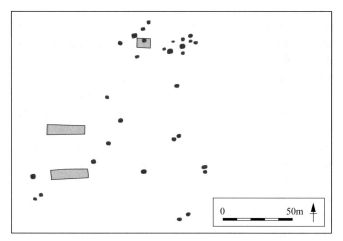

59 Germanic longhouses (grey) and sunken-floored buildings (black) on the site of the former Roman villa at Neerharen-Rekem

analysis of the Roman coins found east of the Rhine indicates that the regions particularly along the river between Mainz and Basel were being supplied with coin continuously until the middle of the fourth century. Most of the areas in the former *Agri Decumates* which were further removed from the Rhine show no continuity of coin supply. This, together with the Alamannic settlement evidence at old Roman sites, whether military or civilian, suggests that the regions immediately bordering on the Rhine frontier were occupied by groups of Alamannic *foederati*. One is reminded of Valentinian's treaty with the Bucinobantes who, under the leadership of their chieftain Macrianus, were charged with protecting the regions east of Mainz. After the civil war between Magnentius and Constantius II from 350 to 353, there is an apparent hiatus in Alamannic federate settlement in the buffer zone along the Rhine, and under Valentinian I the Rhine itself was heavily fortified as the frontier.

By the mid-fifth century northern Gaul and the Rhineland were in Frankish hands. Cologne was taken in 459 and became the seat of a Frankish king. Salvian (*De gubernatione Dei* 6.39) described the situation: Mainz was destroyed, Cologne was full of enemies (Franks) and Trier was sacked. In one of his letters of the time, he described the personal tragedy of one noble Roman family in Cologne who had lost everything, the mother of the family having to work as a servant in Frankish households (*Epistolae* 1.5f.) Nevertheless, the Frankish takeover of Roman territory does not appear to have involved great violence against Roman towns or the remaining civilian Roman population, even if the indigenous Romans were forced to adjust to the new situation. Moreover, the Franks operated within the existing Roman legal and administrative system. The divisions in society were present between Christian and non-Christian, rich and poor, countryside and town dwellers, rather than between barbarians and Romans who by this time were not always clearly distinguishable. In his diatribe against the rapaciousness of the late Roman administration Salvian claimed that both the poor and the rich lived under better conditions and could enjoy greater freedom from Roman state burdens under the new masters, even if they were pagans. The retention of a privileged lifestyle was probably more important to the late Roman land-owning aristocracy than the preservation of imperial control by the government, especially if the government sought to exact taxation and tamper with their fortunes, and any improvement to the conditions of the Roman poor, however slight and wherever it came from, would have been welcomed by those who had been tied to the land and robbed of their freedom.

Settlement continuity and continued use of Roman buildings has been determined in most major and minor towns. Substantial reduction of the Roman urban fabric and demolition of Roman public buildings at Cologne, for example, did not occur until around 1000, although there is little evidence to suggest that Roman private housing survived this long other than as shells or foundations for less substantial timber structures (**colour plate 26**). The Roman Christian communities at Cologne, Bonn, Zürich and Augst were sufficiently strong to build memorial chapels (*cellae memoriae*) in their cemeteries out of which developed parish churches and minsters. The community at Boppard on the Rhine converted the bathhouse within the fortified town into a parish church with a baptistery in the second half of the fifth century, the first of a series of churches on the same site to St Severus. At Jülich, Germanic and late Roman population groups lived side by side in the fifth century, and both were buried in a cemetery 328ft (100m) north of the fortified settlement which until then had been used by the local Roman inhabitants. Not until the early sixth century was a separate cemetery laid out for Frankish newcomers, some of them embracing the Roman funerary custom of sarcophagus burials and making secondary use of older sarcophagi. The evidence suggests that the spread of Germanic settlement and the transformation of the late Roman world into Germanic kingdoms in the fifth century was a continuous process and not an immediate result of a flood of Germanic peoples into the western Empire in 406.

In the mid-fifth century, the Huns had appeared on the scene as the significant 'other' threatening many population groups in the west and uniting them against a common foe. The defeat of the Huns in 451 by combined Roman and Germanic forces under the command of Flavius Aëtius may have been hailed as a Roman victory in Roman chronicles; for Gregory of Tours there was no doubt that 'the army of the Huns was really routed by the prayers of the Bishop' (*Historia Francorum* 2.7). The truth of the matter is that without the allied Frankish and Gothic armies a new (Hunnic) chapter in the history of northern Gaul would have begun. It was a consequence of the Roman loss of territory and of the political situation that Frankish, Alamannic, Burgundian, Saxon and Visigothic kingdoms were established in the sixth century in Gaul and Germany which stood on equal footing with the remains of the Roman Empire. However, their debt to the Roman political, legal, cultural and religious heritage, and even the Latin language, was great, and when Clovis (481-511) ruled as Frankish king he did so with the assistance of Roman advisors and within the context of a Roman administrative structure. During the Carolingian Renaissance, court-based ideology propagated the image of the Frankish kingdom as the reborn Roman Empire, and differences in ethnic origin, language and social standing were united by the Christian Church. The minting of coins by Charlemagne from 806 to 811, which bear a portrait of Charlemagne in the guise of Constantine and with the Latin inscription KAROLUS IMP AUG, indicates, to cite only one example, how late Roman imperial imagery and symbols were appropriated to convey the message of created continuity.

Further reading

Primary Sources
Many of these are available as Penguin Classics and/or in the Loeb Classical Library series
Aelius Aristides, *Orationes, Book 26 (To Rome)*
Ammianus Marcellinus, *Res Gestae (History)*
Anon., *Historia Augusta (Lives of the Caesars)*
Ausonius, *Mosella (Moselle)*
Cassius Dio, *Historia Romana (Roman History)*
Caesar, *De Bello Gallico (Gallic War)*
Cicero, *De Officiis (On Duty)*
Diodorus Siculus, *Bibliotheke Historike (Library of History)*
Florus, *Epitome (Epitome of Roman History)*
Gregory of Tours, *Historia Francorum (History of the Franks)*
Pliny, *Historia Naturalis (Natural History)*
Plutarch, *Vitae (Parallel Lives)*
Prosper of Aquitaine, *De Vocatione Omnium Gentium (On the calling of all peoples)*
Salvian, *De gubernatione Dei (On the government of God)*, *Epistolae (Letters)*
Strabo, *Geographia (Geography)*
Suetonius, *Vitae Duodecim Caesarum (Lives of the Twelve Caesars)*
Tacitus, *Germania (Germany)*, *Annales (Annals)*, *Historiae (Histories)*, *Agricola*
Velleius Paterculus, *Historia Romana (Roman History)*

Collective works, surveys and syntheses

Baatz, D. and Herrmann, F. (eds.), *Die Römer in Hessen* (Stuttgart: 1982)
Bechert, T., *Römisches Germanien zwischen Rhein und Maas: die Provinz Germania Inferior* (Zurich: 1982)
Blagg, T.F.C., and Millett, M. (eds.), *The Early Roman Empire in the West* (Oxford: 1990)
Brandt, R., and Slofstra, J. (eds.), *Roman and Native in the Low Countries. Spheres of Interaction*. BAR International Series 184 (Oxford: 1983)
Creighton, J.D. and Wilson, R.J.A. (eds.), *Roman Germany. Studies in Cultural Interaction* (Portsmouth, Rhode Island: 1999)
Cüppers, H. (ed.), *Die Römer in Rheinland-Pfalz* (Stuttgart: 1990)
Czysz, W., Dietz, K., Fischer, T., and Kellner, H.-J. (eds.), *Die Römer in Bayern* (Stuttgart: 1995)
Drack, W. and Fellmann, R., *Die Römer in der Schweiz* (Stuttgart: 1988)
Drinkwater, J., *Roman Gaul* (London: 1983)
Filtzinger, P., Planck, D., and Cämmerer, B. (eds.), *Die Römer in Baden-Württemberg* (Stuttgart: 1986)
Fischer, T., *Die Römer in Deutschland* (Stuttgart: 1999)
Galsterer, B., and Galsterer, H., *Die römischen Steininschriften aus Köln* (Cologne: 1975)
Horn, H.G. (ed.), *Die Römer in Nordrhein-Westfalen* (Stuttgart: 1987)
Horn, H.G., Hellenkemper, H., Isenberg, G., and H. Koschik (eds.), *Millionen Jahre Geschichte. Fundort Nordrhein-Westfalen* (Cologne: 2000)
King, A., *Roman Gaul and Germany* (London: 1990)
Lenz-Bernhard, G., and Bernhard, H., *Das Oberrheingebiet zwischen Caesars Gallischem Krieg und der flavischen Okkupation (58 v.-73 n. Chr.). Eine siedlungsgeschichtliche Studie* (Speyer: 1991)
Metzler, J., Millett, M., Roymans, N., and Slofstra, J. (eds.), *Integration in the Early Roman West. The role of culture and ideology* (Luxembourg: 1995)
Roymans, N., *Tribal Societies in Northern Gaul. An anthropological perspective* (Amsterdam: 1990)
Roymans, N., and Theuws, F. (eds.), *Images of the Past. Studies on ancient societies in north-western Europe* (Amsterdam: 1991)
Selzer, W., *Römische Steindenkmäler. Mainz in römischer Zeit* (Mainz: 1988)

Wamser, L. (ed.), *Die Römer zwischen Alpen und Nordmeer. Zivilisatorisches Erbe einer europäischen Militärmacht* (Mainz: 2000)

Wightman, E.M., *Gallia Belgica* (London: 1987)

Willems, W.J.H., *Romans and Batavians. A Regional Study in the Dutch East River Area* (Amsterdam: 1986)

Woolf, G., *Becoming Roman. The Origins of Provincial Civilization in Gaul* (Cambridge: 1998)

Celts and Germans

Ament, H., Der Rhein und die Ethnogenese der Germanen, *Prähistorische Zeitschrift* 59, 1984, 35-45

Bazelmans, J., Conceptualising early Germanic political structure: a review of the use of the concept of Gefolgschaft, in Roymans and Theuws (1991) 91-130

Bittel, K., Kimmig, W., and Schiek, S. (eds.), *Die Kelten in Baden-Württemberg* (Stuttgart: 1981)

Collis, J., *Oppida. Earliest Towns North of the Alps* (Sheffield: 1984)

Fichtl, S., *Les Gaulois du Nord de la Gaule* (Paris: 1994)

Fitzpatrick A., Ethnicity and Exchange: Germans, Celts and Romans in the late Iron Age, in C. Scarre and F. Healey (eds.), *Trade and Exchange in Prehistoric Europe. Proceedings of a Conference held at the University of Bristol, April 1992*. Oxbow Monograph 33 (Oxford: 1993) 233-44

Mariën, M.E., Tribes and Archaeological Groupings of the La Tène period in Belgium: some observations, in J. Boardman, M.A. Brown and T.G.E. Powell (eds.), *The European Community in Later Prehistory. Studies in honour of C.F.C. Hawkes* (London: 1971) 213-41

Oesterwind, B.C., *Die Spätlatènezeit und die frühe Römische Kaiserzeit im Neuwieder Becken* (Bonn: 1989)

Scholz, M., Namen von Kelten, 'Römern' und Germanen? Die Bevölkerung von Nida-Heddernheim im Spiegel von Namensgraffiti, in C. Bridger and C. von Carnap-Bornheim (eds.), *Römer und Germanen - Nachbarn über Jahrhunderte*. BAR International Series 678 (Oxford: 1997) 49-57

Steidel, B., Frühe Germanen am unteren Main, *Germania* 74, 1996, 238-47

Todd, M., *The Early Germans* (Oxford: 1992)

Weisgerber, L., *Die Namen der Ubier* (Cologne: 1968)

Wells, C.M., Celts and Germans in the Rhineland, in M.J. Green (ed.), *The Celtic World* (London: 1995) 603-20

Wells, P.S., Identities, Material Culture and Change: "Celts" and "Germans" in Late Iron Age Europe, *Journal of European Archaeology* 3.2, 1996, 169-85

Wells, P.S., *The Barbarians Speak. How the conquered peoples shaped Roman Europe* (Princeton: 1999)

Wild, J.P., The Clothing of Britannia, Gallia Belgica and Germania Inferior, in *Aufstieg und Niedergang der Römischen Welt* II 12.3 (Berlin: 1985) 362-422

Roman military and civilians

Alföldy, G., *Die Hilfstruppen der römischen Provinz Germania Inferior*. Epigraphische Studien 6 (Düsseldorf: 1968)

Becker, A. and Rasbach, G., Der spätaugusteische Stützpunkt Lahnau-Waldgirmes, *Germania* 76, 1998, 672-92

Bellen, H., *Die germanische Leibwache der römischen Kaiser des julisch-claudischen Hauses* (Mainz: 1981)

Carroll, M., New Excavations at the base of the *Classis Germanica* in Cologne (Alteburg), in N. Gudea (ed.), *Roman Frontier Studies. Proceedings of the XVIIth International Congress of Roman Frontier Studies* (Zalau: 1999) 317-24

Carroll, M., and Fischer, T., Archäologische Ausgrabungen 1995/96 im Standlager der römischen Flotte (*Classis Germanica*) in Köln-Marienburg, *Kölner Jahrbuch* 32, 1999 (forthcoming)

Haalebos, J.K., *Castra und Canabae. Ausgrabungen auf dem Hunerberg in Nijmegen 1987-1994* (Nijmegen: 1995)

Kühlborn, J.S. (ed.), *Germaniam pacavi-Germanien habe ich befriedet: Archäologische Stätten augusteischer Okkupation* (Münster: 1995)

Mann, J.C., *Legionary Recruitment and Veteran Settlement during the Principate* (London: 1983)

Reddé, M. (ed.), *L'Armée romaine en Gaule* (Paris: 1996)

Roschinski, H.P., Eine Gefäßscherbe mit aramäischen Namen aus Krefeld-Gellep. *Epigraphische Studien* 13 (Cologne: 1983) 79-86

Trier, B. (ed.), *Die römische Okkupation nördlich der Alpen zur Zeit des Augustus. Akten Kolloquium Bergkamen 1989* (Münster: 1991)

Schlüter, W., and Wiegels, R. (eds.), *Rom, Germanien und die Ausgrabungen von Kalkriese* (Osnabrück: 1999)

Speidel, M.A., *Die römischen Schreibtafeln von Vindonissa* (Brugg: 1996)

Speidel, M.P., *Riding for Caesar. The Roman Emperors' Horse Guard* (London: 1994)

Wells, C.M., *The German Policy of Augustus* (Oxford: 1972)

Wells, C.M., What's New along the Lippe: Recent Work in North Germany, *Britannia* 29, 1998, 457-64

Wigg, A., Confrontation and interaction: Celts, Germans and Romans in the Central German Highlands, in Creighton and Wilson (1999) 35-53

Frontiers

Bechert, T., and Willems, W.J.H. (eds.), *Die römische Reichsgrenze von der Mosel bis zur Nordseeküste* (Stuttgart: 1995)

Beck, W., and Planck, D., *Der Limes in Südwestdeutschland* (Stuttgart: 1980)

Brun, P., van der Leeuw, S., Whittaker, C.R. (eds.), *Frontières d'Empire. Nature et signification des frontières romaines* (Nemours: 1993)

Der römische Limes in Deutschland. Römisch-Germanische Kommission and Verband der Landesarchäologen in der Bundesrepublik Deutschland (Stuttgart: 1992)

Galestin, M.C., Romans and Frisians. Analysis of the strategy of the Roman Army, in Groenmann-van Waateringe, van Beek, Willems and Wynia (1997) 346-53

Groenman-van Waateringe, W., van Beek, B.L., Willems, W.J.H., and Wynia, S.L. (eds.), *Roman Frontier Studies 1995* (Oxford: 1997)

Kunow, J., Relationships between Roman occupation and the *Limesvorland* in the province of Germania Inferior, in Blagg and Millett (1990) 87-96

Schallmayer, E., *Der Odenwaldlimes. Vom Main bis an den Neckar* (Stuttgart: 1984)

Schönberger, H., The Roman frontier in Germany: an archaeological survey, *J. Roman Studies* 59, 1969, 144-97

Whittaker, C.R., *Frontiers of the Roman Empire. A Social and Economic Study* (Baltimore: 1994)

Towns

Bloemers, J.H.F., Lower Germany: *plura consilio quam vi*. Proto-urban settlement developments and the integration of native society, in Blagg and Millett (1990) 72-86

Carroll-Spillecke, M., Neue vorkoloniezeitliche Siedlungsspuren in Köln, *Archäologische Informationen* 18/2, 1995, 143-52

Carroll-Spillecke, M., An early bath house in the suburbs of Roman Cologne, *J. Roman Archaeology* 10, 1997, 263-70

Eck, W., and Galsterer, H. (eds.), *Die Stadt in Oberitalien und in den nordwestlichen Provinzen des römischen Reiches* (Mainz: 1991)

Frézouls, E. (ed.), *Les villes antiques de la France II. Germanie Supérieure 1* (Strasbourg: 1988)

Gechter, M., Small Towns of the Ubii and Cugerni/Baetasii Civitates (Lower Germany), in A.E. Brown (ed.), *Small Towns in Eastern England and Beyond*. BAR British Series (Oxford: 1995) 193-203

Harries, J., Christianity and the city in late Roman Gaul, in J. Rich (ed.), *The City in Late Antiquity* (London: 1992) 77-98

Petit, J.-P., and Mangin, M. (eds.), *Atlas des agglomérations secondaires de la Gaule Belgique et des Germanies* (Paris: 1994)

Petit, J.-P., and Mangin, M. (eds.), *Les agglomérations secondaires de la Gaule Belgique, des Germanies et l'Occident romain. Actes du colloque de Bliesbruck-Rheinheim/Bitche (Moselle)* (Paris: 1994)

Schalles, H.-J., von Hesberg, H., and Zanker, P. (eds.), *Die römische Stadt im 2. Jahrhundert n. Chr. Der Funktionswandel des öffentlichen Raumes* (Cologne: 1992)

Gechter, M., and Schütte, S., Ursprung und Voraussetzungen des mittelalterlichen Rathauses und seiner Umgebung, in W. Geis and U. Krings (eds.), *Köln: Das gotische Rathaus und seine historische Umgebung* (Cologne: 2000) 69-196

Tarpin, M., Colonia, municipium, vicus: Institutionen und Stadtformen, in N. Hanel and C. Schucany (eds.), *Colonia - municipium - vicus. Struktur und Entwicklung städtischer Siedlungen in Noricum, Rätien und Obergermanien*. BAR International Series 783 (Oxford: 1999) 1-10

Woolf, H. Die Kontinuität städtischen Lebens in den nördlichen Grenzprovinzen des römischen Reiches und das Ende der Antike, in Eck and Galsterer (1991) 287-318

Rural settlements and the environment

Bender, H., and Wolff, H. (eds.), *Ländliche Besiedlung und Landwirtschaft in den Rhein-Donau-Provinzen des Römischen Reiches* (Espelkamp: 1994)

Bloemers, J.H.F., *Rijswijk (Z.H.), 'De Bult'. Eine Siedlung der Cananefaten* (Amersfoort: 1978)

Bunnik, F.P.M., Kalis, A.J., Meurers-Balke, J., and Stobbe, A., Archäopalynologische Betrachtungen zum Kulturwandel in den Jahrhunderten um Christi Geburt, *Archäologische Nachrichten* 18/2, 1995, 169-85

Buurman, J., Carbonised Plant Remains and Phosphate Analysis of two Roman period House Plans with Sunken Byres at Oosterhout, *Berichten van de Rijksdienst voor het Oudheidkundig Bodemonderzoek* 40, 1990, 285-96

Ebnöther, C., and Schucany, C., Vindonissa und sein Umland. Die Vici und die ländliche Besiedlung, *Jahresbericht der Gesellschaft Pro Vindonissa* 1998, 67-97

Gaitzsch, W., Grundformen römischer Landsiedlungen im Western der CCAA, *Bonner Jahrbuch* 186, 1986, 397-427

Gechter, M., and Kunow, J., Zur ländlichen Besiedlung des Rheinlandes in römischer Zeit, *Bonner Jahrbuch* 186, 1986, 377-93

Hiddink, H.A., Rural centres in the Roman settlement system of Northern Gallia Belgica and Germania Inferior, in Roymans and Theuws (1991) 201-33

Kreuz, A., Becoming a Roman Farmer: Preliminary report on the environmental evidence from the Romanization project, in Creighton and Wilson (1999) 71-98

Lauwerier, R.C.G.M., Groenewoudt, B.J., Brinkkemper, O., and Laarman, F.J., Between ritual and economics: Animals and plants in a fourth century native settlement at Heeten, the Netherlands, *Berichten van de Rijksdienst voor het Oudheidkundig Bodemonderzoek* 43, 1998/99, 155-98

Lenz, K.H., *Villae rusticae*. Zur Entstehung dieser Siedlungsform in den nordwestlichen Provinzen des römischen Reichs, *Kölner Jahrbuch* 31, 1998, 49-70

Schucany, C., Solothurn and Olten. Zwei Kleinstädte und ihr Hinterland in römischer Zeit, *Archäologie der Schweiz* 22, 1999, 88-95

Slofstra, J., Changing Settlement patterns in the Meuse-Demer-Scheldt area during the Early Roman period, in Roymans and Theuws (1991) 131-99

Van Enckevort, H., Bemerkungen zum Besiedlungssystem in den südöstlichen Niederlanden während der späten vorrömischen Eisenzeit und der römischen Kaiserzeit, in T. Grünewald (ed.), *Germania Inferior. Besiedlung, Gesellschaft und Wirtschaft an der Grenze der römisch-germanischen Welt* (Berlin 2001) 336-96

Van Ossel, P., *Établissements ruraux de l'Antiquité tardive dans le nord de la Gaule*. Gallia Suppl. 51 (Paris: 1992)

Verwers, W.J.H., and L.I. Kooistra, Native house plans from the Roman Period in Boxtel and Oosterhout, *Berichten van de Rijksdienst voor het Oudheidkundig Bodemonderzoek* 40, 1990, 251-84

Industry

Berger, L., *Ein römischer Ziegelbrennofen bei Kaiseraugst, mit einigen Bemerkungen zur Typologie römischer Ziegelbrennöfen* (Basel: 1969)

Carroll, M., Frührömische Töpferöfen in Köln, in Horn, Hellenkemper, Isenberg and Koschik (2000) 328-30

Carroll, M., The early Roman pottery industry in Cologne, Germany: A new kiln site in the *Oppidum Ubiorum, J. Roman Pottery Studies* (forthcoming)

Carroll-Spillecke, M., Die Ausgrabungen im römischen Suburbium an der Jahnstraße in Köln, *Kölner Jahrbuch* 29, 1996, 563-78

Doppelfeld, O., *Römisches and fränkisches Glas in Köln* (Cologne: 1966)

Feller, M., and Brulet, R., Récherches sur les ateliers de céramique gallo-romains en Argonne. *Archaeologia Mosellana* 3, 1998, 229-368

Flügel, C., Handgemachte Grobkeramik aus *Arae Flaviae*-Rottweil, *Fundberichte aus Baden-Württemberg* 21, 1996, 315-400

Fremersdorf, F., Die Anfänge der römischen Glashütten Kölns, *Kölner Jahrbuch* 9, 1966, 24-43

Furger, A.R., Die Bronzewerkstätten in der Augster Insula 30, *Jahresberichte August und Kaiseraugst* 19, 1998, 121-40

Gaitzsch, W., and Wedepohl, K.H., Spätrömische Glashütten im Hambacher Forst. Archäologische Befunde und geochemische Analysen, in Horn, Hellenkemper, Isenberg and Koschik (2000) 298-301

Garbsch, J. *Terra sigillata. Ein Weltreich im Spiegel seines Luxusgeschirrs* (Munich: 1982)

Haupt, D., Römischer Töpfereibezirk bei Soller, Kreis Düren, in D. Haupt (ed.), *Beiträge zur Archäologie des römischen Rheinlandes* 4. Rheinische Ausgrabungen 23 (Cologne: 1984) 391-476

Höpken, C., Die Produktion römischer Gefäßkeramik in Köln, *Kölner Jahrbuch* 32, 1999 (forthcoming)

Hussong, L., and Cüppers, L., *Trierer Kaiserthermen. Die spätrömische und frühmittlelalterliche Keramik* (Trier: 1972)

Reutti, F., Tonverarbeitende Industrie im römischen Rheinzabern, *Germania* 61, 1983, 33-69

Schuler, A., Ein Dolium mit Herstellerangabe aus einer *villa rustica* bei Oberzier, *Archäologie im Rheinland 1992* (Cologne: 1993) 74-75

Symonds, R.P., *Rhenish Wares. Fine dark coloured pottery from Gaul and Germany* (Oxford: 1992)

Economy, trade and exchange

Brandt, R., A brief encounter along the northern frontier, in Brandt and Slofstra (1983) 129-45

Carroll, M., Supplying the Roman Fleet: Native Belgic, Frisian and Germanic pottery from Cologne, *J. Roman Archaeology* 14, 2001 (forthcoming)

Drinkwater, J.F., Money-rents and Food-renders in Gallic Funerary Reliefs, in A. King and M. Henig (eds.), *The Roman West in the Third Century*. BAR International Series 109 (Oxford: 1981) 215-33

Drinkwater, J.F., The Wool Textile Industry of Gallia Belgica and the Secundinii of Igel: Questions and Hypotheses, *Textile History* 13(1), 1982, 111-28

Du Plat Tayor, J., and Cleere, H. (eds.), *Roman shipping and trade: Britain and the Rhine Provinces*. CBA Research Report 24 (London: 1978)

Dusek, S., *Römische Handwerker im germanischen Thüringen* (Stuttgart: 1992)

Kneissl, P., Die utriclarii. Ihre Rolle im gallo-römischen Transportwesen und Weinhandel, *Bonner Jahrbuch* 181, 1981, 169-204

Kunow, J., Die "Dritte Welt" der Römer. Kontakte zwischen dem *Imperium Romanum* und der *Germania libera*, *Archäologie in Deutschland* 1988/4, 34-39

Slippschuh, O., *Die Händler im römischen Kaiserreich in Gallien, Germanien und den Donauprovinzen Rätien, Noricum and Pannonien* (Amsterdam: 1974)

Van Beek, B.L., Salinatores and Sigillata: The coastal areas of North Holland and Flanders and their economic differences in the 1st century A.D., *Helinium* 23, 1983, 3-12

Wierschowski, L., Handels- und Wirtschaftsbeziehungen der Städte in den nordwestlichen Provinzen des römischen Reiches, in Eck and Galsterer (1991) 121-40

Wigg, D.G., *Münzumlauf in Nordgallien um die Mitte des 4. Jahrhunderts n. Chr.* (Berlin 1991)

Wolters, R., Römische Funde in der Germania Magna und das Problem römisch-germanischer Handelsbeziehungen in der Zeit des Prinzipats, in G. Franzius (ed.), *Aspekte römisch-germanischer Beziehungen in der frühen Kaiserzeit* (Espelkamp: 1995) 99-117

Tombs and cemeteries

Andrikopoulou-Strack, J.-N., *Grabbauten des 1. Jahrhunderts n. Chr. im Rheingebiet. Untersuchungen zur Chronologie und Typologie*. Bonner Jahrbuch Beih. 43 (Cologne: 1986)

Balzer, M., Die Alltagsdarstellungen der treverischen Grabdenkmäler, *Trierer Zeitschrift* 46, 1983, 7-151

Böhme, H.W., *Germanische Grabfunde des 4. bis 5. Jahrhunderts zwischen unterer Elbe und Loire* (Munich: 1974)

Bridger, C., *Das römerzeitliche Graberfeld 'An Hinkes Weißhof', Tönisvorst-Vorst, Kreis Viersen* (Cologne: 1996)

Castella, D. *La nécropole gallo-romaine d'Avenches 'En Chaplix'. Fouilles 1987-1992*. Vol. 1: *Études des sépultures* (Lausanne: 1999)

Fasold, P., Fischer, T., von Hesberg, H., and Witteyer, M. (eds.), *Bestattungssitte und kulturelle Identität. Grabanlagen und Grabbeigaben der frühen römischen Kaiserzeit in Italien und den Nordwest-Provinzen* (Cologne: 1998)

Ferdière, A. (ed.), *Mondes des Mort, Monde des vivants en Gaule rurale. Actes du Colloque Archéa/Ager (Orléans)* (Tours: 1993)

Gabelmann, H., Römische Grabbauten der Nordprovinzen im 2. und 3. Jh. n. Chr., in H. von Hesberg and P. Zanker (eds.), *Römische Graberstraßen. Selbstdarstellung, Status, Standard* (Munich: 1987) 291-308

Haffner, A., *Gräber - Spiegel des Lebens. Zum Totenbrauchtum der Kelten und Römer* (Trier: 1989)

Müller, G., *Die römischen Gräberfelder von Novaesium*. Novaesium Vol. 7 (Berlin: 1977)

Neu, S., Römische Reliefs vom Kölner Rheinufer, *Kölner Jahrbuch* 22, 1989, 241-364

Päffgen, B., *Die Ausgrabungen in St Severin zu Köln* (Cologne: 1992)

Struck, M. (ed.), *Römerzeitliche Gräber als Quellen zu Religion, Bevölkerungsstruktur und Sozialgeschichte* (Mainz: 1993)

Religion

Bauchhenß, G., and Neumann, G. (eds.), *Matronen und verwandte Gottheiten* (Cologne: 1987)

Brunaux, J.-L. (ed.), *Les sanctuaires celtiques et leur rapports avec le monde meditéranéen* (Paris :1991)

Derks, T., The perception of the Roman pantheon by a native elite: the example of votive inscriptions from Lower Germany, in Roymans and Theuws (1991) 235-65

Derks, T., *Gods, Temples and Ritual Practices. The transformation of religious ideas and values in Roman Gaul* (Amsterdam: 1998)

Eck, W., Zur Christianisierung in den nordwestlichen Provinzen des Imperium Romanum, in Eck and Galsterer (1991) 251-61

Fishwick, D., *The imperial cult in the Latin West* (Leiden: 1987)

Trunk, M., *Römische Tempel in den Rhein- und westlichen Donauprovinzen* (Augst: 1991)

Late Roman Defence

Bridger, C. and Gilles, K.-J. (eds.), *Spätrömische Befestigungsanlagen in den Rhein- und Donauprovinzen.* BAR International Series 704 (Oxford: 1998)

Brulet, R., Le *litus saxonicum* continental, in V.A. Maxfield and M.J. Dobson (eds.), *Roman Frontier Studies 1989. Proceedings of the XVth International Congress of Roman Frontier Studies* (Exeter: 1991) 155-69

Brulet, R., Verteidiger und Verbündete des Römischen Reiches. Germanen in römischen Diensten und das spätantike Befestigungssystem, in Wieczorek, Périn, von Welck and Menghin (1997) 85-90

Carroll-Spillecke, M., Das römische Militärlager *Divitia* in Köln-Deutz, *Kölner Jahrbuch* 26, 1993, 321-444

Carroll-Spillecke, M., The late Roman frontier fort *Divitia* in Cologne-Deutz and its garrisons, in Groenman van Waateringe, van Beek, Willems and Wynia (1997) 143-50

Fischer, T., Materialhorte des 3. Jhs. in den römischen Grenzprovinzen zwischen Niedergermanien und Noricum, in *Das mitteleuropäische Barbaricum und die Krise des römischen Weltreiches im 3. Jahrhundert* (Brno: 1999) 19-50

Gilles, K.-H., *Spätrömische Höhensiedlungen in Eifel und Hunsrück* (Trier: 1985)

Hoffmann, D., *Das spätrömische Bewegungsheer und die Notitia dignitatum*. Epigraphische Studien 7 (Düsseldorf: 1970)

Rüger, C.B, Die spätrömische Großfestung in der Colonia Ulpia Traiana, *Bonner Jahrbuch* 179, 1979, 499-524

Schallmayer, E. (ed.), *Der Augsburger Siegesaltar. Zeugnis einer unruhigen Zeit*. Saalburg-Schriften 2 (Bad Homburg: 1995)

Schwarz, P.-A., Die spätrömischen Befestigungsanlagen in *Augusta Raurica* - Ein Überblick, in Bridger and Gilles (1998) 105-112

Strobel, K., *Raetia amissa?* Raetien unter Gallienus: Provinz und Heer im Licht der neuen Augsburger Siegesinschrift, in Bridger and Gilles (1998) 83-94

Romans and barbarians in the late Roman period

Anderson, T., Roman military colonies in Gaul, Salian ethnogenesis and the forgotten meaning of *Pactus Legis Salicae* 59.5, *Early Medieval Europe* 4, 1995, 129-44

Bernhard, H., Germanische Funde der Spätantike zwischen Strassbourg and Mainz, *Saalburg-Jahrbuch* 38, 1982, 72-109

Brulet, R., *La Gaule septentrionale au Bas-Empire. Nordgallien in der Spätantike* (Trier: 1990)

Buchet, L., Die Landnahme der Franken in Gallien aus der Sicht der Anthropologen, in Wieczorek, Périn, von Welck and Menghin (1997) 662-67

Drinkwater, J., and Elton, H. (eds.), *Fifth-Century Gaul: A Crisis of Identity?* (Cambridge: 1992)

Drinkwater, J., Ammianus, Valentinian and the Rhine Germans, in J.W. Drijvers and D. Hunt (eds.), *The Late Roman World and its Historian, Interpreting Ammianus Marcellinus* (London: 1999) 127-37

Geuenich, D., Zum gegenwärtigen Stand der Alemannenforschung, in Staab (1994) 159-69

James, E., *The Franks* (Oxford: 1988)

Knight, J.K., *The End of Antiquity. AD 235-700* (Stroud: 1999)

Moreland, J., and van de Noort, R., Integration and social reproduction in the Carolingian Empire, *World Archaeology* 23/3, 1992, 320-33

Müller-Wille, M., and Schneider, R. (eds.), *Ausgewählte Probleme europäischer Landnahmen des Früh- und Hochmittelalters* (Sigmaringen: 1993)

Pilet, C., *La nécropole de Frénouville*. BAR International Series 83 (Oxford: 1980)

Pirling, R., *Römer and Franken in Krefeld-Gellep* (Mainz: 1986)

Schallmayer, E., Germanen in der Spätantike im hessischen Ried mit Blick auf die Überlieferung bei Ammianus Marcellinus, *Saalburg Jahrbuch* 49, 1998, 139-54

Staab, F. (ed.), *Zur Kontinuität zwischen Antike und Mittelalter am Oberrhein* (Sigmaringen: 1994)

Stribrny, K., Römer rechts des Rheins nach 260 n. Chr. Kartierung, Strukturanalyse und Synopse spätrömischer Münzreihen zwischen Koblenz und Regensburg, *Bericht der Römisch-Germanischen Kommission* 70, 1989, 349-505

Swift, E., *The End of the Western Roman Empire: an archaeological investigation* (Tempus 2000)

Thoen, H., and Vermeulen, F., Phasen der Germanisierung in Flandern in der mittel- und spätrömischen Zeit, in Bridger and Gilles (1998) 1-12

Wieczorek, A., Périn, P., von Welck, K., and Menghin, W. (eds.), *Die Franken -Wegbereiter Europas. 5. bis 8. Jahrhundert n. Chr.* (Mainz: 1997)

Identity and Nationalism

Brunt, P.A., The Revolt of Vindex and the Fall of Nero, *Latomus* 18, 1959, 531-39

Brunt, P.A., Tacitus on the Batavian Revolt, *Latomus* 19, 1960, 494-517

Collis, J., Celts and Politics, in Graves-Brown, Jones and Gamble (1996) 167-78

Diaz-Andreu, M., and Champion, T., *Nationalism and Archaeology in Europe* (London: 1996)

Dietler, M. "Our ancestors the Gauls": Archaeology, Ethnic Nationalism and the Manipulation of Celtic Identity in Modern Europe, *American Anthropology* 96, 1994, 584-605

Fleury-Ilett, B., The identity of France: archetypes in Iron Age studies, in Graves-Brown, Jones and Gamble (1996) 196-208

Geary, P.J., *Before France and Germany. The creation and transformation of the Merovingian World* (Oxford: 1988)

Graves-Brown, P., Jones, S., and Gamble, C., *Cultural Identity and Archaeology. The Construction of European Communities* (London: 1996)

Hedeager, L., The Creation of Germanic Identity: A European Origin-Myth, in Brun, van der Leeuw and Whittaker (1993) 121-31

Jenkins, R., *Rethinking Ethnicity: arguments and explorations* (London: 1997)

Okun, M.L., Pluralism in Germania Superior, in V.A. Maxfield and M.J. Dobson (eds.), *Roman Frontier Studies 1989. Proceedings of the XVth International Congress of Roman Frontier Studies* (Exeter: 1991) 345-38

Roymans, N., Romanization, cultural identity and the ethnic discussion. The integration of lower Rhine populations in the Roman Empire, in Metzler, Millett, Roymans and Slofstra (1995) 47-64

Smith, A.D., *National Identity* (London: 1991)

Veit, U., Ethnic concepts in German prehistory: a case study on the relationship between cultural identity and archaeological objectivity, in S. Shennan (ed.), *Archaeological Approaches to Cultural Identity* (London: 1994) 35-56

Wiwjorra, I., German archaeology and its relation to nationalism and racism, in Diaz-Andreu and Champion (1996) 164-188.

Index

Figure numbers are in brackets after the main entries